William J Fay

TAKAMITSU MURAOKA

CLASSICAL SYRIAC FOR HEBRAISTS

TAKAMITSU MURAOKA

CLASSICAL SYRIAC FOR HEBRAISTS

1987

OTTO HARRASSOWITZ · WIESBADEN

CIP-Kurztitelaufnahme der Deutschen Bibliothek

Muraoka, Takamitsu:
Classical Syriac for Hebraists / Takamitsu Muraoka.
– Wiesbaden: Harrassowitz, 1987.
ISBN 3-447-02585-9

Publication of this book was supported by grants from
the Committee on Research and Graduate Studies
and Maurice David Goldman Publication Fund,
both University of Melbourne, Australia

Phototypesetting, reproduction and binding:
Imprimerie Orientaliste, Leuven
Printed in Belgium

To Prof. M. H. Goshen-Gottstein

CONTENTS

Part III: MORPHOSYNTAX AND SYNTAX

PREFACE

The present writer has been aware for some time that the only currently and readily available introductory Syriac grammar written in English is the fourth edition of Theodore H. Robinson's *Paradigms and Exercises in Syriac Grammar* as revised by L. H. Brockington and published in 1962 (the first edition appeared in 1915). With due respect to these noted scholars of the past, the work leaves much to be desired both scientifically and pedagogically. Despite the author's and reviser's reference to the standard grammars by Nöldeke and Duval [1], the structure of the language could have been presented in a substantially different form at many a point, if fuller account had been taken of the two last-mentioned grammars. This is nothing to say of advances made since 1898, when the second edition of Nöldeke's grammar appeared.

A learner might find Robinson's work less than stimulating, particularly with its plentiful, but tedious and often boring Exercises.

Another matter which we believe to be of some pedagogical importance is that many who take up the study of this rich and important Semitic language will already have some acquaintance with Hebrew or Arabic, or perhaps both. It seems to us that by assuming such knowledge of the cognate language a study of Syriac can be made more interesting and efficient.

With these two considerations uppermost in our mind, we decided to prepare the present work, believing that a Hebraist or beginning Comparative Semitist would be its most likely user.

It is only fair to acknowledge our debt to the above-mentioned grammars by Nöldeke and Duval together with C. Brockelmann's *Syrische Grammatik mit Paradigmen, Literatur, Chrestomathie und Glossar*, 9th ed. (Leipzig, 1962). Indeed, it ought to be stressed that every serious student of Syriac grammar would find it necessary and profitable to make constant reference to these standard works, especially Nöldeke. Yet the present writer would like to believe that his own study of Syriac documents has enabled him to incorpo-

1 Theodor Nöldeke, *Kurzgefasste syrische Grammatik* (Leipzig, [2]1898) [repr. with additional materials: Darmstadt, 1966]; R. Duval, *Traité de grammaire syriaque* (Paris, 1881). The former was translated, with the addition of a useful index of passages, into English by J. A. Crichton as *Compendious Syriac Grammar* (London, 1904). The German reprint also includes the index.

rate in this work some new insights and perhaps improvements on his predecessors' description of the language.

As the principal aim of this brief grammar is to help the student acquire a reasonable measure of facility in reading Syriac documents, whether pointed (vocalised) or not, we make the practical suggestion that he should first thoroughly study the asterisked paragraphs or parts of a paragraph and then proceed to the appended chrestomathy. As he reads along, he will find, in footnotes, references to the grammar section, including unasterisked paragraphs which deal in greater detail with finer points of orthography, morphology, morphosyntax, and syntax. Having read the first three or four pieces, the student would profitably commence a gradual study of the entire grammar as he continues to read the remaining pieces of the chrestomathy.

Some bibliographical information

Dictionaries:

J. Payne Smith, *A Compendious Syriac Dictionary* (Oxford, 1903).

L. Costaz, *Dictionnaire syriaque-français/Syriac-English Dictionary/Qamus suryani-ʿarabi* (Beyrouth, 1963).

C. Brockelmann, *Lexicon Syriacum* (Halle, ²1928) [repr.: Hildesheim, 1966).

R. Payne Smith, *Thesaurus Syriacus*, 2 vols. (Oxford, 1879-1901) with J. P. Margoliouth's *Supplement* (Oxford, 1927).

For those who wish to read further texts in Brockelmann's grammar there is available an English edition of his glossary with some additional materials: M. H. Goshen-Gottstein, *A Syriac-English Glossary with Etymological Notes* (Wiesbaden, 1970). Another readily available collection of Syriac texts may be found in Part II of F. Rosenthal (ed.), *An Aramaic Handbook* (Wiesbaden, 1967).

Dr S. P. Brock has written a highly useful and stimulating chapter on Syriac studies in J. H. Eaton (ed.), *Horizons in Semitic Studies: Articles for the Student* (Dept. of Theology, University of Birmingham: Birmingham, 1980), pp. 1-33.

For questions of Syriac linguistics, see also F. Rosenthal, *Aramaistische Forschung seit Th. Nöldekes Veröffentlichungen* (Leiden, 1939), pp. 179-211.

W. Wright's *A Short History of Syriac Literature* (London, 1894), R. Duval's *La littérature syriaque* (Paris, ³1907), and especially A. Baumstark's *Geschichte der syrischen Literatur* (Bonn, 1922; repr., Bonn, 1968) may be found useful. The last-mentioned is a rich mine of bibliographical data. See also "Literatur" in Brockelmann's *Grammatik*, pp. 150-84, and C. Moss, *Catalogue of Syriac Printed Books and Related Literature in the British Museum* (London, 1962), supplemented by S. P. Brock's classified bibliography in *Parole de l'Orient*, 4 (1973), 393-465. See also I. Ortiz de Urbina, *Patrologia syriaca* (Rome, ^{2}1965).

Examples cited in the section Morphosyntax and Syntax are taken from Nöldeke's grammar if references are not given. Otherwise, note the following abbreviations:

'P,' 'C,' 'S' with Gospel references indicate Peshitta, Curetonian, Sinaiticus respectively (see for details pp. 71, 94)
Aphr. = Aphrahat, *Demonstrationes*, ed. Parisot (see p. 83)
Acta Thomae = as found in W. Wright, *Apocryphal Acts of the Apostles* etc., 2 vols. (London, 1871)
Addai = G. Phillips, *The Doctrine of Addai, the Apostle* etc. (London, 1876)
Bardaisan = H. J. W. Drijvers, *The Book of the Laws of Countries. Dialogue on Fate of Bardaisan of Edessa* (Assen, 1965).
Josh. St. = W. Wright, *The Chronicle of Joshua the Stylite* etc. (Cambridge, 1882)
Spic. = W. Cureton, *Spicilegium syriacum* etc. (London, 1885).

It is a pleasant duty to acknowledge the valuable assistance given by Messers. G.R. Clark and R.G. Jenkins in the way of improving the English style of the grammar and presentation of its materials; the former in particular worked under most trying personal circumstances. I am also obliged to put on record that my research in connection with the present work has been greatly facilitated by A. Bonus's concordance to the entire Peshitta New Testament, a manuscript of which is in our Department's possession. The Research and Graduate Studies Committee of the University of Melbourne and Maurice David Goldman Publication Fund have defrayed a substantial portion of the cost of production of the present work. Last, but not least, Dr Helmut Petzolt of Harrassowitz has been uncommonly supportive and encouraging since the initial approach was made to the publisher. My thanks are due to the Imprimerie Orientaliste, Leuven (Belgium) for their superb technical execution and to Mr R. Friedrich of Harrassowitz for his tireless efforts in mediating between the publisher and the printer.

May, 1987

Takamitsu Muraoka

Dept. of Middle Eastern Studies,
University of Melbourne,
Parkville, Victoria 3052,
AUSTRALIA.

INTRODUCTORY

§ 1 *Syriac as a Semitic language*

Syriac is a form of Aramaic, a branch of the Semitic language family with great historical and geographical spread [2]. Among the great variety of Aramaic dialects, Syriac belongs to the so-called Eastern Aramaic group along with Mandaic and the Aramaic of the Babylonian Talmud. Historically, it dates to the period called by Fitzmyer "Late Aramaic," [3] roughly 200-700 A.D., when distinct local varieties of *written* Aramaic began to take shape. The language blossomed between the third and the seventh centuries A.D. The advance of Islam dealt a virtual death blow to Syriac as a viable spoken idiom, although it managed to maintain some lingering existence even down to the thirteenth century, as is eloquently testified to by that well-known prolific polymath, Barhebraeus (1226-86).

Geographically, at one point or another of its history, Syriac was spread over a vast area comprising Lebanon, Northern Syria, Eastern Turkey, Iraq, and Western Iran. It is still used in modern forms as a second language in tiny pockets of population in the Middle East and by their expatriates around the world. With the active encouragement of Western Christian missionaries in the latter half of the nineteenth century, attempts were made, with a measure of success, to revive the use of a form of Syriac even as a means of written communication [4].

The famous Christological controversy of the fifth century led to the gradual development of dialectal traits distinguishing Eastern (Nestorian) from Western (Jacobite) Syriac. The two differed in phonetics and phonology, and also developed two alphabets (see below). However, our present scanty knowledge does not enable us to determine whether they differed significantly in grammar, vocabulary and other matters [5].

2 See F. Rosenthal, "Aramaic studies during the past thirty years", *Journal of Near Eastern Studies*, 37 (1978), 81-92.

3 J. A. Fitzmyer, "The phases of the Aramaic language", in his *A Wandering Aramean: Collected Aramaic Essays* (Missoula, Mont., 1979), pp. 57-84.

4 See R. Macuch and E. Panouss, *Neusyrische Chrestomathie* (Wiesbaden, 1974).

5 J. P. P. Martin, "Les deux principaux dialectes araméens", *Journal Asiatique*, 6ᵉ série, 19 (1872), 305-483.

Apart from some epigraphic materials[6] and translations from classical authors and the like, the extant Syriac literature is mostly ecclesiastical or theological in its contents, and its quantity is enormous; this has important implications for the study of relatively poorly documented idioms of Aramaic. All in all, we have in Syriac the best attested and most intensively studied[7] Aramaic idiom.

6 Some examples may be found in H. J. W. Drijvers, *Old Syriac (Edessean) Inscriptions* (Leiden, 1972) and T. Muraoka, "Two Syriac inscriptions from the Middle Euphrates", *Abr-Nahrain*, 23 (1984-85), 83-89.

7 See W. Strothmann, *Die Anfänge der syrischen Studien in Europa* (Wiesbaden, 1971).

Part I: ORTHOGRAPHY AND PHONOLOGY

§ 2* *The Alphabet*

The Syriac alphabet contains, as in Hebrew, twenty-two letters and comes in three varieties: Estrangela (also Estrangelo)[8], Nestorian, and Jacobite (also known as *serṭa* [*serṭo*][9]). The first, an offshoot of the Palmyrene branch of the Aramaic alphabet[10], represents the earliest phase; the latter two are subsequent Eastern and Western dialectal varieties respectively[11]. All three scripts are cursive, and fourteen of the letters must be joined both to the right and to the left, whilst the remaining eight can be joined only to the right. In this work we shall present the grammar and texts in the Estrangela script, with a sample of the remaining scripts appended at the end of the chrestomathy.

A close study of the table of the alphabet on the following page would show that special care is required not to confuse the following pairs:

ܕ	(Daleth)	:	ܪ	(Resh)
ܚ	(Ḥeth)	:	ܝܝ	(double Yodh),
			ܢܝ	(Nun + Yodh),
			ܢܢ	(double Nun)
ܠ	(Lamadh)	:	ܥ	(ʿE)
ܢ	(Nun)	:	ܝ	(Yodh)

As Syriac, in common with Hebrew and Arabic, is written from right to left, the general direction of writing strokes is from top to bottom and right to left.

§ 3* The *pronunciation* adopted in this grammar is a scientifically reconstructed one with a mixture of conventional practice. In comparison with the "academic" pronunciation of Biblical Hebrew, one may note the twofold pronunciation of ܒ, ܓ, ܕ, ܟ, ܦ, ܬ, as in the Tiberian pronunciation of Beghadhkephath.

8 From Gk στρογγύλη "round".

9 Syr. word meaning "incised line; script *par excellence*, i.e. Jacobite script".

10 See J. Naveh, *Early History of the Alphabet* (Jerusalem, 1982), pp. 143-51.

11 Actual manuscripts sometimes mix different scripts, as can be easily seen in some samples given in W. H. P. Hatch, *An Album of Dated Syriac Manuscripts* (Boston, 1946), Plate CI.

Table of the Alphabet

	Estrangelo				Serṭa	Nestorian	Hebrew
Name	Unattached	Joined to the left	Joined to the right and left	Joined to the right			
Alaf	ܐ	ܐ			ܐ ܐ	ܐ ܐ	א
Beth	ܒ	ܒ	ܒ	ܒ	ܒ ܒ ܒ ܒ	ܒ ܒ ܒ ܒ	ב
Gamal	ܓ	ܓ	ܓ	ܓ	ܓ ܓ ܓ ܓ	ܓ ܓ ܓ ܓ	ג
Dalath	ܕ	ܕ			ܕ ܕ	ܕ ܕ	ד
He	ܗ	ܗ			ܗ ܗ	ܗ	ה
Waw	ܘ	ܘ			ܘ ܘ	ܘ ܘ	ו
Zai(n)	ܙ	ܙ			ܙ ܙ	ܙ ܙ	ז
Ḥeth	ܚ	ܚ	ܚ	ܚ	ܚ ܚ ܚ ܚ	ܚ ܚ ܚ ܚ	ח
Ṭeth	ܛ	ܛ	ܛ	ܛ	ܛ ܛ ܛ ܛ	ܛ ܛ ܛ ܛ	ט
Yodh	ܝ	ܝ	ܝ	ܝ	ܝ ܝ ܝ ܝ	ܝ ܝ ܝ ܝ	י
Kaf	ܟ	ܟ	ܟ	ܟ	ܟ ܟ ܟ ܟ	ܟ ܟ ܟ ܟ ܟ	כ, ך
Lamadh	ܠ	ܠ	ܠ	ܠ	ܠ ܠ ܠ ܠ	ܠ ܠ ܠ ܠ	ל
Mim	ܡ	ܡ	ܡ	ܡ	ܡ ܡ ܡ ܡ	ܡ ܡ ܡ ܡ	מ, ם
Nun	ܢ	ܢ	ܢ	ܢ	ܢ ܢ ܢ ܢ	ܢ ܢ ܢ ܢ	נ, ן
Semkath	ܣ	ܣ	ܣ	ܣ	ܣ ܣ ܣ ܣ	ܣ ܣ ܣ ܣ	ס
ʿE	ܥ	ܥ	ܥ	ܥ	ܥ ܥ ܥ ܥ	ܥ ܥ ܥ ܥ	ע
Pe	ܦ	ܦ	ܦ	ܦ	ܦ ܦ ܦ ܦ	ܦ ܦ ܦ ܦ	פ, ף
Ṣadhe	ܨ	ܨ			ܨ ܨ	ܨ ܨ	צ, ץ
Qof	ܩ	ܩ	ܩ	ܩ	ܩ ܩ ܩ ܩ	ܩ ܩ ܩ ܩ	ק
Resh	ܪ	ܪ			ܪ ܪ	ܪ ܪ	ר
Shin	ܫ	ܫ	ܫ	ܫ	ܫ ܫ ܫ ܫ	ܫ ܫ ܫ ܫ	ש
Taw	ܬ	ܬ			ܬ ܬ	ܬ ܬ	ת

A) As mentioned above, Eastern and Western Syriac differ at times in matters of phonetics and phonology alike [12]. It is believed that the former tradition has often preserved a more primitive state, as we shall note from time to time.

§ 3a B) The following table showing correspondence of consonants between Syriac, Biblical Aramaic (BA), Hebrew, Arabic, and Proto-Semitic (PS) may be found of some interest.

	Syr.	BA	Heb.	Arab.	PS	
a)	ܕ	ד	ד	د	/d/	(a
b)			ז	ذ	/ḏ/	(b
c)	ܚ	ח	ח	ح	/ḥ/	(c
d)				خ	/ḫ/	(d
e)	ܛ	ט	ט	ط	/ṭ/	(e
f)			צ	ظ	/ṯ̣/	(f
g)	ܣ	ס	ס	س	/s/	(g
h)		שׂ	שׂ	ش	/ś/	(h
i)	ܥ	ע	ע	ع	/ʿ/	(i
j)		(ק)	צ	ض	/ḏ̣/	(j
k)		ע	ע	غ	/g̱/	(k
l)	ܨ	צ	צ	ص	/ṣ/	(l
m)	ܫ	שׁ	שׁ	س	/š/	(m
n)	ܬ	ת	ת	ت	/t/	(n
o)			שׁ	ث	/ṯ/	(o

12 On some details of the Nestorian pronunciation, see Theodor Weiss, *Zur ostsyrischen Laut- und Akzentlehre auf Grund der ostsyrischen Massorah-Handschrift des British Museum mit Facsimiles von 50 Seiten der Londoner Handschrift* (Stuttgart, 1933), and J. P. P. Martin, art. cit. (n. 5) above.

Examples:

a)	ܕܶܒܳܐ /*debbā*/	דֹּב	דֹּב	دُبّ	"bear"
b)	ܕܪܳܥܳܐ /*drā'ā*/	דְּרָעָא	זְרֹעַ	ذِرَاع	"arm"
c)	ܚܰܟܺܝܡ /*ḥakkim*/	חַכִּים	חָכָם	حَكِيم	"wise"
d)	ܚܰܡܪܳܐ /*ḥamrā*/	חַמְרָא	חֶמֶר	خَمْر	"wine"
e)	ܛܰܒܳܚܳܐ /*ṭabbāḥā*/	טַבָּחָא	טַבָּח	طَبَّاخ	"cook"
f)	ܛܶܠܳܠܳܐ /*ṭellālā*/ Root	טלל	צֵל	ظِلّ	"shade"
g)	Root ܣܓܕ (SGD)	סגד	סגד	سجد	"prostrate"
h)	ܥܣܰܪ /*'sar*/	עֲשַׂר	עֶשֶׂר	عَشْر	"ten"
i)	ܥܰܝܢܳܐ /*'aynā*/	עַיִן	עַיִן	عَيْن	"eye"
j)	ܐܰܪܥܳܐ /*'ar'ā*/	אַרְקָא	אֶרֶץ	أَرْض	"earth"
k)	ܬܰܪܥܳܐ /*tar'ā*/	תַּרְעָא	שַׁעַר	ثَغْر	"gate; (Arb.) opening"
l)	ܨܶܒܥܳܐ /*ṣev'ā*/	אֶצְבְּעָא	אֶצְבַּע	إِصْبَع	"finger"
m)	ܫܡܰܝܳܐ /*šmayyā*/	שְׁמַיָּא	שָׁמַיִם	سَمَاء	"heaven"
n)	Root ܟܬܒ (KTB)	כתב	כתב	كتب	"write"
o)	ܬܠܳܬ /*tlāṯ*/	תְּלָת	שָׁלוֹשׁ	ثَلَاث	"three"

* EXERCISE 1

1. Transliterate, disregarding the vowel signs, the first five lines of Text no. 2 in the chrestomathy.
2. Transcribe the following paragraphs in Syriac (Estrangela) characters:

1) ויצא אחד אל השדה ללקט ארת וימצא גפן שדה וילקט ממנו
פקעת שדה מלא בגדו ויבא ויפלח אל סיר הנזיד כי לא ידעו
(2 Kg 4.39)

2) ואלישע ישב בביתו והזקנים ישבים אתו וישלח איש מלפניו
בטרם יבא המלאך אליו והוא אמר אל הזקנים הראיתם כי שלח בן
המרצח הזה להסיר את ראשי ראו כבא המלאך סגרו הדלת ולחצתם
אתו בדלת הלוא קול רגלי אדניו אחריו (ib. 6.32)

3) ויבאו המצרעים האלה עד קצה המחנה ויבאו אל אהל אחד
ויאכלו וישתו וישאו משם כסף וזהב ובגדים וילכו ויטמנו וישבו
ויבאו אל אהל אחר וישאו משם וילכו ויטמנו (ib. 7.8)

§4* As was the case in North West Semitic in general, the vowel notation in Syriac developed gradually in the course of several centuries, starting with the use of *matres lectionis*, i.e. Waw, Yodh and Alaf, and proceeding to the development of special vowel symbols ("points")[13]. A Syriac text, when fully pointed, does not present a picture of ideal economy.

Two sets of vowel symbols are in use: Nestorian and Jacobite. We show them as attached to the consonant ܣ /*s*/, and give the pronunciation of the syllable (as well as the name of the vowel sign).

	Nestorian (ES)[14]		Jacobite (WS)	
/*sā*/	ܣܵ	(zeqāfā)	ܣܳ	(zeqofo)
/*sa*/	ܣܲ	(petāḥā)	ܣܰ	(petoḥo)
/*si*/	ܣܝܼ	(ḥevāṣā)	ܣܺܝ	(ḥevoṣo)
/*su*/	ܣܘܼ	(ʿeṣaṣā ʿalliṣā)	ܣܽܘ	(ʿeṣoṣo)
/*sē*/	ܣܹ	(revāṣā karyā)	ܣܶܝ / ܣܶ	(revoṣo)
/*se*/	ܣܸ	(revāṣā 'arrikā)		
/*so*/	ܣܘܿ	(ʿeṣāṣā rewiḥā)		

The dots of the Nestorian system occur in the fixed positions, whilst the symbols of the Jacobite system, developed from the Greek vowel letters, may be positioned either above or below the letter concerned. The vowel symbols are turned through 180°, when they are placed below; thus ܣܴ ܣܱ ܣܻܝ ܣܾܘ ܣܷ.

The phonological structure of vowels of the two traditions differs:

Nestorian	Jacobite
/*sā*/ corresponds to	/*så*/[15]
/*sē*/ corresponds to	/*se*/ or /*si*/[16]
/*so*/ corresponds to	/*su*/

Scholars believe that the ES tradition represents the more archaic pronunciation, especially in the correspondence between ES /*ē*/ and /*o*/ and WS /*i*/ and /*u*/ respectively[17]. Accordingly, we shall follow the useful convention adopted by Brockelmann and others, and use on the following pages those

13 J. B. Segal, *The Diacritical Point and the Accents in Syriac* (London, 1953).

14 ES = Eastern Syriac; WS = Western Syriac.

15 Presumably equivalent to the American pronunciation of *so*ft.

16 The conditions for this two-way correspondence are not altogether clear. See J. Blau, "The origin of the open and closed *e* in Proto-Syriac", *Bulletin of the School of Oriental and African Studies*, 32 (1969), 1-9.

17 That is to say, as far as Syriac is concerned. Cf. Nöldeke, §48, 1st paragraph.

two Nestorian vowel symbols in words which are largely vocalised with the Jacobite vowel symbols: thus ܢܐܡܰܪ "he or we will say" (= pure WS: ܢܶܐܡܰܪ) and ܢܶܪܡܽܘܢ "they shall throw" (= pure WS: ܢܶܪܡܽܘܢ)[18].

The macron in /sā/ and /sē/ is used as a merely artificial device to indicate that they differ somewhat from /sa/ and /se/ respectively. In other words, the sounds so marked do not probably represent prolonged articulation of the sounds written without a macron[19]. Many other details of Syriac phonetics of the classical period are still rather obscure[20].

Neither system has a symbol for *shewa*, whether *mobile* ("vocalic") or *quiescent* ("silent"). Nor does there exist a special symbol equivalent to the Tiberian *dagesh forte*. Although we do not believe that Classical Syriac possessed a "vocal shewa" as a distinct phoneme, actual pronunciation would be facilitated by inserting some such indistinct vowel in cases like /*wmalkā*/ (to be pronounced [wəmalkā]) or /*neqṭlun*/ ([neqṭəlun]).

§ 5* *Other noteworthy graphic symbols*

1) A dot is placed above ܒ ܓ ܕ ܟ ܦ ܬ to indicate their hard pronunciation ([b g d k p t]) — called /*quššāyā*/ "hardening" by the native grammarians — and below those letters to indicate their soft (aspirate) pronunciation ([v g̠ d̠ k̠ f t̠]) — /*rukkāk̠ā*/ "softening". This is of course similar to the Tiberian *dagesh lene* point and the *rafe* stroke as in בּ = [b] versus בֿ = [v]. E.g.,

ܡܰܠܟ݁ܳܐ	/*malkā*/	"king"
ܕܰܗܒ݂ܳܐ	/*dahvā*/	"gold"

2) A horizontal stroke, called *linea occultans* "obscuring line", is written above a non-final silent consonant. This occurs most commonly with the enclitic use of the verb ܗ̄ܘܳܐ /*wā*/ "he was" and some pronouns such as ܐ̄ܢ̄ܬ /*'at*/ "you", ܐ̄ܢܳܐ /*nā*/ "I", ܡܰܠܟܰ̈ܘܗ̄ܝ /*malkaw*/ "his rulers".

18 Vocalised manuscripts, even those dealing with Syriac grammar, display a considerable degree of fluctuation, which is particularly true of the Nestorian distinction between the two kinds of *e*. Hence in our transliteration we shall use a macron (ē) only when it corresponds to the Jacobite /*i*/.

19 Cf. H. Birkeland, "The Syriac phonematic vowel systems", *Festskrift til Professor Olaf Broch på hans 80 Årsdag* (Oslo, 1947), pp. 13-39, and Sh. Morag, *The Vocalization Systems of Arabic, Hebrew and Aramaic* ('s-Gravenhage, 1962), pp. 45-59.

20 Cf. Nöldeke, §§ 2, 20-22, 26-39, 42-55.

§6 3) The same symbol, but called by native grammarians *marheṭana*, is sometimes used in the manner of a *shewa*, whether vocalic or silent: ܦܠܓܘ /*pleg*/ "were divided" vs. ܠܚܡܝ /*laḥm*/ "my bread"[21].

4) A sublinear stroke, *mehaggeyana* "articulator", may indicate that a murmured vowel is to be pronounced in a sequence of the structure -CCCV-[22]: ܚܟܡܬܐ /*ḥekəmṯā*/ "wisdom". In this grammar, we shall not use this symbol, but only the supralinear stroke, and that as *linea occultans*.

* 5)* Two dots placed horizontally above a word, called *seyame*, may be found with plural forms of nouns and the like: e.g., ܡ̈ܠܟܐ /*malke*/ "kings"[23].

6) The *seyame* originally emerged as a diacritical device to distinguish sequences of letters graphically identical but phonetically (and hence also semantically) different: e.g., ܡܠܟܐ /*malkā*/ "king" vs. ܡ̈ܠܟܐ /*malke*/ "kings". This was subsequently generalised, being applied to a plural form which was graphically distinct from its singular equivalent as in ܡ̈ܠܟܘܗܝ /*malkaw*/ "his kings". If a word contains a Resh, its diacritical point and the *seyame* usually blend into ܪ̈, thus ܬܪ̈ܝܢ /*tren*/ "two".

It stands to reason that the sign developed at a time when the vowel points or symbols were not yet in existence. As a similar primitive reading aid there was also used a single diacritical dot, which was written above the consonant concerned to signify the fuller, stronger pronunciation of the following vowel and below the consonant to denote the finer, weaker pronunciation: the former covered roughly the range of vowels like *a*, *ā*, *o*, and the latter *e*, *i*, *u*. Thus ܡܢ = /*mān*/ "what?" or /*man*/ "who?" vs. ܡܢ = /*men*/ "from"; ܡܠܟܐ = /*malkā*/ "king" vs. ܡܠܟܐ = /*melkā*/ "advice"; ܗܘ = /*haw*/ "that" vs. ܗܘ = /*hu*/ "he"[24]. In this light one can appreciate why the ES sign for /*ā*/ is placed where it is in relation to the sign of the same shape for /*ē*/: ܣ /*sā*/ vs. ܣ /*sē*/. Compare also ܣܘ /*so*/ with ܣܘ /*su*/ on the one hand, and note the sublinear position of the signs as in ܣ ܣ, ܣܝ on the other.

It will be seen that a fully vocalised text does not require the use of these diacritical marks including the *seyame*[25]. However, many late manuscripts,

21 See Duval, §148-50.

22 C = consonant; V = vowel. See Duval, §143-47.

23 For details of the use of the symbol, see Nöldeke, §16.

24 See Nöldeke, §7, for further details.

25 Indeed, a *mehaggeyana* is not usually written if the symbol for the helping vowel is also added (Duval, §143 end).

especially of the Scriptures, do present a full array of these extraneous signs coupled with those for cantillation similar to the familiar Tiberian accents[26].

7) The most commonly used punctuation marks are a single dot (.) and .:., the latter to mark the end of a paragraph.

* Exercise 2

Transcribe the Hebrew of Genesis 1.1-10 in the Estrangela script, adding the *quššaya/rukkaka* point in such a way as it would correspond to the presence or absence of the *dagesh*.

§7 *Some remarks on phonology*

A) *Vowel Deletion Rule*

In the course of inflectional modifications, the vowels /*a*/, /*e*/, and /*o*/ are deleted when the syllable containing them becomes an open syllable, i.e. a syllable ending in a vowel. For example, in the pair ܫܒܚ /*šabbaḥ*/ "he praised" and ܫܒܚܬ /*šabbḥat*/ "she praised", the process can be formulated as: /*šabbaḥ*/ + /*-at*/ → */*šabbaḥat*/ → /*šabbḥat*/. Likewise ܡܩܒܠ /*mqabbel*/ "receiving" (m. sg.) — ܡܩܒܠܐ /*mqabblā*/ (f. sg.); ܬܩܛܘܠ /*teqṭol*/ "you (m. sg.) shall kill" — ܬܩܛܠܘܢ /*teqṭlun*/ "you (m. pl.) shall kill". In these examples, two of the three vowels concerned are found in contiguous open syllables. It is the second of those vowels which is deleted.

This rule, which is valid in many Aramaic idioms, accounts for the morphological changes that occur when the definite article is appended to certain nouns: e.g. ܨܠܡ /*ṣlem*/ "image" becomes ܨܠܡܐ /*ṣalmā*/ "the image". Here both forms can be derived from the underlying */*ṣalem*/: */*ṣalem*/ → /*ṣlem*/ and */*ṣalemā*/ → /*ṣalmā*/.

The rule, in addition to comparative Semitic etymology, enables us on occasion to postulate gemination: ܡܠܬ "the word of", which can be construed only as /*mellat*/, for a single /*l*/ would necessarily lead to /*mlat*/ (< */*melat*/)[27].

26 The development of these symbols as well as vowel signs is traced in Segal's monograph (cited in n. 13) on the basis of manuscript evidence. See also the monograph by Weiss (n. 12 above), pp. 27-46.

27 The WS, however, appears to have given up gemination very early in its development. Moreover, it appears that the vowel deletion rule had ceased to operate when the feature mentioned under (I) below set in.

B) /e/ → /a/ before /r/ or a guttural

This is a pan-Aramaic feature. Examples are: ܫܳܡܰܥ /šāma'/ "hearing" < */šāme'/; ܫܰܒܰܚ /šabbaḥ/ "he praised" < */šabbeḥ/; ܕܳܒܰܪ /dāvar/ "leading" < */dāver/; ܒܰܪ /bar/ "a son" < */ber/ (cf. Heb. /bēn/).

C) The primitive Semitic *diphthongs*, /ay/ and /aw/ [28], mostly remain stable in comparison with Hebrew and Biblical Aramaic. Thus: ܐܰܘܕܰܥ /'awda'/ vs. BA /hōḏa'/ and BH /hōdia'/ "he made known"; ܐܰܠܳܗܰܝܟܽܘܢ /'alāhaykon/ vs. BA /'ĕlāhēḵōn/ "your gods".

D) In contrast with BA, the Beghadhkephath following one of /ay/, /aw/ or /ā/ is *not* spirantised: e.g., ܒܰܝܬܳܐ /baytā/ vs. BA /bayṯā/ and ܟܳܬܒܳܐ /kāṯbā/ as against BA /kāṯvā/ "writing" (ptc. f. sg.).

E) Where the analogy of Tiberian Hebrew leads one to expect something equivalent to a *ḥafef* vowel with a guttural, Syriac shows a vowel only with a syllable-initial Alaf: ܐܶܟܰܠ /'eḵal/ vs. BA /'ăḵal/ "he ate"; ܐܰܠܳܗܳܐ /'alāhā/ vs. BH /'ĕlōhim/ "god", but ܥܒܳܕܳܐ /'vāḏā/ vs. BH /'ăvōdā/ "work, service"; ܚܠܰܡ /ḥlam/ "he dreamed" vs. BH /ḥălōm/ "a dream" [29].

F) Where the historical grammar would require a *shewa* with a syllable-initial Yodh, Syriac has a full vowel /i/: e.g., ܝܺܕܰܥ /yiḏa'/ "he came to know"; ܝܺܗܽܘܕܳܐ /yihuḏā/ vs. יְהוּדָה "Judah". Such forms are often spelled with an Alaf, indicating the shift /yi/ > /i/: ܐܺܝܕܳܐ /'iḏā/ "a hand". Cf. BH בִּיהוּדָה < *בִּיְהוּדָה.

G) *Proclitics*

Like the Hebrew inseparable prepositions, the monophthongal (or: one-letter) grammatical words ܒ "in", ܠ "to", ܘ "and", and ܕ "that, which, of" phonetically form an integral part with the immediately following word and are spelled as part of the latter. Thus ܒܒܰܝܬܳܐ /bvaytā/ "at home"; ܘܡܰܠܟܳܐ /wmalkā/ "and the king".

If the immediately following consonant lacks a vowel, the preceding particle receives a helping vowel /a/ [30]: e.g., ܒ + ܫܡܰܝܳܐ /šmayyā/ → ܒܰܫܡܰܝܳܐ /bašmayyā/ "in the sky". The same rule is applied also when two or more of such particles follow one another as in ܠܰܕܒܰܫܡܰܝܳܐ /laḏvašmayyā/ "to what (or: who) is in the sky".

H) *Enclitics*

a) A word-initial Alaf, He or Ḥet is regularly elided in pronunciation (and often in writing as well) in some grammatical words which form a close

28 ES consistently has /āw/: e.g. ܝܰܘܡܳܐ /yāwmā/.

29 But cf. § 6,(4) above on *mehaggeyana*, though its use is not confined to gutturals.

30 Tiberian Hebrew would show a *ḥiriq* /i/ in such a case.

phonetic unit with the immediately preceding word. Such are (i) the Alaf of the independent personal pronouns in the first and second persons (ܐܢܳܐ /'enā/, ܐܢ̱ܬ /'at/ "you" [m. sg.], ܐܢ̱ܬܝ /'at/ [f. sg.], ܐܢ̱ܬܘܢ /'atton/ [m. pl.], ܐܢ̱ܬܝܢ /'atten/ [f. pl.]), (ii) the He of the third person pronouns ܗ̇ܘ /hu/ "he, it", ܗ̇ܝ /hi/ "she, it" and the Perfect tense of the verb ܗܘܳܐ /hwā/ "he was, there was", and (iii) the Ḥet of the first person pl. pronoun ܚܢܰܢ /ḥnan/.

b) The consonants thus elided may be left out altogether in writing as in ܩܳܛܶܠܢܳܐ /qāṭelnā/ "I murder" (< ܩܳܛܶܠ ܐܢܳܐ) or they would carry a *linea occultans*: ܩܳܛܶܠ ܐ̱ܢܳܐ.

c) As can be seen from the last example, in the case of the first person pronoun, not only the consonant but also the following vowel is elided. In the third person pronouns /hu/ and /hi/, the /u/ and /i/ are retained as such respectively if preceded by a consonant, but as /w/ and /y/ if preceded by a vowel. Thus ܐܢ̱ܬ ܗ̇ܘ ܡܰܠܟܳܐ /'attu malka/ "you are the king"; ܡܰܠܟܳܐ ܗ̇ܘ ܐܢ̱ܬ /malkaw 'at/ "you are king"; ܐܢ̱ܬܝ ܗ̇ܝ ܡܰܠܟܬܳܐ /'atti malkṯā/ "you are the queen"; ܫܰܦܺܝܪܳܐ ܗ̇ܝ ܡܰܠܟܬܳܐ /šappirāy malkṯā/ "the queen is beautiful".

d) A similar development has occurred in some isolated words: apart from the ancient ܚܰܕ /ḥaḏ/ "one", note ܐ̱ܢܳܫ /nāš/ "man, people"; ܐ̱ܚܪܺܢ /ḥrēn/ "another"; ܐ̱ܚܪܳܝܳܐ /ḥrāyā/ "last"; ܚܰܪܬܳܐ /ḥarṯā/ "end"; ܚܳܬܳܐ /ḥāṯā/ "sister"; ܗ̱ܕܶܝܢ /den/ "then" (cf. BA אֱדַיִן and BH אֱזַי).

I) Elision of Alaf in sequence C'V

If an Alaf preceded by a vowelless consonant is elided, its vowel is then taken over by the preceding consonant. Thus * ܐܶܬܐܶܟܶܠ /'eṯ'eḵel/ "it was eaten" → /'eṯeḵel/. This also applies to cases of proclisis (G above): ܠ + ܐܰܪܥܳܐ → * ܠܐܰܪܥܳܐ → ܠܐܰܪܥܳܐ /lar'ā/ "to the land"; ܡܐܰܣܝܳܐ /masse/ < */m'asse/ "healing"[31].

J) Elision of Alaf in sequence V'C

Examples are: ܢܶܐܟܘܿܠ /neḵol/ "we will eat" (< */ne'kol/); ܬܐܡܰܪ /tēmar/ "she shall say". Cf. BH לֵאכֹל, BA יֵאמַר, and BH לֵאלֹהִים.

§ 8 K) The position of tone or stress differs between the ES and WS in their respective traditional pronunciation, the former preferring penultimate stress, the latter stress on the ultima. However, the tone is not a phonemic feature, as it is in Hebrew, and hence does not distinguish forms which are phonetically

31 Some printed editions do not always adhere to this rule.

identical saving the position of the tone. There is, in Syriac, nothing corresponding to Heb. בָּנוּ */bắnu/* "in us" as against */bānú/* "they built", where changing the position of the tone causes a change in the meaning.

Here again the Nestorian tradition seems to have preserved the more primitive state of affairs, for only the penultimate stress would satisfactorily account for the loss of final vowels as in ܩܛܰܠܘ */qṭal/* "they murdered" and ܐܰܢ̄ܬܝ */'at/* "you" (f. sg.).

L) The rules governing the alternation between the hard (*quššaya*) and soft (*rukkaḵa*) pronunciations of BGDKPT are comparable to those applicable to Tiberian Hebrew, although there are in Syriac some signs of nascent phonematisation of the two sets of allophones.

§* Exercise 3

Practise reading aloud Text no. 1 in the chrestomathy until you can read it with ease, even when you are covering the accompanying transliteration.

Part II: MORPHOLOGY

§ 9* *Independent Personal Pronouns*

	Separate		Enclitic	
sg. 1	ܐܶܢܳܐ	/'enā/	ܐܶܢܳܐ ܢܳܐ	
2 m	ܐܰܢ݇ܬ݁	/'at/	ܬ݁	
f	ܐܰܢ݇ܬ݁ܝ	/'at/	ܬ݁ܝ	
3 m	ܗܽܘ	/hu/	ܗܽܘ ܘ	/aw/ or /u/ (§ 7H, c)
f	ܗܺܝ	/hi/	ܗܝ	/ay/ or /i/ (ib.)
pl. 1 m	ܚܢܰܢ	/ḥnan/ (ܐܢܚܢܢ)	ܢܰܢ	
2 m	ܐܰܢ݇ܬ݁ܽܘܢ	/'atton/	ܬ݁ܽܘܢ	
f	ܐܰܢ݇ܬ݁ܶܝܢ	/'atten/	ܬ݁ܶܝܢ	
3 m	ܗܶܢܽܘܢ	/hennon/	ܐܶܢܽܘܢ	/'ennon/
f	ܗܶܢܶܝܢ	/hennen/	ܐܶܢܶܝܢ	/'ennen/

§ 10 The enclitic forms for the first and second persons, and those for the third person to a lesser extent, are used as weakened subjects in nominal clauses following the predicate: e.g., ܡܰܠܟ݁ܳܐ ܐܶܢܳܐ /malkā nā/ "I am a king", ܟ݁ܳܬ݂ܒ݁ܰܬ݁ܝ /kāṯbat/ "you (f. sg.) write" (also spelled fully ܟ݁ܳܬ݂ܒ݁ܳܐ ܐܰܢ݇ܬ݁ܝ /kāṯbā 'at/). The third person singular enclitic forms, however, are more commonly employed to give varying degrees of prominence to a part of the sentence as in ܐܰܢ݇ܬ݁ ܗܽܘ ܡܰܠܟ݁ܳܐ /'attu malkā/ "you are the king"; ܡܰܠܟ݁ܳܐ ܗܽܘ ܩܛܰܠܬ݁ /malkaw qṭalt/ "it is the king that you murdered" or as an enclitic subject as in ܐܰܢ݇ܬ݁ ܡܰܠܟ݁ܳܐ ܗܽܘ /'at malkaw/ "you are king"[32]. The third person pl. enclitic forms are mainly used as direct objects "them" of a verb form other than a participle: ܩܛܰܠ ܐܶܢܽܘܢ /qṭal 'ennon/ "he killed them."

See § 7H a-c and Nöldeke, § 64.

§ 11* *Suffixed Personal Pronouns*

The following are attached to a singular noun or to a feminine plural noun, with possessive meaning "my, your" etc., and also to certain prepositions[33]:

32 For more details on these questions, see the section on syntax (§ 105 f.).

33 The forms used with a masculine plural noun are given in § 26 below.

sg. 1	ܝ silent[34]		and after vowels	ܝ /y/
2 m	ܟ /āḵ/			ܟ /ḵ/[35]
f	ܟܝ /eḵ/			ܟܝ /ḵ/
3 m	ܗ /eh/			ܗܝ /y/
f	ܗ /āh/			ܗ /h/
pl. 1	ܢ /an/			ܢ /n/
2 m		ܟܘܢ /ḵon/		
f		ܟܝܢ /ḵen/		
3 m		ܗܘܢ /hon/		
f		ܗܝܢ /hen/		

§12* *Object Suffixes*[36]

sg. 1	ܢܝ /an/		and after vowels	ܢܝ /n/
2 m	ܟ /āḵ/			ܟ /ḵ/
f	ܟܝ /eḵ/			ܟܝ /ḵ/
3 m	ܗ /eh/		ܝܗܝ, ܘܗܝ and ܗܝ	/y/
f	ܗ /āh/			ܗ /h/
pl. 1	ܢ /an/			ܢ /n/
2 m		ܟܘܢ /ḵon/		
f		ܟܝܢ /ḵen/		
3 m	The enclitics ܐܢܘܢ and ܐܢܝܢ are used (§10).			

§13* *Demonstrative Pronouns* (Nöldeke, §67)

a) For what is nearer: "this, these":

sg.m.	ܗܳܢܳܐ (rarely ܗܳܢ)	/hānā/
f.	ܗܳܕܶܐ	/hāḏe/
pl.c.	ܗܳܠܶܝܢ	/hāllen/

In conjunction with the enclitic ܗܝ (f. sg.), ܗܳܕܶܐ changes to ܗܝ ܗܳܕܳܐ /hāḏāy/.

34 With two of the prepositions, it *is* pronounced: ܒܝ /bi/ "in me" and ܠܝ /li/ "to me", but not in ܕܝܠܝ /dil/ "my, mine".

35 E.g. ܐܒܘܟ /'avuḵ/ "your father".

36 On these, more later: §56.

b) For what is more distant: "that, those":

sg.m.	ܗܰܘ /*haw*/	pl.m.	ܗܳܢܽܘܢ /*hānnon*/
f.	ܗܳܝ /*hāy*/	f.	ܗܳܢܶܝܢ /*hānnen*/

§ 14* *Interrogatives* (Nöldeke, § 68)

"who?": ܡܰܢ
"what?": ܡܳܢܳܐ[37] (less commonly: ܡܳܢ, ܡܽܘܢ, ܡܳܐ)[38]
"which, what?": m. sg. ܐܰܝܢܳܐ /*'aynā*/, f. ܐܰܝܕܳܐ /*'aydā*/, pl. ܐܰܝܠܶܝܢ /*'aylen*/
"where?": ܐܰܝܟܳܐ /*'aykā*/
"when?": ܐܶܡܰܬܝ /*'emmat*/
"why?": ܠܡܳܢܳܐ /*lmānā*/
"how?": ܐܰܝܟܰܢܳܐ /*'aykannā*/ (less commonly ܐܰܝܟܰܢ)
"how much?": ܟܡܳܐ /*kmā*/

Most of these can be followed by an enclitic as in ܡܰܢܽܘ , ܡܰܢ ܗܽܘ /*manu*/ "who is he?, who is it that ...?"; ܐܰܝܟܰܘ /*'aykaw*/ "where is he?, where is it that ...?," etc.

§ 15* The *relative pronoun* is ܕ . For its pronunciation, see § 7G and I.

§ 16 A series of *independent possessive pronouns* is formed by combining the relative ܕ in its primitive form (ܕܝ) with the preposition ܠ and the appropriate pronoun suffix: ܕܺܝܠܝ /*dil*/ "my", ܕܺܝܠܳܟ /*dilāk*/ "your (m. sg.)", ܕܺܝܠܗܽܘܢ /*dilhon*/ "their (m.)" etc. For their use, see below: § 87.

§ 17* *Declension of Nouns and Adjectives* (Nöldeke, § 70-91)

The declensional categories of Syriac nouns and adjectives are roughly the same as those for Hebrew, namely, two genders, two numbers[39], but three *states*. In addition to the basic form called status absolutus and st. construc-

37 Also adjectivally: ܡܳܢܳܐ ܒܰܝܬܳܐ "what house?, what sort of house?".

38 For distributional differences between /*mā*/ and /*mānā*/, see Nöldeke, § 232.

39 The dual is virtually extinct, preserved only in the numerals "two" m. ܬܪܶܝܢ /*tren*/, f. ܬܰܪܬܶܝܢ /*tarten*/, and ܡܳܐܬܶܝܢ /*maten*/ "two hundred".

tus, Syriac possesses a third form known as *emphaticus* (or: *determinatus*), which in Classical Aramaic was equivalent to the form of a noun with the proclitic definite article in Hebrew.

Since a grammatically feminine noun can, as in Hebrew, lack a specifically feminine ending and conversely a masculine plural noun may not be marked as such, we illustrate below the declension of Syriac nouns by using an adjective, which does not present such ambiguity. The endings are as follows:

	sg.			pl.		
	st. abs.	cst.	emph.	abs.	cst.	emph.
m.	—	—	*/-ā/*	*/-in/*	*/-ay/*	*/-e/*
f.	*/-ā/*	*/-at̲/*	*/-tā/* or */-t̲ā/*	*/-ān/*	*/-āt̲/*	*/-āt̲ā/*

Apllied to the adjective ܒܝܫ */biš/* "evil":

	sg.			pl.		
	st. abs.	cst.	emph.	abs.	cst.	emph.
m.	ܒܝܫ */biš/*	ܒܝܫ */biš/*	ܒܝܫܐ */bišā/*	ܒܝܫܝܢ */bišin/*	ܒܝܫܝ */bišay/*	ܒ̈ܝܫܐ */biše/*
f.	ܒܝܫܐ */bišā/*	ܒܝܫܬ */bišat̲/*	ܒܝܫܬܐ */bištā/*	ܒ̈ܝܫܢ */bišān/*	ܒ̈ܝܫܬ */bišāt̲/*	ܒ̈ܝܫܬܐ */bišāt̲ā/*

§ 18 The st. abs. and cst. are rather infrequently used. The normal form of any given noun is that of the st. emph. Hence the citation form of a Syriac noun is normally that of the st. emph. sg., although older dictionaries such as those of Payne Smith use the st. abs. form.

§ 19 The st. emph. morpheme is invariably */-ā/* except in the m. pl. and, with some exceptions, its form is derived from the st. cst. form by application of the vowel deletion rule, if appropriate. Thus */bišat̲/* + */-ā/* ⟶ **/bišat̲ā/* ⟶ */bištā/*; pl. */bišāt̲/* + */-ā/* ⟶ */bišāt̲ā/*.

§ 20 Whether the sg. f. emph. ending is to be pronounced */tā/* or */t̲ā/* is an extremely complicated question. See a discussion in Nöldeke, § 23E.

§ 21 A limited number of nouns and certain classes of adjective have their pl. m. emph. forms ending in the archaic */-ayyā/* as in ܫ̈ܢܝܐ */šnayyā/* "years"; ܒ̈ܢܝܐ */bnayyā/* "sons"; ܩ̈ܫܝܐ */qšayyā/* from ܩܫܐ */qše/* "hard".

§ 22 Some nouns and adjectives add /-y/ to form the feminine bases: ܙܥܘܪ /zʿor/ "small" — f. sg. abs. ܙܥܘܪܝܐ, cst. ܙܥܘܪܝܬ (but emph. ܙܥܘܪܬܐ), pl. ܙܥܘܪܝܢ etc.; ܡܣܟܢ /meskēn/ "poor", ܡܣܟܝܢܝܐ, ܡܣܟܢܝܢ, ܡܣܟܝܢܝܬܐ.
See Nöldeke, § 71, and cp. BA אָחֳרָי, אֵימְתָנִי.

§ 23 Nouns (and adjectives) with /y/ or /w/ as their third etymological radical are declined as follows.

sg. abs.	ܬܫܥܝ	"story"	ܡܠܟܘ	*"kingdom"*
cst.	ܬܫܥܝܬ		ܡܠܟܘܬ	
emph.	ܬܫܥܝܬܐ		ܡܠܟܘܬܐ	
pl. abs.	ܬܫܥܝܢ		ܡܠܟܘܢ	
cst.	ܬܫܥܝܬ		ܡܠܟܘܬ	
emph.	ܬܫܥܝܬܐ		ܡܠܟܘܬܐ	

In other words, /y/ and /w/ are restored in the plural to their original consonantal value.

§ 24 The expansion of the plural base by means of the added /w/ is also observable in other types of noun: ܐܪܝܐ "lion" — ܐܪܝܘܬܐ; ܟܘܪܣܝܐ "throne" — ܟܘܪܣܘܬܐ; ܠܠܝܐ "night" — ܠܠܝܘܬܐ; ܐܬܪܐ "place" — ܐܬܪܘܬܐ; ܢܗܪܐ "river" — ܢܗܪܘܬܐ; ܣܦܬܐ "lip" — ܣܦܘܬܐ.
A fuller treatment of this type of noun may be found in Nöldeke, § 75-79.

§ 25 A detailed description of various patterns of the Syriac noun and adjective may be found in Nöldeke, § 92-140.

§ 26 *Attachment of the Possessive Suffix Pronouns*

The suffix pronouns given in § 11, when attached to a m. pl. noun, undergo some modifications. It is convenient to think that there are two sets of suffix possessive pronouns. The first set is what was given in § 11, and is used with singular nouns, whether masculine or feminine, *and* feminine plural nouns.
The second set, used with masculine plural nouns, is as follows:

sg. 1	ـܝ	/ay/	pl.	ـܝܢ	/ayn/
2 m	ـܝܟ	/ayk/		ـܝܟܘܢ	/aykon/
f	ـܝܟܝ	/ayk/		ـܝܟܝܢ	/ayken/

3 m	ܘܗܝ	/*aw*/	ܝܗܘܢ	/*ayhon*/
f	ܗ	/*eh*/	ܝܗܝܢ	/*ayhen*/

N.B. 1. The Yodh for 1 sg. *is* pronounced.

2. The Kaf for 2 m. and 2 f., both sg. and pl., is pronounced hard, in contrast to the other set. See § 7D.

3. Note the peculiar form for the 3 m.sg. "his".

4. "his" with a singular noun and a pl.f. noun on the one hand and "her" with a m.pl. noun sound the same, though the latter has a Yodh before the final He: e.g., ܡܠܬܗ /*mellteh*/ "his word" vs. ܡܠܝܗ /*melleh*/ "her words".

5. It is of utmost importance to remember that 'masculine' and 'feminine' in this context refer to the typical endings (*form*) associated with each of the two genders. A considerable number of nouns which are *grammatically* feminine, i.e. are treated as such in terms of the choice of verb, numeral, demonstrative pronoun etc., are not *formally* marked as such in the singular (e.g., f. sg. abs. ܐܪܥ, emph. ܐܪܥܐ "earth"), and there are also nouns whose plural form does not reveal their grammatical gender (e.g., f. pl. abs. ܡܠܝܢ, emph. ܡܠܐ "words"; m. pl. abs. ܐܒܗܢ, emph. ܐܒܗܬܐ "fathers"). As far as the attachement of the suffix pronouns is concerned, the first set must be applied to ܐܪܥ and ܐܒܗܢ, and the second set to ܡܠܝܢ. Thus ܐܪܥܗ "his land" and ܐܒܗܬܗ "his forefathers" but ܡܠܘܗܝ "his words".

§ 27* Here are the possessive pronouns as applied to the noun ܕܝܢܐ "judgement".

sg. noun ("my judgement", "your judgement" etc.)

ܕܝܢܝ	/*din*/	my
ܕܝܢܟ	/*dinā<u>k</u>*/	your (m. sg.)
ܕܝܢܟܝ	/*dine<u>k</u>*/	your (f. sg.)
ܕܝܢܗ	/*dineh*/	his
ܕܝܢܗ	/*dināh*/	her
ܕܝܢܢ	/*dinan*/	our
ܕܝܢܟܘܢ	/*din<u>k</u>on*/	your (m. pl.)
ܕܝܢܟܝܢ	/*din<u>k</u>en*/	your (f. pl.)
ܕܝܢܗܘܢ	/*dinhon*/	their (m.)
ܕܝܢܗܝܢ	/*dinhen*/	their (f.)

pl. noun ("my judgements", "your judgements" etc.)

ܕܝܢܝ	/*dinay*/	my
ܕܝܢܝܟ	/*dinayk*/	your (m. sg.)

ܕܺܝܢܰܝܟܝ	/*dinayk*/	your (f. sg.)
ܕܺܝܢܰܘܗܝ	/*dinaw*/	his
ܕܺܝܢܶܗ	/*dineh*/	her
ܕܺܝܢܰܝܢ	/*dinayn*/	our
ܕܺܝܢܰܝܟܽܘܢ	/*dinaykon*/	your (m. pl.)
ܕܺܝܢܰܝܟܶܝܢ	/*dinayken*/	your (f. pl.)
ܕܺܝܢܰܝܗܽܘܢ	/*dinayhon*/	their (m.)
ܕܺܝܢܰܝܗܶܝܢ	/*dinayhen*/	their (f.)

§28 The suffix pronouns are attached[40] to the base of a noun which can be obtained by dropping the st. emph. morpheme /*ā*/ or /*e*/.

1) Plural noun: attach the appropriate pronoun directly to the base.

E.g. ܡ̈ܶܠܶܐ "words"; ܡ̈ܶܠܰܝ /*mellay*/ "my words"
ܢܰܦ̈ܫܳܬܳܐ "souls"; ܢܰܦ̈ܫܳܬܗܽܘܢ /*nafšāṯhon*/ "their souls"
ܫܡܳܗ̈ܳܬܳܐ "names"; ܫܡܳܗ̈ܳܬܟܽܘܢ /*šmāhāṯkon*/ "your (pl.) names"

2) Singular noun

a. If the base ends in -C$\bar{V}$C[41], -CVCC or -CV$\breve{C}$[42], attach the suffix pronoun to it.

E.g. ܪܺܫܳܐ	/*rēšā*/:	ܪܺܫܶܗ	/*rēšeh*/	"his head"
ܠܒܽܘܫܳܐ	/*lvušā*/:	ܠܒܽܘܫܝ	/*lvuš*/	"my garment"
ܟܶܣܦܳܐ	/*kespā*/:	ܟܶܣܦܰܢ	/*kespan*/	"our silver"
ܠܶܒܳܐ	/*lebbā*/:	ܠܶܒܶܟܝ	/*lebbeḵ*/	"your (f. sg.) heart"

Here the feminine morpheme /*t*/ counts as final C. Thus

ܩܪܺܝܬܳܐ	/*qriṯā*/:	ܩܪܺܝܬܳܟ	/*qriṯāḵ*/	"your (m. sg.) field"
ܬܰܘܕܺܝܬܳܐ	/*tawdiṯā*/:	ܬܰܘܕܺܝܬܰܢ	/*tawdiṯan*/	"our praising"[43]
ܝܳܠܶܕܬܳܐ	/*yāledṯā*/:	ܝܳܠܶܕܬܶܗ	/*yāledṯeh*/	"his mother"

40 For further details and some exceptions, see Nöldeke, § 145.

41 $\bar{V}$ signifies one of the vowels /*ā, ē, i, u, o*/, that is, all vowels other than /*a, e*/.

42 $\breve{C}$ signifies the gemination of a consonant. However, whether the consonant is doubled or not is not always apparent. See above (§ 7A end). In a case like ܠܶܒܳܐ, the vowel deletion rule coupled with the *quššaya* of the Beth would enable one to identify the root as L-B-B. Comparison with Heb. (לִבִּי/לֵב) also helps. In contrast, the knowledge of Heb. אֵם with its אִמִּי etc. alone can settle the case of ܐܶܡܳܐ "mother".

43 Root: Y-D-Y. Cf. Heb. /*tōdā*/.

b. If the stem ends in -CCC or -CC, either /*a*/ or /*e*/ — invariably /*a*/ if the final C is the feminine morpheme /*t*/ — must be inserted[44] between the last two consonants before the suffix of the 1st. sg., 2nd or 3rd pl. is attached. Thus

ܡܰܠܟܬܳܐ /*malkṯā*/: ܡܰܠܟܬܳܗ /*malkṯāh*/ "her queen", but
ܡܰܠܟܰܬܗܽܘܢ /*malkaṯhon*/ "their (m.) queen"

ܚܰܘܒܬܳܐ /*ḥawbṯā*/: ܚܰܘܒܬܰܢ /*ḥawbṯan*/ "our debt", but
ܚܰܘܒܰܬܝ /*ḥawbaṯ*/ "my debt"[45]

ܡܰܣܒܳܐ /*massvā*/[46]: ܡܰܣܒܳܗ /*massvā*/ "her taking", but
ܡܰܣܰܒܟܽܘܢ /*massavḵon*/ "your (m. pl.) taking"

ܓܰܢܬܳܐ /*ganntā*/: ܓܰܢܬܶܗ /*gannṯeh*/ "his garden", but
ܓܰܢܰܬܗܽܘܢ /*gannaṯhon*/ "their garden"

ܕܽܘܟܬܳܐ /*dukkṯā*/: ܕܽܘܟܬܳܟ /*dukkṯāḵ*/ "your (m. sg.) place" but
ܕܽܘܟܰܬܝ /*dukkaṯ*/ "my place".

c. The vowel insertion as detailed in the preceding paragraph is due to the development of a cluster of three consonants at the end of a base; or alternatively, the cluster is of two consonants if we regard the first consonant as forming a syllable together with the preceding vowel. A number of monosyllabic nouns with the delectable vowel /*a*/ or /*e*/ lend themselves to such a description.

ܫܡܳܐ /*šmā*/: ܫܡܶܗ /*šmeh*/ "his name", but ܫܶܡܝ /*šem*/ "my name"

ܕܡܳܐ /*dmā*/: ܕܡܳܗ /*dmāh*/ "her blood", but ܕܶܡܗܽܘܢ /*demhon*/ "their blood"

ܒܪܳܐ /*brā*/: ܒܪܰܢ /*bran*/ "our son", but ܒܶܪܝ /*ber*/ "my son"[47]

ܙܢܳܐ /*znā*/: ܙܢܶܗ /*zneh*/ "his kind", but ܙܰܢܟܽܘܢ /*zanḵon*/ "your kind".

§29 There is another large group of nouns which are also subject to the vowel deletion rule. They may be conveniently considered under two sub-groups.

44 Rather 'restored', etymologically speaking.
45 It will be seen that /*w*/ of /*aw*/ and /*y*/ of /*ay*/ count as consonants.
46 Root: N-S-B "take" with the assimilation of Nun.
47 But the sg.abs. and cst. is ܒܰܪ.

A) Nouns with two deletable vowels whose underlying pattern is CV̆CV̆C[48]. In the sg. st. abs. and cst. forms they take the shape CCV̆C, whilst in all other forms, including those with the suffixed personal pronoun, they show the shape CVCC-. Examples:

ܓܡܠ /gmal/: ܓܡܠܐ, ܓܡܠܝ /gaml/ "my camel", pl. ܓܡ̈ܠܐ

ܣܒܪ /svar/: ܣܒܪܐ, ܣܒܪܢ /savran/ "our hope"

ܕܗܒ /dhav/: ܕܗܒܐ /dahvā/, ܕܗܒܟ /dahvāk/ "your gold"

ܐܪܥ /'ara'/: ܐܪܥܐ /'ar'ā/, ܐܪܥܗ /'ar'eh/ "his earth", pl. ܐܪ̈ܥܬܐ

ܡܠܟ /mlek/: ܡܠܟܐ /malkā/, pl. cst. ܡܠ̈ܟܝ /malkay/, ܡܠ̈ܟܝܢ /malkayn/ "our kings"

ܟܬܦ /ktef/: ܟܬܦܐ /katpā/, ܟܬܦܗ /katpāh/ "her shoulder"

ܢܦܫ /nfeš/: ܢܦܫܐ /nafšā/, ܢܦܫܗ /nafšeh/ "his soul", pl. ܢܦ̈ܫܬܐ

ܟܣܦ /ksef/: ܟܣܦܐ /kespā/, ܟܣܦܟܘܢ /kespkon/ "your silver"

ܪܓܠ /rgel/: ܪܓܠܐ /regl/ ܪܓܠܝ /regl/ "my foot"

ܩܕܘܫ /qdoš/: ܩܘܕܫܐ /qudšā/, ܩܘܕܫܗ /qudšeh/ "his holiness"[49]

Whether a Beghadhkephath as the third root sound is to be pronounced soft or hard is unpredictable. Etymology is not always a sure guide.

B) Nouns of the underlying type CV̄CV̆C or CVCCV̆C in which the first vowel is not deletable, but the second is. Here the unsuffixed form is identical with the underlying pattern, whilst all remaining forms show the base CV̄CC- or CVCCC-. Examples:

ܥܠܡ /'ālam/ "eternity": sg. emph. ܥܠܡܐ, pl. abs. ܥܠܡܝܢ

ܣܠܩ /sāleq/ "ascending": f. sg. abs. ܣܠܩܐ, pl. f. abs. ܣܠܩܢ

ܡܫܟܚ /meškaḥ/ "finding": f. sg. abs. ܡܫܟܚܐ, pl. m. abs. ܡܫܟܚܝܢ

ܡܫܟܢ /maškan/ "tent": sg. emph. ܡܫܟܢܐ; ܡܫܟܢܗ "his tent".

One may include here nouns such as ܝܠܕܐ /yāldā/ "mother" and ܢܫܡܐ /nešmā/ "soul", but here the sg. emph. shows the second short vowel, whilst in all other forms it is deleted. Thus

48 V̆ = "short", i.e. deletable vowel.

49 The student will recognise some nouns listed here as equivalent to Hebrew segholates, but he will also see that the stem vowel of a given Syriac "segholate" does not always agree with that of its Hebrew analogue: so ܪܓܠܐ // רֶגֶל with its רַגְלוֹ.

ܡܰܠܟܬܳܐ vs. ܡܰܠܟܳܐ, ܡܰܠܶܟ

ܢܥܡܬܐ vs. ܢܥܡܐ, ܢܥ̈ܡܬܐ

ܡܟܝܟܬܐ "low" vs. ܡܟܝ̈ܟܬܐ etc.

It will be seen that in all nouns treated in this paragraph (§ 29) one needs to know both the sg. abs. and emph. forms in order to be able to decline them fully. In particular, in nouns with two deletable vowels (CV̆CV̆C type like ܕܗܒܐ) none of the actual manifestations of them shows both vowels: one needs to know both ܕܗܒ and ܕܗܒܐ, for since neither vowel is predictable; the forms *ܕܗܒ and * ܕܗܒܐ are, in theory, both possible.

§ 30 *List of Important Irregular Nouns* (Nöldeke, § 146)

		cst.	sg. w. suf.	pl.
father	ܐܒܐ	?	ܐܒܝ ܐܒܘܟ ܐܒܘܗܝ etc.	ܐܒܗ̈ܬܐ / ܐܒ̈ܗܐ
brother	ܐܚܐ	?	ܐܚܝ ܐܚܘܟ ܐܚܘܗܝ etc.	ܐܚ̈ܐ
sister	ܚܬܐ	?	ܚܬܝ ܚܬܟ etc.	ܐܚ̈ܘܬܐ
other m.	ܐܚܪܢܐ	ܐܚܪܝܢ	ܐܚܪܢܢ ܐܚܪܢܟ etc.	ܐܚܪ̈ܢܐ
f.	ܐܚܪܢܬܐ	ܐܚܪܢܝܬ	ܐܚܪܢܬܝ ܐܚܪܢܬܟ etc.	ܐܚܪ̈ܢܝܬܐ
woman	ܐܢܬܬܐ /'attā/	ܐܢܬܬ	ܐܢܬܬܝ ܐܢܬܬܗ etc.	ܢܫ̈ܐ
son	ܒܪܐ	ܒܪ	ܒܪܝ ܒܪܟ ܒܪܟܘܢ etc.	ܒܢ̈ܝܐ
daughter	ܒܪܬܐ	ܒܪܬ	ܒܪܬܝ ܒܪܬܟ ܒܪܬܟܘܢ etc.	ܒܢ̈ܬܐ
house	ܒܝܬܐ	ܒܝܬ	ܒܝܬܝ ܒܝܬܟ etc.	ܒ̈ܬܐ
hand	ܐܝܕܐ	ܐܝܕ / ܝܕ[50]	ܐܝܕܝ ܐܝܕܟ etc.	ܐܝ̈ܕܝܐ / ܐܝ̈ܕܬܐ
night	ܠܠܝܐ	?	?	ܠܠܘ̈ܬܐ
lord	ܡܪܝܐ / ܡܪܐ[51]	ܡܪܐ	ܡܪܝ ܡܪܗ etc.	ܡܪ̈ܘܢ
field	ܚܩܠܬܐ	ܚܩܠ ܚܩܘܠ	ܚܩܠܝ ܚܩܠܟ etc.	ܚܩ̈ܠܐ
year	ܫܢܬܐ	ܫܢܬ	?	ܫ̈ܢܐ

50 /yaḏ/ in prepositional phrases like ܒܝܕ /byaḏ/; /'iḏ/ "hand of".

51 /māryā/ of the God of Israel and Christ.

§ 31 *Numerals* (Nöldeke, § 148-54)

A) *Cardinals*

	m.	f.		m.	f.
1	ܚܰܕ	ܚܕܳܐ	2		ܬܰܪ̈ܬܶܝܢ
3	ܬܠܳܬܳܐ	ܬܠܳܬ	4	ܐܰܪܒܥܳܐ	ܐܰܪܒܰܥ
5	ܚܰܡܫܳܐ	ܚܰܡܶܫ	6	ܐܶܫܬܳܐ / ܫܬܳܐ	ܫܶܬ
7	ܫܰܒܥܳܐ	ܫܒܰܥ	8	ܬܡܳܢܝܳܐ	ܬܡܳܢܶܐ
9	ܬܶܫܥܳܐ	ܬܫܰܥ	10	ܥܶܣܪܳܐ	ܥܣܰܪ

11 *m.* ܚܕܰܥܣܰܪ
f. ܚܕܰܥܶܣܪܶܐ , ܚܕܰܥܣܪܶܐ
12 m. ܬܪܶܥܣܰܪ
f. ܬܪܬܰܥܣܪܶܐ , ܬܪܬܰܥܶܣܪܶܐ
13 m. ܬܠܳܬܰܥܣܰܪ
f. ܬܠܳܬܰܥܣܪܶܐ , ܬܠܳܬܰܥܶܣܪܶܐ
14 m. ܐܰܪܒܰܬܰܥܣܰܪ, ܐܰܪܒܰܥܣܰܪ, ܐܰܪܒܰܥܬܰܥܣܰܪ
f. ܐܰܪܒܰܥܣܪܶܐ (ܐܰܪܒܰܥܶܣܪܶܐ, ܐܰܪܒܰܥܬܰܥܣܪܶܐ)
15 m. ܚܰܡܫܰܥܣܰܪ, ܚܰܡܶܫܬܰܥܣܰܪ
f. ܚܰܡܫܰܥܣܪܶܐ, ܚܰܡܫܰܥܶܣܪܶܐ
16 m. ES ܫܬܬܰܥܣܰܪ, ܫܬܬܰܥܣܰܪ WS ܫܬܬܰܥܣܰܪ
f. ES ܫܬܬܰܥܣܪܶܐ, ܫܬܬܰܥܶܣܪܶܐ WS ܫܬܬܰܥܣܪܶܐ
17 m. ܫܒܰܥܬܰܥܣܰܪ, ܫܒܰܥܬܰܥܣܰܪ (ܫܒܰܥܣܰܪ)
f. ܫܒܰܥܣܪܶܐ (ܫܒܰܥܶܣܪܶܐ , ܫܒܰܥܬܰܥܣܪܶܐ)
18 m. ܬܡܳܢܬܰܥܣܰܪ (ܬܡܳܢܰܥܣܰܪ)
f. ܬܡܳܢܰܥܣܪܶܐ, ܬܡܳܢܰܥܶܣܪܶܐ
19 m. ܬܫܰܥܬܰܥܣܰܪ, ܬܫܰܥܬܰܥܣܰܪ (ܬܫܰܥܣܰܪ)
f. ܬܫܰܥܣܪܶܐ, ܬܫܰܥܶܣܪܶܐ

20	ܥܣܪܝܢ	60	ܫܬܝܢ ܐܫܬܝܢ
30	ܬܠܬܝܢ	70	ܫܒܥܝܢ
40	ܐܪܒܥܝܢ	80	ܬܡܢܝܢ (also spelled ܬܡܐܢܝܢ)
50	ܚܡܫܝܢ	90	ܬܫܥܝܢ
100	ܡܐܐ 200 ܡܐܬܝܢ	300	ܬܠܬܡܐܐ
1000	ܐܠܦ (pl. ܐܠܦܝܢ)		

A composite number displays the descending order as in English: thus 7377 = ܫܒܥܐ ܐܠܦܝܢ ܘܬܠܬܡܐܐ ܘܫܒܥܝܢ ܘܫܒܥܐ.

B) *Ordinals*

1st	ܩܕܡܝܐ, also ܩܕܡܝܐ, st. abs. ܩܕܡ	6th	ܫܬܝܬܝܐ (WS ܫܬܝܬܝܐ)
2nd	ܬܪܝܢܐ f. ܬܪܝܢܝܬܐ	7th	ܫܒܝܥܝܐ
	also ܬܢܝܢܐ f. ܬܢܝܢܬܐ		
3rd	ܬܠܝܬܝܐ	8th	ܬܡܝܢܝܐ
4th	ܪܒܝܥܝܐ	9th	ܬܫܝܥܝܐ
5th	ܚܡܝܫܝܐ	10th	ܥܣܝܪܝܐ

Alternatively, Syriac also has a structure such as ܕܬܪܝܢ as in ܐܝܘܒ ܕܬܪܝܢ "the second Job". Apparently the two structures are free variants: see Gn 2.13 ܢܗܪܐ ... ܬܢܝܢܐ 14 ܢܗܪܐ ܕܬܠܝܬܝܐ. Cf. also ib. 41.5 ܕܬܪܬܝܢ ܙܒܢܝܢ "for a second time".

§ 32* Like some Hebrew prepositions, the following Syriac *prepositions*, when followed by pronouns, take those of the second set as given in § 26 above.
ܥܠ; e.g., ܥܠܘܗܝ "upon him/it", ܥܠܝܗܘܢ "upon them" etc.

ܬܚܝܬ "under"; ܠܘܬ "with, towards"; ܩܕܡ "before in the presence of"; ܚܠܦ "instead of"; ܒܠܥܕ "without".

The following three are subject to the vowel deletion rule:

ܒܣܬܪ "behind": ܒܣܬܪ, ܒܣܬܪܟ, ܒܣܬܪܗܘܢ etc.

ܒܬܪ "after": ܒܬܪ, ܒܬܪܗ, ܒܬܪܗܘܢ etc.

ܠܘܩܒܠ "against, opposite": ܠܘܩܒܠܗ, ܠܘܩܒܠܟ, but ܠܘܩܒܠܝܗܘܢ etc.

Verb

§ 33* The inflection of the Syriac verb is, in its basic structure, virtually analogous to that of the Hebrew, the only noteworthy difference consisting in verb patterns, conjugations, or *binyanim*, as shown in the comparative table below.

Syriac		Hebrew	
P'al	Ethpᶜel	Qal	
Paᶜᶜel	Ethpaᶜᶜal	Piᶜᶜel(-Puᶜᶜal)	Hithpaᶜᶜel
Afᶜel	Ettafᶜal [52]	Hifᶜil(-Hufᶜal)	
		Nifᶜal	

A) It is immediately apparent that Syriac, compared with Hebrew, presents a much neater and more symmetrical scheme than Hebrew, since each of the three non-prefixed patterns has a corresponding *eth-* prefixed, so-called reflexive pattern.

B) The internal passive, Pual and Hufal of Hebrew, has been preserved only in the participle of Pael and Afel contrasting with its active counterpart by virtue of an *Ablaut* [53] as in Hebrew: e.g.,
Passive

Pael:	Active	ܡܩܰܒܶܠ	"receiving"
	Passive	ܡܩܰܒܰܠ	"received"
Afel:	Active	ܡܰܥܡܶܕ.	"baptising"
	Passive	ܡܰܥܡܰܕ.	"baptised"

The Syriac passive participle of Peal is as distinct from the active participle as its Hebrew counterpart is:

Act.	ܩܳܛܶܠ	קֹטֵל
Pass.	ܩܛܺܝܠ	קָטוּל

C) The meanings or functions of the different patterns in Syriac in relation to one another are just as fully or little known as in Hebrew. Note however the comparative table above. The *eth*-prefixed patterns are often passive, reflexive or ingressive, i.e. signifying entry into a new state or acquisition of a new property or characteristic.

52 Partly in accordance with the widespread practice and partly for simplicity's sake, we shall hereafter refer to these patterns as Pe(al), Pa(el), Af(el), Ethpe(el), Ethpa(al), and Ettaf(al).

53 A German word meaning a change in inflectional categories marked by a vowel change.

D) The inflection of verbs with four or more root consonants follows exactly the pattern of Pael and its corresponding Ethpaal. Thus

ܫܥܒܕ.	"to enslave";	ܐܫܬܥܒܕ.	"to be enslaved" [54]
ܒܠܒܠ	"to confuse";	ܐܬܒܠܒܠ	"to get confused"
ܬܠܡܕ.	"to teach"	ܐܬܬܠܡܕ.	"to be taught"
ܥܪܓܠ	"to roll (tr.)"	ܐܬܥܪܓܠ	"to roll (intr.)".

§ 34 Ettafal is of rather rare occurrence. Not a few Afel verbs show their *eth*-pattern as Ethpe or Ethpa: e.g. ܐܟܪܙ "to preach, proclaim" vs. ܐܬܟܪܙ "to be preached"; ܐܗܠ "to mock" vs. ܐܬܗܠܠ "to be mocked"; ܐܫܟܚ "to find" [55] vs. ܐܫܬܟܚ "to be found" [56].

In Biblical Aramaic Šafel appears to be extraneous to the system of verb conjugation patterns, being virtually confined to those verbs which happen to have Šafel counterparts in Akkadian. Syriac, however, makes a more productive use of the pattern: ܫܡܠܝ "to fulfil", ܫܘܕܥ "to announce", ܫܘܫܛ "to lead", ܫܥܒܕ "to enslave", ܐܫܬܘܕܝ "to promise".

§ 35 Where an internal passive participle (§ 33B above) and its corresponding *eth*-passive are attested side by side, the former emphasises a result, the latter a process: ܒܢܐ "built (i.e. the building is complete)" vs. ܡܬܒܢܐ "under construction".

The passive participle of Peal also underlines a result or state; this is particularly true of intransitive verbs: e.g. Gn 29.2 ܪܒܝܥ "lying, crouching" [57].

§ 36* The following *inflectional affixes* are applicable irrespective of pattern and inflexional class with the exception of Third-Yodh verbs, which, as we shall see later, require some modification as in Hebrew. See Nöldeke, § 158.

54 With the characteristic metathesis due to the sibilant /š/, as in Hebrew.

55 With an atypical change of the initial /'a/ to /'e/.

56 For * ܐܫܬܟܚ (§ 7B).

57 See an example cited in Nöldeke, § 278A: ܠܐ ܚܬܝܡܢ ܡܠܐ ܗܠܝܢ ... ܘܠܐ ܡܬܚܬܡܢ "these words are not yet sealed ... and are not to be sealed".

Perfect

sg. 3 m	–		pl.	ܘ	(silent) [; –, ܘܢ]
f	ܬ	/*at*/		–	[; ܝ (silent); ܝܢ]
2 m	ܬ	/*t*/		ܬܘܢ	/*ton*/
f	ܬܝ	/*t*/		ܬܝܢ	/*ten*/
1	ܬ	/*et*/		ܢ	/*n*/ [; ܢܢ /*nan*/]

Imperfect

sg. 3 m	ܢ	pl.	ܢ . . . ܘܢ
f	ܬ		ܢ . . . ܢ
2 m	ܬ		ܬ . . . ܘܢ
f	ܬ . . . ܝܢ		ܬ . . . ܢ
1	ܐ		ܢ

Imperative

sg. m	–	pl.	ܘ	(silent) [; ܘܢ]
f	ܝ		ܝܢ	; ܝ (silent)

Participle

sg. m	–	pl.	ܝܢ
f	ܐ		ܢ

N.B.: The /*n*/ of the Impf. 3 m. sg. and 3 pl. prefix is highly characteristic, one of the hallmarks of Eastern Aramaic.

Note that the shorter forms, which are the more primitive, for Perf. 3 m. and f. pl. are phonetically identical with each other as well as with that for the 3 m.sg., and also that the forms for Perf. 2 m. and f. sg. are phonetically identical. In the Imperative, one form with no suffix can serve for all the four categories [58].

§ 37* Study the *Infinitive* forms in Paradigm I, noting that, unlike in Hebrew, the preposition Lamadh is invariably prefixed except on rare occasions when the same form is used in the manner of the Hebrew infinitive absolute [59], and also that the forms for the "derived" patterns, i.e. patterns other than Peal, share the feature /*-ā-u*/.

58 The suffixation of the object pronouns has preserved the primitive distinction: see below § 56.

59 But note also a case like Gn 19.33 ܒܡܕܡܟܗ̇ ܘܒܡܩܡܗ̇.

§38 In addition to the participle, which like its Hebrew counterpart can also be used as a noun signifying an actor, a person habitually performing the action denoted by the verb, Syriac possesses for each pattern a category known as *nomen agentis* "actor noun". In Peal the form is ܦܳܥܽܘܠ, whereas in the remaining patterns the form can be derived by adding the suffix /*-ān*/ to the m. sg. participle concerned: e.g. ܡܩܰܒܠܳܢ "one who receives" from ܡܩܰܒܶܠ (with vowel deletion); ܡܒܰܪܟ݂ܳܢ "one who blesses" from ܡܒܰܪܶܟ݂; Af. ܡܰܚܛܝܳܢ "one who sins" from ܡܰܚܛܶܐ.

By extension, *nomen agentis* may also be used adjectivally, verbal adjectives, as in ܡܶܬ݂ܚܙܝܳܢ "visible"; Aphr. I 101.4 ܕܳܪܳܐ ܡܚܰܒܠܳܢܳܐ "a corrupt (lit. corrupting) generation"; ib. I 156.5 ܦܽܘܡܳܐ ܐܳܟ݂ܽܘܠܳܐ "a voracious mouth"; Josh St. 4.2 ܨܠܰܘܳܬ݂ܳܟ݂ ܡܦܰܨܝܳܢܝܳܬ݂ܳܐ "your saving prayers". Some dictionaries (e.g. Brockelmann) do not always list *nomina agentis* as separate entries.

§39* In comparison with Hebrew, the conjugation of the Syriac verb in the derived patterns is simple in that the vowel sequence is constant and unchanged throughout a given pattern, which is true of the Pf., Impf., Impv., and Ptc. (Active)[60]. Thus, the principal forms of the causative (Afel) of ܠܒܫ "to clothe" are: Pf. ܐܰܠܒܶܫ, Impf. ܢܰܠܒܶܫ Impv. ܐܰܠܒܶܫ, Ptc. ܡܰܠܒܶܫ.

In contrast, the corresponding Hebrew forms are: הִלְבִּישׁ, יַלְבִּישׁ, הַלְבֵּשׁ, מַלְבִּישׁ. Even the infinitive and the nomen agentis display basically the same pattern: ܠܡܰܠܒܳܫܽܘ, ܡܰܠܒܫܳܢ.

§40 Syriac has lost the special modal forms such as the jussive (יָקֹם) and cohortative (אָקוּמָה) of Hebrew, although we can identify traces of the primitive distinction. Thus Pe. Impv. f. sg. ܦܽܘܩܽܘܕܝ with the medial vowel preserved is to be contrasted with the corresponding Impf. 2 f. sg. ܬܶܦܩܕܺܝܢ with the vowel deletion, which is to be compared with the situation still prevailing in Biblical Aramaic יֵאבַדוּ vs. יְהוֹבְדוּן[61]. One can similarly account for the retention of the vowel before the third radical as in ܫܡܰܥܰܝܢܝ "hear me" (Impv. m. sg.), ܢܰܛܰܪܶܝܗ "observe her" (Pael Impv. m. sg.)[62] and

60 On the passive participle, see above, §33B.

61 See my observation in *Revue de Qumran*, no. 29 (1972), 28 f.

62 For further examples, see Nöldeke, §190B. Hence hardly an artificial device, as claimed by A. Mingana, *Clef de la langue araméenne ou grammaire complète et pratique des deux dialectes syriaques occidental et oriental* (Mossoul, 1905), p. 16, n. 2, and p. 17, §41.

also for the fact that the second form, with the medial vowel, of Pe. Impf. 2 m.sg. with an object suffix such as ܬܩܛܘܠܝܘܗܝ (in contrast to ܬܩܛܠܝܘܗܝ) "serves properly to denote prohibition" (Nöldeke, § 188).

§ 41* *Triliteral regular verb*

Study the Peal conjugation in Paradigm I.

A) As in Hebrew Qal, Peal shows a variety of vowel *Ablauts*

	Perfect	Imperfect and Imperative
1.	*a*	*o* [63]
2.	*a*	*e*
3.	*a*	*a*
4.	*e*	*a*
5.	*e*	*o* [63]
6.	*e*	*e* [64]

Whilst the type to which a given verb belongs is not always predictable— such information can be gained from a dictionary—the following observations may be made.

a. Type 1 (*a-o*) is by far the most common: ܩܛܠ, ܢܩܛܘܠ.

b. Type 2 (*a-e*) is attested by two verbs, ܥܒܕ "to make" and ܙܒܢ "to buy" as well as by some First-Nun verbs like ܢܦܠ "to fall", ܢܦܨ "to shake": ܙܒܢ, ܢܙܒܢ; ܢܦܠ, ܢܦܠ.

c. Type 3 (*a-a*) is not confined to Third-Guttural verbs, but also found in regular verbs: ܫܠܛ "to rule"— ܢܫܠܛ; ܠܐܐ "to toil"— ܢܠܐܐ.

d. Type 4 (*e-a*), intransitive *par excellence*, is fairly common: ܕܡܟ "to sleep"— ܢܕܡܟ. In other words, verbs with an /*e*/ in the Pf. which are not any of the small number of verbs belonging to either Type 5 or 6 all have an /*a*/ in the Impf.

e. Type 5 (*e-o*) is attested only by ܣܓܕ "to worship" (ܢܣܓܘܕ), ܫܬܩ "to keep silence" (ܢܫܬܘܩ), ܩܪܒ "to be near" (ܢܩܪܘܒ), ܢܚܬ "to descend" (ܢܚܘܬ with the assimilation of the first Nun).

f. Type 6 (*e-e*) is confined to ܝܬܒ "to sit" (ܢܬܒ) [65].

63 This vowel appears as /*u*/ in Western Syriac.

64 Two rare verbs attest to the /*o-o*/ class: ܣܡܘܪ "to bristle" and ܐܟܡܘܡ "to be black" (Nöldeke, § 160B).

65 For a comparative Semitic description, see J. Aro, *Die Vokalisierung des Grundstammes im semitischen Verbum* (Helsinki, 1964).

§42* As can be seen from the above table, the Peal Perfect can appear with either /*a*/ or /*e*/ as its stem vowel. The distinction between the two is maintained throughout except for 1 sg. and 3 f. sg. Thus

3 sg. m	ܩܛܠ	"he killed"	ܕܚܠ	"he feared"
f	ܩܛܠܬ		ܕܚܠܬ	
2 sg. m	ܩܛܠܬ		ܕܚܠܬ	
1 sg.	ܩܛܠܬ		ܕܚܠܬ	
3 pl. m	ܩܛܠܘ		ܕܚܠܘ	

§43* *Beghadhkephath*

a) As in Hebrew, a Beghadhkephath is pronounced soft when it occurs as the second member of a consonant cluster at the beginning of a word or of a syllable: ܫܬܩ /*št̲eq*/ "he was silent"; ܡܒܣܡ /*mvassem*/ "delectable" (Pa. ptc.); ܐܬܟܬܒ /*'et̲kt̲ev*/ "it was written" (Ethpe. Pf.).

b) In Peal, the third radical, if a Beghadhkephath, becomes hard in Pf. 3 f. sg. and 1 sg.: ܥܒܕ /*'vad̲*/ "he made", but ܥܒܕܬ /*'evdat̲*/ "she made" and ܥܒܕܬ /*'evdet̲*/ "I made".

In the Peal participle, the third radical, if a Beghadhkephath, is pronounced hard when an ending is added: ܥܒܕ /*'āved̲*/, but f. ܥܒܕܐ /*'āvdā*/, pl. m. ܥܒܕܝܢ /*'āvdin*/.

In Ethpeel, the third radical, if a Beghadhkephath, becomes hard whenever the helping vowel[66] /*a*/ is inserted after the first radical. This happens, for instance, in Pf. 3 f. sg. and 1 sg., Impf. 2 f. sg., 2 and 3 pl., Ptc. (except m. sg.): e.g. ܐܬܟܬܒܬ /*'et̲kat̲bat̲*/ "it was written"; ܢܬܟܬܒܘܢ /*net̲kat̲bun*/.

c) In Pael and Ethpaal, the doubled second radical, if a Beghadhkephath, is of course pronounced hard: ܩܒܠ /*qabbel*/ "he received", ܠܡܩܒܠܘ /*lamqabbālu*/ "to receive" (Inf.); ܐܬܩܒܠܬ /*'et̲qabblat̲*/ "she was received"; ܬܬܩܒܠܝܢ /*tet̲qabblin*/ (Impf. 2 f. sg.).

In these two patterns, the third radical is *always* pronounced soft. Hence the distinction between ܡܬܥܒܕܐ /*met̲'avdā*/ Ethpe. Ptc. f. and ܡܬܩܪܒܐ /*met̲qarrvā*/ Ethpa. Ptc. f.

In Pa. Impf. 1 sg., the first radical is exceptionally pronounced hard (or geminated): ܐܒܪܟ /*'ebbarrek̲*/ "I will bless".

66 It may be more accurate to say that the vowel is, historically speaking, primitive; hence the pattern can be designated Ethpa'al, which has changed to Ethp'el by virtue of the vowel deletion rule.

§44 *Verbs with gutturals* (Nöldeke, §169-70)
Unlike in Hebrew a guttural or /*r*/ as second or third radical does not automatically result in an /*a*/ as the stem vowel of the Impf. and Impv. Peal. Thus alongside ܢܶܨܘܰܚ "he shall cry out" and ܢܶܫܡܰܥ "he shall hear" we also find ܢܶܗܦܽܘܟ݂ "he shall overthrow" and ܢܶܛܒܽܘܥ "he shall immerse".

§45* More importantly, a guttural or /*r*/ as the third radical regularly occasions the change of /*e*/ to /*a*/ (§7B above), which takes place in Pael, Afel and Ethpeel as well as Peal active participle. Thus Pa. ܫܰܕܰܪ "he sent"; Af. ܐܰܫܡܰܥ "he announced"; Ethpe ܐܶܬ݂ܦܬܰܚ "it was opened"; Pe. ptc. ܫܳܡܰܥ "listening".
As a consequence the vowel contrast between the active and passive participles in Pa. and Af. may be neutralised: ܡܫܰܕܰܪ can mean either "sending" or "sent".

§46 *Second-Alaf verbs* (Nöldeke, §171)
The phonological rule given above in §71 governs the conjugation of the common verb ܫܐܠ: Pe. Pf. ܫܶܐܠ < *ܫܐܶܠ "he demanded"; Impf. ܢܶܫܐܰܠ < *ܢܶܫܐܰܠ; Inf. ܠܡܶܫܐܰܠ; Ptc. pass. ܫܐܺܝܠ; Ethpe. Pf. ܐܶܫܬܶܐܠ.

§47 *Third-Alaf verbs* (Nöldeke, §172)
A small number of verbs are conjugated as if their original final /'/ retained its guttural sound, though it is actually a mute letter. The vowel /*e*/ preceding this Alaf changes to /*a*/ in accordance with §7B. E.g., Pf. Pa. ܒܰܝܰܐ /*bayya*/ "he consoled" (< */*bayye'*/), Impf. ܢܒܰܝܰܐ /*nvayya*/, Ptc. act. and pass. ܡܒܰܝܰܐ /*mvayya*/. Also ܛܰܡܰܐ "defiled". For details, see Nöldeke, §172, and also below §51A.

§48 *First-Nun verbs* (Nöldeke, §173)
The /*n*/ of the first radical is assimilated under the same conditions as in Hebrew Pe-Nun verbs; this occurs in certain forms of Peal and throughout Afel and Ettafal. Also as in Hebrew, a second radical /*h*/ prevents the assimilation, and the Nun is lost in the Imperative of most of these verbs. Study the following synopsis:

Peal Pf.	ܢܦܰܩ	"go out"	ܢܣܰܒ	"take"	ܢܓܰܕ	"draw"
Impf.	ܢܶܦܽܘܩ		ܢܶܣܰܒ		ܢܶܓܶܕ	
Impv.	ܦܽܘܩ		ܣܰܒ		ܓܶܕ	

Afel ܐܰܘܩܶܕ, ܐܰܘܩܶܕܬ݂; ܢܰܘܩܶܕ, ܢܰܘܩܕܽܘܢ; ܡܰܘܩܶܕ; ܠܡܰܘܩܳܕܽܘ.
Ettafal ܐܶܬ݁ܬ݁ܰܘܩܰܕ, ܐܶܬ݁ܬ݁ܰܘܩܕܶܬ݂.

§49* *First-Alaf verbs* (Nöldeke, §174)

A) In accordance with §7E, the initial Alaf must take a full vowel, which is /e/ in Pe. Pf. and in the whole of Ethpe., but /a/ in Pe. ptc. pass.: ܐܶܟ݂ܰܠ "he ate"; ܐܶܬ݂ܐܶܟ݂ܶܠ "it was eaten"; ܐܰܟ݂ܺܝܠ "eaten".

B) In Ethpeel and Ethpaal, remember §71. Thus ܐܶܬ݁ܬ݁ܶܟ݂ܶܠ < *ܐܶܬ݂ܐܶܟ݂ܶܠ and ܐܶܬ݁ܬ݁ܰܠܺܝ < *ܐܶܬ݂ܐܰܠܺܝ "he was oppressed".

The following forms also lend themselves to similar explanation: ܢܰܠܶܦ Pa. Impf. < *ܢܐܰܠܶܦ "he shall teach", Ptc. ܡܰܠܶܦ. Cf. also ܐܰܠܺܝ, which is Pa. Pf. "he oppressed" and also Pa. Impf. 1 sg. (< *ܐܐܰܠܶܐ).

C) The prefix vowel of the Pe. Impf. and Impv. coalesces with the initial Alaf into /ē/: ܢܶܐܒܰܕ /nēvad/ "he shall perish"; ܢܶܐܡܰܪ /nēmar/ "he shall say"; ܢܶܐܟ݂ܽܘܠ /nekol/ "he shall eat". See §7J above.

West Syriac shows /i/ where the stem vowel is /a/ or when a verb has /y/ as third radical. Thus ܢܺܐܡܰܪ; ܢܺܐܬܶܐ (from ܐܶܬ݂ܳܐ "to come").

D) Verbs with /o/ in the stem take /a/ as the vowel of the initial /'/ in the Impv., whilst the others take /e/: ܐܰܟ݂ܽܘܠ, but ܐܶܡܰܪ.

E) In Afel and Ettafal, the initial Alaf appears as /w/. Thus ܐܰܘܟ݂ܶܠ "he fed"; ܐܰܘܒܶܕ "he destroyed". This is part of the process whereby this class of verbs passed over to that of First-Yodh verbs.

F) The Ethpeel of ܐܶܚܰܕ usually shows the assimilation of the initial Alaf, resulting in a spelling like ܐܶܬ݁ܬ݁ܚܶܕ (or simply ܐܶܬ݁ܚܶܕ)[67].

Study the following synopsis:

Peal

Pf. ܐܶܟ݂ܰܠ, ܐܶܟ݂ܠܶܬ݂, ܐܶܟ݂ܰܠܘ

Impf. ܢܶܐܟ݂ܽܘܠ, ܬܶܐܟ݂ܽܘܠ, ܬܶܐܟ݂ܠܺܝܢ, ܐܶܟ݂ܽܘܠ; ܬܶܐܡܰܪ, ܬܶܐܡܪܺܝܢ, ܐܶܡܰܪ, ܢܶܐܡܰܪ

Impv. ܐܰܟ݂ܽܘܠ, ܐܰܟ݂ܽܘܠܝ; ܐܶܡܰܪ, ܐܶܡܰܪܝ

67 Cf. Nöldeke, §174D and G. Widengren, "Aramaica et Syriaca", in A. Caquot and M. Philonenko (eds.), *Hommages à André Dupont-Sommer* (Paris, 1971), pp. 221-23, and H. Yalon, *Pirque lashon* [in Heb.] (Jerusalem, 1971), pp. 62-75.

Inf. ܠܡܐܟܠ ; ܠܡܐܡܪ
Ptc. pass. ܐܟܝܠ ; ܐܡܝܪ

Ethpeel

Pf. ܐܬܐܟܠ, ܐܬܐܟܠܬ Impf. ܢܬܐܟܠ, ܢܬܐܟܠܘܢ
Impv. ܐܬܐܟܠ Ptc. ܡܬܐܟܠ, ܡܬܐܟܠܐ Inf. ܠܡܬܐܟܠܘ

Pael

Pf. ܐܠܦ Impf. ܢܐܠܦ, ܐܠܦ Impv. ܐܠܦ
Ptc. act. ܡܐܠܦ; pass. ܡܐܠܦ Inf. ܠܡܐܠܦܘ

Ethpaal

Pf. ܐܬܐܠܦ Impf. ܢܬܐܠܦ Impv. ܐܬܐܠܦ
Ptc. ܡܬܐܠܦ Inf. ܠܡܬܐܠܦܘ

Afel ܐܘܟܠ
Ettafal ܐܬܬܘܟܠ } see under First-Yodh verbs (§ 50).

§ 50* *First-Yodh verbs* (Nöldeke, § 175)

A) In accordance with § 7E, the initial Yodh is provided with the full vowel /*i*/ where a regular verb would have no vowel. Thus ܝܬܒ "he sat"; Ethpe. ptc. ܡܬܝܠܕ "is born". The former and the like may also be spelled ܐܝܬܒ.

B) The stem vowel in Pe. Pf. is /*e*/ unless the third radical is a guttural or /*r*/: ܝܬܒ, but ܝܕܥ "he realised".

C) In the Impf. and Inf., the two most common verbs of this class, ܝܬܒ and ܝܕܥ, behave like First-Nun verbs: ܢܬܒ /*nettev*/ and ܢܕܥ /*nedda'*/[68], and lose the initial Yodh in the Impv.: ܬܒ and ܕܥ (so also ܗܒ "give"[69]). The remainder behave like First-Alaf verbs: ܬܐܠܕ (WS ܬܐܠܕ) "she shall give birth"; ܢܐܒܫ (WS ܢܐܒܫ) "it shall be dry".

D) In Afel and Ettafal, the initial Yodh, as in Hebrew, appears as Waw: ܐܘܒܫ "he dried something up"; ܐܘܕܥ "he informed". But ܐܝܢܩ "he suckled" (from ܝܢܩ) and ܐܝܠܠ "he wailed" retain the original /*y*/, again as in Hebrew (הֵינִיק, הֵילִיל).

68 Cf. BA יִנְדַּע and יְדַע .
69 See below § 55E.

Study the following synopsis:

Peal

Pf. ܝܙܰܦ ("borrow"), ܝܶܙܦܰܬ, ܝܙܰܦܬ etc.

Impf. ܢܺܐܙܽܘܦ, ܢܺܐܙܦܽܘܢ etc. Impv. ܙܽܘܦ, ܙܽܘܦܝ etc.

ܢܺܬܶܒ, ܢܺܬܒܽܘܢ etc. ܬܶܒ, ܬܶܒܝ etc.

ܢܺܕܰܥ, ܢܺܕܥܽܘܢ etc. ܕܰܥ, ܕܰܥܝ etc.

Inf. ܠܡܺܐܙܰܦ ; ܠܡܺܬܰܒ ; ܠܡܺܕܰܥ

Ethpeel

Pf. ܐܶܬܺܝܙܶܦ, ܐܶܬܺܝܙܦܰܬ, ܐܶܬܺܝܙܶܦܬ Impf. ܢܶܬܺܝܙܶܦ, ܢܶܬܺܝܙܦܽܘܢ

Inf. ܠܡܶܬܺܝܙܳܦܽܘ

Afel

ܐܰܘܙܶܦ ("he lent") — ܢܰܘܙܶܦ — ܡܰܘܙܶܦ — ܠܡܰܘܙܳܦܽܘ

Ettafal

ܐܶܬܬܰܘܙܰܦ — ܢܶܬܬܰܘܙܰܦ — ܡܶܬܬܰܘܙܰܦ — ܠܡܶܬܬܰܘܙܳܦܽܘ

§ 51* *Third-Yodh verbs* (Nöldeke, § 176)

Taking note of the following points, make a careful study of Paradigm II.

A) Most originally Third-Alaf verbs are conjugated like Third-Yodh verbs: so ܡܠܳܐ. For a few exceptions, see above § 47.

B) As in Hebrew, this verb-class is highly important, comprising a large number of verbs and deviating significantly from the regular pattern.

C) In the basic form, viz. Pf. Pe. ms. sg., what corresponds to Hebrew Lamed-He verbs is spelled with an Alaf at the end.

D) As in the case of the triliteral regular verb (§ 42), there are attested a small number of verbs of the type ܚܕܺܝ "he rejoiced", which deviates from the majority type ܪܡܳܐ "he threw" in the Pe. Pf. Other examples are: ܨܗܺܝ "to thirst"; ܣܪܺܝ "to stink"[70]; ܠܐܺܝ /lī/ for */l'ī/ (§ 71) "to get tired".

E) The Taw of the second person, both m. and f., sg. and pl., whether preceded by a plain vowel (e.g. ܚܕܺܝܬ /ḥḏīt/) or a diphthong (ܪܡܰܝܬ

70 ܐܶܫܬܺܝ "to drink" also belongs here, with a secondary prosthetic Alaf, which is confined to the Pf. and Impv.

/*rmayt*/), is consistently pronounced hard in contrast to the soft Taw of 1 sg. (ܚܕܺܝܬ /*ḥdiṯ*/; ܪܡܶܝܬ /*rmēṯ*/ [WS ܪܡܺܝܬ /*rmiṯ*/]).

F) The Impf. 2/3 m. pl. ending /*on*/ appears in WS as /*un*/: ܢܶܪܡܽܘܢ /*nermon*/ as against ܢܶܪܡܘܿܢ /*nermun*/.

G) The conjugation in the Pf. in the derived patterns is modelled on the ܚܕܺܝ type.

H) This is the only verb-class in which the Waw of the Pf. 3 m.pl. and Impv. m. pl. *is* pronounced: ܪܡܰܘ /*rmaw*/, ܚܕܺܝܘ /*ḥdiw*/, etc.

I) The infinitive of the derived patterns has reinstated the original /*y*/: Pa. ܠܡܪܰܡܳܝܽܘ, Af. ܠܡܰܪܡܳܝܽܘ etc. So in the Pe. infinitive when a pronoun suffix is attached as in ܠܡܶܪܡܝܳܗ /lmermyāh/ "to throw her".

J) The same /*y*/ is in evidence in other forms such as Pe. Pf. 2 m. sg. ܪܡܰܝܬ /*rmayt*/, Ptc. f. sg. ܪܳܡܝܳܐ /*rāmyā*/, pl. ܪܳܡܝܳܢ /*rāmyān*/, Impv. f. sg. ܪܡܳܝ /*rmāy*/.

K) The infinitive of the derived patterns receives /*ṯ*/ before a pronoun suffix is attached: ܠܡܰܪܡܳܝܽܘܬܰܢ /*lmarmāyuṯan*/ "to throw us".

§ 52 L) The Ettafal is excluded from the paradigm on account of its extreme rarity.

M) In the Impv. Ethpe. the West-Syrians have ܐܶܬܪܡܝ as against the East-Syrians' ܐܶܬܪܡܺܝܢ, which is modelled on the regular verb.

N) As against the standard /*i*/ ending of the Impv. m. sg., a few verbs have preserved the archaic /*ay*/: ܝܡܰܝ "swear" alongside of ܝܡܺܝ; ܐܶܫܬܺܝ "drink" (with a prosthetic Alaf).

§ 53* *Second-Waw or Yodh verbs* (Nöldeke, § 177)
Study Paradigm III.

A) The deviation from the regular type is observed in Peal, Afel, Ethpeel and Ettafal, whilst in Pael and Ethpaal the conjugation is fashioned after the regular class, /*y*/ serving as middle radical as in ܩܰܝܶܡ "establish" and ܐܶܬܩܰܝܰܡ.

B) Like Heb. מֵת , ܡܺܝܬ is the only example showing the stem vowel /*i*/ in the Perfect, whereas in the Impf. and Impv. ܣܺܝܡ "to place" is the only example with the stem vowel /*i*/.

C) In contrast to Hebrew, the long /*ā*/ is maintained throughout Peal Pf.: cf. Heb. קָם, but קַמְתָּ.

D) The Ethpeel has been replaced by Ettafal: thus ܐܶܬܬܩܺܝܡ.

§ 54* *Geminate verbs* (Nöldeke, § 178) [70a]
Study Paradigm IV.

A) In prefixed forms, i.e. Pe. Impf. and Inf., the whole of Afel and Ettafal, verbs of this class are conjugated like First-Nun verbs, whose Nun is assimilated. Thus ܢܒܘܙ /*nebboz*/ "he shall plunder"; ܐܥܠ /*'a''el*/ Af. "he introduced".

B) Where the two identical radicals have no vowel in between, a shorthand spelling is used as in Pe. Pf. 3 f. sg. ܒܙܬ < *ܒܙܙܬ /*bezzat̲*/; Ptc. act. f. sg. ܒܙܐ < *ܒܙܙܐ /*bāzzā*/.

C) In Pe. Impf. there are also /*a*/ and /*e*/ patterns: e.g. ܢܪܓ "to desire" [71] and ܢܛܥ "to stray" (the only attested example of the /*e*/ pattern).

D) Note that a Beghadhkephath as a geminate radical is pronounced hard in Pe. ptc. act. pl.: ܦܐܕܝܢ, ܦܕܝܢ (/*pād̲din*/ → /*pāddin*/ [assimilation]).

E) In Ethpeel the second and third radicals are kept apart: ܐܬܒܙܙ, not ܐܬܒܙ, although the above-mentioned short-hand spelling is occasionally found as in ܡܬܩܨܐ for ܡܬܩܨܨܐ /*met̲qaṣṣā*/.

§ 55* *List of anomalous verbs* (Nöldeke, § 179, 183)

A) ܐܫܟܚ Af. "to find" for the anticipated *ܐܫܟܚ.

B) ܐܬܐ Pe. "to come". Impv. m. ܬܐ, f. ܬܝ /*tāy*/, pl. m. ܬܘ /*taw*/, f. ܬܝܢ /*tāyen*/. Af. ܐܝܬܝ "he brought", with /*'ay*/ like ܐܝܢܩ (§ 50D).

C) ܐܙܠ Pe. "to go". When the Zay has no vowel, the Lamadh is dropped, and the vowel of the latter is thrown back: ܐܙܠܬ /*'ezet̲*/ "I went"; ܢܐܙܠܘܢ /*nēzun*/ "they (m.) shall go"; ܐܙܠܐ /*'āzā*/, Ptc. f. sg., etc. Impv. ܙܠ, but Impf. with /*a*/: ܢܐܙܠ /*nēzal*/.

D) ܣܠܩ "to ascend". In the sequence /*-sl-*/, the /*l*/ is assimilated to the /*s*/. Thus in Pe. Impf., Inf., Af. and Ettaf.: Pe. Impf. ܢܣܩ /*nessaq*/, Inf. ܠܡܣܩ /*lmessaq*/; Af. ܐܣܩ /*'asseq*/. The Pe. Impv. is derived from the Impf.: ܣܩ, ܣܩܝ, ܣܩܘ, all /*saq*/.

E) ܝܗܒ /*yav*/ "to give". In the Pe. Pf. the verb retains the /*h*/ only in 3 f. sg. ܝܗܒܬ and 1 sg. ܝܗܒܬ; otherwise ܝܗܒ, ܝܗܒܬ etc. Impv. ܗܒ ܗܒܝ, ܗܒܘ, ܗܒܝܢ. Ptc. act. ܝܗܒ, ܝܗܒܐ etc., pass. ܝܗܝܒ. The Impf. and Inf. are

70a Cf. also J. L. Boyd III, "The development of the West Semitic Qal Perfect of the double-'ayin verb with particular reference to its transmission in Syriac", *J. of Northwest Semitic Languages*, 10 (1982), 11-23.

71 *Pace* Brockelmann, *Lexicon Syriacum*, which indicates /*nerrog*/.

supplied by a hypothetical root ܢܬܠ as ܢܶܬܶܠ, ܠܡܶܬܰܠ. Ethpe. is regular: ܐܶܬܺܝܗܶܒ.

F) ܚܝܐ "to live, be alive". The Pf. is regular; ܚܝܐ, ܚܝܬ, ܚܝܝܬ etc. So also Impv.: ܚܝܝ, ܚܝܝ, ܚܝܘ. But the Impf. is formed as if the root were ܢܚܐ (N-Ḥ-Y): ܢܚܐ, ܬܚܐ, ܢܚܘܢ etc. Likewise the Inf. and the whole of Afel: ܐܚܝ, ܐܚܝܬ, ܐܚܝܘ /'aḥḥiw/; ܢܚܐ; Ptc. ܡܚܐ, pass. ܡܚܝ; Inf. ܠܡܚܝܘ.

G) ܗܘܐ "to be". It is perfectly regular except that as an enclitic (§71) it always loses its /h/ as in ܗܘܐ /wā/ ܩܛܠ "he was killing"; ܗܘܘ /waw/ ܛܒܝܢ "they were good".

§56* *Verbs with object-suffixes* (Nöldeke, §184-98)

Whilst Hebrew either attaches an object-suffix directly to the verb (like שְׁלַחְתִּיךָ) or expresses the same notion as two distinct units (שְׁלַחְתִּי אֹתְךָ), the latter analytical option is virtually unavailable in Syriac — or at least the two modes are not freely interchangeable —[72] thus rendering essential the knowledge of the rules of fusion, which are no less complicated than those applicable to Hebrew. The following is a summary of the more important rules; for details see Nöldeke, §184-98. Study the rules with reference to Paradigms V and VI.

A) In many a case the verb with an object-suffix has preserved the more archaic shape:

2 m. sg. ending /tā/ as in ܩܛܠܬܢܝ /qṭaltān/ "you killed me"

2 f. sg. ending /ti/ as in ܩܛܠܬܝܢܝ /qṭaltin/ "you killed me"

3 m. pl. ending /u/ as in ܩܛܠܘܢܝ /qaṭlun/ "they killed me"

3 f. pl. ending /ā/ as in ܩܛܠܢܝ /qaṭlān/ "they killed me"

the hard /t/ of 1 sg. as against soft /ṯ/ of 3 f. sg. as in ܩܛܠܬܟ /qṭaltāk/ "I killed you" vs. ܩܛܠܬܟ /qṭalṯāḵ/ "she killed you"

the initial /a/ in a form like ܩܛܠܗ "he killed her".

B) The pl. "them" is always expressed by means of the enclitics: m. ܐܢܘܢ, f. ܐܢܝܢ. But a participle requires ܠܗܘܢ or ܠܗܝܢ.

C) The forms of the object suffixes may be found in §12.

D) Whenever a verb form itself ends in /n/, the latter is followed by /ā/ before the suffix with the exception of ܟܝ (2 f. sg.). This happens in Pf. 1 pl., 2 pl.; Impf. 2 f. sg., and 3 pl.; longer Impv. pl. with /n/. Thus ܩܛܠܬܘܢܢܝ

72 For details, see below §95B,C.

/*qṭaltonān*/ "you (m. pl.) killed me"; ܢܶܩܛܠܽܘܢܳܟ݂ܽܘܢ "they shall kill you (m. pl.)" etc.

E) The 3 m. sg. suffix takes a variety of forms[73]. If the verb ends in a consonant, it is ܗ̄ /*eh*/: e.g. ܩܶܛܠܰܬ݂ܶܗ "she killed him". If preceded by a vowel, however, it is spelled, ܗ and pronounced in a variety of ways:

after /*ā*/ — ܝܗ̄ /*āy*/ as in ܩܛܰܠܬܳܝܗ̄ /*qṭaltāy*/ "you (m. sg.) killed him"
after /*i*/ — ܝܽܘܗ̄ܝ /*iw*/ as in ܩܛܰܠܬܺܝܘܗ̄ܝ /*qṭaltiw*/ "you (f. sg.) ..."
after /*e*/ — ܝܘܗ̄ܝ /*ew*/ as in ܢܶܓܠܶܝܘܗ̄ܝ /*neglew*/ "he shall reveal it".

F) The Impf. forms ending in the third consonantal radical, i.e. 3 m. and f. sg., 2 m. sg., 1 sg. and pl., insert an /*i*/ before the 3 sg. suffixes: ܢܶܩܛܠܺܝܘܗ̄ܝ /*neqṭliw*/ (see E above) "he shall kill him" and ܢܶܩܛܠܺܝܗ̇ /*neqṭlih*/ "he shall kill her".

G) The Impv. m. sg., if ending in the third consonantal radical, inserts either /*ā*/ or /*ay*/: ܩܛܘܿܠܰܝܢܝ /*qṭolayn*/ "kill me"; ܩܛܘܿܠܳܝܗ̄ /*qṭolāy*/ "kill him".

H) Third-Yodh verbs (Paradigm VI) retain in Pe. the /*a*/ of the 3 m. sg. before suffixes. Likewise with the vowel endings of the root in the Impf. and Impv. The /*i*/ of the Pf. (Pa. 3 m. sg.) and the /*a*/ of the Inf. change to /*y*/ except before ܟܽܘܢ and ܟܶܝܢ. Note also the shift of the /*aw*/ in Pf. 3 m. pl. and Impf. m. pl. to /*a'u*/, and the /*iw*/ of Pa. Pf. 3 m. pl. to /*yu*/, and the /*āy*/ of Impf. f. sg. to /*ā'i*/.

Note that the /*t*/ of the Pf. 1 sg. is pronounced soft, unlike that of a non-Third-Yodh verb (A above).

The phonological rules D and E given above are equally applicable to Third-Yodh verbs.

73 Cf. J. Wesselius, "The spelling of the third person masculine singular suffixed pronoun in Syriac", *Bibliotheca Orientalis*, 39 (1982), 251-54.

Part III: MORPHOSYNTAX AND SYNTAX

§57 *Noun*: *Gender* (Nöldeke, §201, 254)

The feminine may be used to refer to "things" (neuter): ܐܚܪܢܝܬܐ "something else", ܛܒܬܐ "the good". Likewise the pronoun ܗܕܐ "this (thing, matter)" and a verb form as in ܡܕܡ ܕܡܫܟܚܐ ܗܘܐ ܠܡܕܒܪܘܬܗ "something that he can manage". But the use of the masculine is not uncommon: ܐܘ ܠܛܒ ܐܘ ܠܒܝܫ "whether for the better or for the worse", ܡܛܠ ܗܢܐ "because of this". With the plural, however, only the feminine is allowed: ܛܒܬܐ "good things", ܗܠܝܢ ܬܪܬܝܗܝܢ "these two (things)".

§58 *Noun*: *State* (Nöldeke, §202-204)[74]

Since the emphatic state in Syriac has weakened so much that a form such as ܡܠܟܐ is ambiguous, meaning either "a king" or "the king", the use of the original st. absolutus is severely curtailed, being confined chiefly to the following instances[75]:

A) Distributive repetition as in ܡܢ ܫܢܐ ܠܫܢܐ "from year to year"; ܩܝܡܝܢ ܗܘܘ ܟܢܫܝܢ ܟܢܫܝܢ "they stood there in groups"; ܘܫܪܝܘ ܗܘܘ ܠܡܡܠܠܘ ܠܫܢ ܠܫܢ Ac 2.4 "they began to speak, each in his own tongue". Belonging here also are such cases as Gn 11.3 ܘܐܡܪܘ ܓܒܪ ܠܚܒܪܗ "they said to each other".

B) After ܟܠ and numerals[76]: ܬܪܝܢ ܥܠܡܝܢ "two worlds"; ܒܟܠ ܚܦܝܛܘ "with all zeal". Similarly ܟܡܐ ܙܒܢܝܢ "how many times?".

C) In negative expressions as in ܠܝܬ ܝܘܬܪܢ "there is no gain", and especially after ܕܠܐ as in ܕܠܐ ܡܢܝܢ "without number, innumerable".

D) In certain idiomatic phrases with a preposition: ܡܢ ܫܠܝ /men šel/ "suddenly"; ܠܥܠܡ "for ever".

E) Adjectival predicate of a nominal clause: ܥܝܢܟ ܒܝܫܐ "your eye is evil". Likewise ܐܫܬܟܚܬ ܒܛܢܐ "she was found to be pregnant".

74 Cf. §17-18 above.

75 Even here, however, the emphatic state *is* occasionally employed.

76 See further §78.

§ 59 As a consequence of the weakening of the emphatic state, a demonstrative pronoun, especially the series ܗܘ, may be added: so Gn 37.15 ܓܒܪܐ ܗܘ (= /hā'iš/); Ex 4.9 (/hammayim/) ܣܒ ܡܢ ܡܝܐ ܕܢܗܪܐ .. ܗܢܘܢ ܡܝܐ ܕܬܣܒ ܐܢܬ. This is especially common where the demonstrative so used is analogous in function to the anaphoric definite article. On the other hand, the addition of a numeral "one" may have the effect of weakening the emphatic to that of the primitive absolute state: ܓܒܪܐ ܚܕ Lk 14.28PC (S om ܚܕ) (= ἄνθρωπός τις)

§ 60 Some forms which look like those of the f. sg. cst. are in reality the residue of the archaic st. abs. used adverbially: ܪܒܬ "exceedingly"; ܩܕܡܝܬ "firstly"[77].

§ 61 Whilst the typical Semitic status constructus cannot be said to have died out, the *analytical structure* with the proclitic linking word ܕ- *is far more common*[78]. The use of the former is obligatory in some standing expressions —compound nouns—like ܪܒܝ ܟܘܡܪܐ "chief priests", ܦܣܩ ܕܝܢܐ "a verdict" or with adjectives and passive participles like ܚܣܝܪ ܗܘܢܐ "mindless"; ܐܢܬܬܐ ܫܦܝܪܬ ܚܙܘܐ "a good-looking woman".

§ 62 *Interrogatives* + — ܕ = *Relative pronouns*

ܡܢ "who?" ——— ܡܢ ܕ "whoever"

ܡܢܐ "what?" ——— ܡܐ ܕ "whatever, that which"[79]

ܐܝܟܐ "where?" ——— ܐܝܟܐ ܕ "wherever, where"

ܐܡܬܝ "when?" ——— ܐܡܬܝ ܕ "whenever, when"

ܐܝܟܢܐ "how?" ——— ܐܝܟ ܕ "as (of comparison), in such a way as"

ܐܝܢܐ "which?" ——— ܐܝܢܐ ܕ "whichever, one who/which"

For example: ܡܐ ܕܐܝܬ ܠܝ ܕܝܠܗ ܗܘ "what I have is his".

§ 63 *Prepositions* + — ܕ = *Conjunctions*

ܩܕܡ "before" (of time) ——— ܩܕܡ ܕ "before"

77 See Brockelmann, *Syr. Gram.*, § 163.

78 See Nöldeke, § 205-10.

79 The combination also means "when", especially referring to the future, even followed by a Perfect.

ܒܳܬ݂ܰܪ (ܡܶܢ) "after" (of time) ——— ܒܳܬ݂ܰܪ ܕ (ܡܶܢ) "after"

ܡܶܛܽܠ "because of" ——— ܡܶܛܽܠ ܕ "because"

ܐܰܝܟ /'ak/ "as, like" ——— ܐܰܝܟ ܕ "just as"[80]

Cf. also — ܕ ܥܰܠ "because"; ܟܰܕ "because"; — ܕ ܡܶܢ "after". ܥܰܕ "until"[81] is peculiar in that it functions as a conjunction without the particle —ܕ, though it then also means "while; before"[82].

E.g., ܡܶܛܽܠ ܟܰܦܢܳܐ "because of a famine"; ܡܶܛܽܠ ܕܐܺܝܬ ܗܘܳܐ ܟܰܦܢܳܐ "because there was a famine".

§64 Some prepositions display interesting morphosyntactic distribution ܡܶܛܽܠ with a noun ܡܶܛܽܠ ܡܶܛܪܳܐ "because of the rain"), but — ܡܶܛܽܠܳܬ݂ with a pronoun (ܡܶܛܽܠܳܬ݂ܟ݂ܽܘܢ "on account of you"), ܐܰܝܟ with a noun (ܐܰܝܟ ܦܽܘܩܕܳܢܶܗ "like [= in accordance with] his order"), but — ܐܰܝܟܘܳܬ݂ with a pronoun (ܐܰܝܟܘܳܬ݂ܰܢ "like us") and — ܕ ܐܰܝܟ with a prepositional phrase or an adverb (ܐܰܝܟ ܕܒܝܰܘܡܳܐ ܗܰܘ "as on that day"). ܒܶܝܬ݂ 'between, amongst": never with a pronoun suffix, for which one uses either ܒܶܝܢܳܬ݂ or ܒܶܝܢܰܝ[83].

§65 *Impersonal passive*

When there is no need or desire to name the actor, the m. sg. of a passive form may be used in order to highlight the mere fact that something has happened[84]. E.g., Addai 5.12 ܐܶܫܬܰܥܝ ܗܘܳܐ ܥܠܰܘܗܝ، ܒܦܽܘܡܳܗ ܕܟܽܠܳܗ ܟܪܰܟ݂ܳܐ "he became the talk of the whole town"; Mt 7.2 ܢܶܬ݂ܬܟ݂ܺܝܠ ܠܟ݂ܽܘܢ "(the appropriate amount) will be measured out to you".

§66 *Perfect* (Nöldeke, §255-63)

The Perfect indicates something that happened, has happened or had happened, thus essentially a preterital tense. Some Pf. verbs, mainly stative, may have the translation value of the present: Gn 7.2 ܒܥܺܝܪܳܐ ܕܠܳܐ ܗܘܳܬ݂

80 The phrase, when followed by an Imperfect (and occasionally an Infinitive), also indicates a purpose or result.

81 Also ܥܰܕ ܠ- and ܥܕܰܡܳܐ ܠ-.

82 However, "until" as a conjunction must be rendered by ܥܕܰܡܳܐ ܠ-.

83 On the rich variety of expressions for "between"—no less rich than in Hebrew—see Nöldeke, §251.

84 Cf. Arb. *yusāru 'ilayhi* "someone travelled to his place", and Lv 4.20 /*wnislaḥ lāhem*/ "and forgiveness will be granted to them".

ܕܟܝܐ "an animal which is not clean"; ܝܕܥܢ "we know, i.e. we have come to know, we have realised"[85]. The use of the Pf. after — ܡܐ ܕ referring to a future event is easily understandable: Addai 4.16 "when I have gone up (ܡܐ ܕܣܠܩܬ) to him, I will send to thee one of my disciples".

The Pf. is also commonly used in conditional sentences.

§67 *Imperfect* (Nöldeke, §264-68)

The use of the Imperfect for pure future is rather uncommon.

In independent, i.e. non-subordinated clauses, it often adds a certain modal nuance: Gn 3.2 "from the fruit of any tree in the garden we *may* eat (ܢܐܟܘܠ); ib. 15.8 "how *could/would* I know (ܐܕܥ) that I am going to inheret it?"; ib. 43.4 "we are *willing* to go down (ܢܚܘܬ)" vs. ib. 43.5 "we are not going down (ܠܐ ܢܚܬܝܢܢ)"; Lk 18.32S "the son of man is going to be delivered ... so that they may mock (ܘܢܒܙܚܘܢ) him". Of course the prohibitive Impf. with ܠܐ belongs here: ܠܐ ܬܟܬܘܒ "Don't write".

Much use is made of the Impf. in subordinate clauses: in conditional clauses, in clauses complementing another verb[86] such as ܫܪܝ ، (ܫܪܝ ܕܢܡܠܠ) ، "he began to speak"), ܨܒܐ (ܨܒܐ ܕܢܐܟܘܠ "he desired to eat"), ܡܫܟܚ (ܡܫܟܚ ܐܢܐ ܕܐܟܬܘܒ "I am able to write"), in clauses introduced by ܩܕܡ ܕ— or ܥܕ ܠܐ "they ruled the land of Edom before a king ruled (ܩܕܡ ܕܢܡܠܟ) over the children of Israel", or in purpose clauses introduced by — ܕ as in Jn 3.21P "so that their works may become known (ܕܢܬܝܕܥܘܢ)".

§68 *Participle* (Nöldeke, 269-76)

The participle may be used to indicate what is happening now (Actual Present) or what often or habitually happens (General Present).

More importantly, it may also express the idea of futurity, intention (Prospective Present) or immediacy and certainty of fulfilment in the manner of the English construction *be going to* + Infinitive. E.g., Gn 1.20 ܕܢܚܙܐ ܡܢܐ ܩܪܐ ܗܘܐ ܠܗܘܢ "in order to see what he was going to call them"; ib. 15.2 "he is going to inherit (ܝܪܬ ܠܝ) me" in contrast to ib. 15.4 "that one shall not inherit you (ܢܐܪܬܟ)"; ib. 18.17 ܡܕܡ ܕܥܒܕ ܐܢܐ "what I am going to do".

85 "we know" in the sense of "we are aware of, we know about" is ܝܕܥܝܢ ܚܢܢ (ptc.).

86 See further §97.

However, the line between the participle and the imperfect referring to a future event can become fine, as one may see from the following examples of fluctuation: Gn 2.7 ܒܝܘܡܐ ܕܬܐܟܘܠ ܡܢܗ ܡܘܬܐ ܬܡܘܬ "on the day you eat of it you will surely die" as against ib. 3.5 ܒܝܘܡܐ ܕܐܟܠܝܢ ܐܢܬܘܢ ܡܢܗ ܡܬܦܬܚܢ ܥܝܢܝܟܘܢ "on the day you eat of it your eyes are going to open"; Addai 4.16 ܗܐ ܐܢܐ ܫܕܪ ܐܢܐ ܠܟ ܚܕ ܡܢ ܬܠܡܝܕܝ "I [= Jesus] am going to send you one of my disciples" (similarly in 5.17, 6.14) as against 5.22 ܐܫܕܪ ܠܟ ܚܕ ܡܢ ܬܠܡܝܕܝ.

As in Modern Hebrew, the participle may indicate what has been going on for some time up to the moment of speaking as in Lk 13.7 S ܗܐ ܬܠܬ ܫܢܝܢ ܐܬܐ ܐܢܐ ܒܥܐ ܐܢܐ ܦܐܪܐ ܒܬܬܐ ܗܕܐ "Look, I have been coming the past three years, looking for fruit on this fig tree".

The use of the participle to indicate contemporaneity with the main verb is easily understood: Gn 2.25 "Adam and his wife were naked, without feeling shame (ܠܐ ܒܗܬܝܢ)". This is especially common in clauses introduced by ܟܕ, which would be equivalent to a circumstantial clause, or after verbs of perception: Ex 14.10 ܘܚܙܘ ܠܡܨܪܝܐ ܟܕ ܐܬܝܢ "they saw the Egyptians coming" (but also without the conjunction as in Gn 21.9 ܚܙܬ ܣܪܐ ܠܒܪܗ ܕܗܓܪ ... ܡܓܚܟ "Sarah saw the son of Hagar... mocking"); Lk 21.31 ܡܐ ܕܚܙܝܬܘܢ ܗܠܝܢ ܕܗܘܝܢ "when you have seen these things happening".

One also finds the participle used in conditional sentences, in both protasis and apodosis.

§ 69 *Participle: passive* (Nöldeke, § 278-80)

a) The passive participle emphasises the result of some past action: ܟܬܝܒ "it is written". Note the contrast in Aphr. 101.5 "these words are not sealed (ܚܬܝܡܢ) ... and will not be sealed (ܡܬܚܬܡܢ)".

b) Especially noteworthy is the syntagm ܩܛܝܠ ܠ-, which corresponds to the Perfect in English expressing a result, and what follows the preposition represents the *subject* of the action[87]: Mt 27.23 ܡܢܐ ܕܒܝܫ ܥܒܝܕ ܠܗ "what wrong has he done?", not "what injustice was done to him?"; Acta Thomae 207.3 ܣܓܝܐܢ ܐܢܝܢ ܐܝܠܝܢ ܕܫܡܝܥܢ ܠܝ "many are things

87 On this syntactic feature typical of Eastern Aramaic, see E. Y. Kutscher, "Two 'passive' constructions in Aramaic in the light of Persian", *Proceedings of the International Conference on Semitic Studies Held in Jerusalem, 19-23 July 1965* (Jerusalem, 1969), pp. 132-51.

that we have done"; Addai 2.17 ܫܪܟܐ ܕܥܒ̈ܕܐ ܕܥܒܝܕܢ. ܗܘܐ ܠܗ ܬܡܢ "the rest of the things that he had done there"; Acta Thomae 199.18 ܐܝܠܝܢ ܕܥܒܝܕܢ ܠܟ ܟܠܗܝܢ ܕܐܫܬܥܒܕܘ ܠܟ "those things which thou hast done were subject to thee" (Wright's translation, p. 172); ib. 174.19-20 ܐܦ ܡܠܟܐ ܫܒܝܩܝܢ ܠܗ ܠܟܪ̈ܘܙܐ ܕܢܟܪܙܘܢ "the king has also permitted heralds to proclaim ..."[88]. This syntagm may also be found with a passive participle in Pael or Afel: Addai 49.19 ܐܝܟ ܦܘܩܕܢܐ ܘܝܘܠܦܢܐ ܕܡܩܒܠ ܗܘܐ ܠܗܘܢ ܡܢܗ ܕܐܕܝ، "in accordance with the commandment and instruction which they had received from Addai"; ib. 6.22 ܡܫܠܡܐ ܕܫܝܢܐ ܕܡܫܡ ܠܝ ܥܡ ܡܪܢ ܩܣܪ "the peace treaty which I have concluded with our lord the Emperor". Note the following case in which the participle does not agree with the nucleus in gender and number: Bedjan, *Acta Martyrum et Sanctorum syriace*, IV 657.21 ܡܬܝܚ ܠܗ ܩܫܬܗ "he has drawn his bow".

c) The passive participle may of course retain its original force as in Mt 9.2 ܫܒܝܩܝܢ ܠܟ ܚܛܗܝܟ "your sins have been forgiven"[89].

d) The resultative force of passive participles is conspicuous in cases where they are used like active participles: Acta Thomae 177.3 ܫܘܫܒܝܢܝܗ ܚܕܪܝܢ ܠܗ "her groomsmen are around her, i.e. having encircled her". Ib. 176.1 ܩܢܝܐ ܕܩܢܝܐ ܒܐܝܕܗ ܐܚܝܕ ܗܘܐ therefore does not mean "a reed-branch was grasped in his hand", but "he held a reed-branch in his hand, i.e. having seized it". Cf. § 35 above.

§ 70 *Compound tense*: ܩܛܠ ܗܘܐ (Nöldeke, § 263)

The Perfect used in narrative and immediately followed by the enclitic ܗܘܐ has exactly the same range of time reference as the simple Perfect: ܟܬܒܘ ܗܘܘ "they wrote", "have written", or "had written"[90].

88 This is preferable to seeing here a Lamadh of agent, "permitted by".

89 The context alone can decide that the same syntagm has a different meaning in cases like Lk 17.10P ܟܠܗܝܢ ܐܝܠܝܢ ܕܦܩܝܕܢ ܠܟܘܢ "all that you have been commanded".

90 It is not correct to say that this compound form corresponds to the English Past Perfect 'they had written'; one often finds a compound form where the Past Perfect is not intended, and conversely the simple Perfect where the Past Perfect is intended. The use of this particular syntagm is possibly a matter of individual style. Moreover, it seems to be uncommon in direct speech.

§71 *Compound tense*: ܩܛܠ ܗܘܐ (Nöldeke, §263)
The highly frequent structure (Ptc. act + enclitic ܗܘܐ) signifies an on-going, repeated or habitual action in the past: ܡܙܒܢܝܢ ܗܘܘ "they were selling, kept selling"; Mk 10.13 "they were bringing (ܡܩܪܒܝܢ ܗܘܘ) him children, when the disciples started rebuking them". What may look like the Inceptive Imperfect of Greek is not essentially different: Mk 1.21 "when he entered Capernaum, he was straightaway *seen* teaching (ܡܠܦ ܗܘܐ) on sabbaths in their synagogues".

This syntagm also indicates what was destined to happen: Addai 40.15 "he contracted a disease from which he was (later) to depart (ܢܦܩ ܗܘܐ) from this world". This is most likely an application of the participle used for the future tense.

Also in hypothetical clauses: *Spic*. 1.9 "with this his will would be fulfilled (ܡܫܬܡܠܝܐ ܗܘܐ); Jn 14.28 ܐܠܘ ܪܚܡܝܢ ܗܘܝܬܘܢ ܠܝ ܚܕܝܢ ܗܘܝܬܘܢ "if you loved me, you should rejoice …".

§72 *Compound tense*: ܗܘܐ ܩܛܠ (Nöldeke, §260-61)
This structure indicates a wish, advice or obligation of general and universal applicability, but not an order for some immediate action. An adjective may be found for a participle: e.g., Gn 24.41 "if they will not give her to you, you ought to consider yourself not bound (ܗܘܝܬ ܡܚܣܝܐ) by my oaths"; Mk 11.25S "you ought to forgive" (ܗܘܝܬܘܢ ܫܒܩܝܢ)[91]; *Spic*. 1.9 "they ought to be always doing (ܗܘܘ ܥܒܕܝܢ) what is good". Similarly in subordinate clauses after verbs of wishing, commanding and the like in the Perfect: Aphr. I 621.23 f. ܨܒܝܢ ܗܘܘ ܕܢܗܘܘܢ ܫܩܠܝܢ ܠܗ "they were wanting to carry it".

§73 *Compound tense*: ܢܩܛܘܠ ܗܘܐ (Nöldeke, §268)
This compound tense is sometimes used in a past context, and in a subordinate clause, instead of the simple Imperfect: Addai 2.18 ܩܕܡ ܕܢܐܙܠܘܢ ܗܘܘ ܠܬܡܢ "before they went there"; "you implored that your offerings be accepted (ܢܬܩܒܠܘܢ ܗܘܘ)". Likewise in conditional or associated clauses: ܐܢ ܐܢܫ ܢܐܡܪ ܗܘܐ "should someone say so"; ܡܢ ܐܥܒܕ ܗܘܝܬ "what should I have done?".

91 The syntagm is synonymous with the plain Imperative, which is found in the Peshitta version here and in the parallel Mt 5.24. Compare also Lk 10.28 ܗܕܐ ܥܒܕ with ib. 37 ܗܟܢܐ ܗܘܝܬ ܥܒܕ.

§74 *Compound tense*: ܢܗܘܐ ܩܛܠ (Nöldeke, §300)
This compound form is occasionally used in place of the simple Imperfect: "Women should never enter (ܢܗܘܝܢ ܥܐܠܢ) their monasteries". It freely alternates with the simple Impf.: e.g., Aphr. I 41.20-22 "they will be speaking (ܢܡܠܠܘܢ) new languages and casting out (ܢܗܘܘܢ ܡܦܩܝܢ) demons and laying (ܢܗܘܘܢ ܣܝܡܝܢ) their hands on the sick"[92].

§75 *Noun expanded*

A nucleus noun may be expanded in a variety of ways with addition of further elements. Such additions are placed before the nucleus more frequently in Syriac than in Hebrew.

§76 An *attributive adjective* usually follows the nucleus noun: ܡܠܟܐ ܛܒܐ "a/the good king". But it may on occasion precede: ܩܕܡܝܬܐ ܫܬܐܣܬܐ "the first foundation". So frequently with honorific, laudatory or condemnatory epithets such as ܛܘܒܢܐ ܡܪܝ ܐܦܪܝܡ "the blessed Mar Ephrem", ܪܫܝܥܐ ܝܘܠܝܢܘܣ "the wicked Julian", although it is not easy to decide with certainty whether these are cases of nominalised adjectives in apposition. Such an uncertainty, however, hardly exists with adjectival quantifiers or some pseudo-adjectives like ܣܓܝ, ܐܚܪܢ, ܦܠܢ as in ܣܓܝܐܬܐ ܢܦܫܬܐ "many souls"; ܐܚܪܢܐ ܡܬܠܐ "another parable"; ܦܠܢ ܨܒܘܬܐ "such and such matter". Cp. Mk 15.41 ܐܚܪܢܝܬܐ ܣܓܝܐܬܐ (ἄλλαι πολλαί) with Jn 20.30S ܣܓܝܐܬܐ ܐܚܪܢܝܬܐ (P tr and ἄλλα πολλά). It seems, however, that a preceding ܐܚܪܢܐ emphasises the notion of addition, "more, another" (Mt 13.24 ܐܚܪܢܐ ܡܬܠܐ "another parable"; ib. 4.21 ܐܚܪܢܐ ܐܚܐ ܬܪܝܢ "two more brothers"), but a following ܐܚܪܢܐ underlining the notion of difference ("other, different"), somewhat similarly to ἄλλος vs. ἕτερος. See esp. 2 Cor 11.4 ܐܚܪܢܐ ܝܫܘܥ ... ܐܚܪܬܐ ... ܪܘܚܐ ܐܚܪܬܐ ... ܣܒܪܬܐ ܐܚܪܬܐ (ἄλλον Ἰησοῦν ... πνεῦμα ἕτερον ... εὐαγγέλιον ἕτερον).
Cf. Nöldeke, §211.

92 A quotation from Mk 16.17 f., where P uses the Impf. in all three cases. An example such as Ac 5.15 ܐܦܢ, ܕܢܗܘܐ ܐܬܐ ܫܡܥܘܢ "should Peter come" does not fit any of Nöldeke's (§300) categories: "dauernde oder sich wiederholende oder doch gesetzlich bestimmte Handlungen".

§ 77 A *demonstrative pronoun* may either precede or follow the nucleus noun: ܡܠܟܐ ܗܢܐ or ܗܢܐ ܡܠܟܐ "this king". Whether the difference in sequence is conditioned by some factor or other is not known[92a].

§ 78 Likewise *numerals*. However, the preceding numeral 'one' tends to emphasise the notion of unity or oneness, or is contrastive, whilst the following numeral 'one' has its force weakened to that of the indefinite article[93]: Gn 2.26 ܚܕ ܒܣܪ "one flesh"; Mt 26.40 ܐܦ ܚܕܐ ܫܥܐ "even one hour"; Jn 5.5 ܓܒܪܐ ܚܕ "a man" (τις ἄνθρωπος).

In contrast, no such functional distinction is discernible with other numerals, though the preceding noun generally appears in st. emph., the following one in st. abs.: ܬܪܝܢ ܝܘܡܝܢ vs. ܝܘܡܬܐ ܬܪܝܢ "two days". That no significance is necessarily to be attached to either the difference in sequence or form of the noun (abs. vs. emph.) seems to be proven by an example like Mk 15.33P ܥܕܡܐ ܠܫܥܬܐ ܬܫܥ "until the ninth hour" followed immediately in the next verse by ܒܬܫܥ ܫܥܝܢ "at the ninth hour"[94].

See our study, "Remarks on the syntax of some types of noun modifier in Syriac", *Journal of Near Eastern Studies*, 31 (1972), 192-94.

§ 79 When a noun is qualified by both an adjective and the numeral 'one', the numeral appears either immediately before or after the noun: 1 Sm 6.7 ܥܓܠܬܐ ܚܕܐ ܚܕܬܐ "a new wagon"; Mk 12.6 ܚܕ ܒܪܐ ܚܒܝܒܐ "the only beloved son"[95].

§ 80 The same holds true of a demonstrative pronoun as a qualifier additional to an adjective: Dt 4.6 ܥܡܐ ܗܢܐ ܪܒܐ (MT: */haggōy haggādōl hazze/*); Addai 3.23 ܗܠܝܢ ܬܕܡܪܬܐ ܪܘܪܒܬܐ "these great wonders"[96].

§ 81 Notwithstanding the want of an extensive study[97], it appears that similar cohesion exists between other numerals and the nucleus noun, an additional

92a See I. Avinery, "The position of the demonstrative pronoun in Syriac", *J. of Near Eastern Studies*, 34 (1975), 123-27.

93 See above § 59.

94 In the Greek the numeral precedes in both cases, whereas S has ܬܫܥ ܫܥܝܢ in both.

95 See art. cit. (§ 78).

96 See art. cit. (§ 78). An apparent exception is Ex 2.23 ܒܝܘܡܬܐ ܣܓܝܐܐ ܗܢܘܢ but ܣܓܝ is atypical anyway (§ 76).

97 The entire Syriac New Testament (Peshitta) has been looked at for the numerals 1 to 100 with the aid of Bonus's concordance.

modifier such as an adjective, demonstrative pronoun, and ܐܚܪ̈ܢܝܢ being prevented from intervening. So Mt 12.45PC ܫܒܥ ܪ̈ܘܚܐ ܐܚܪ̈ܢܝܢ (ἑπτὰ ἕτερα πνεύματα) "seven other spirits"; Gn 21.29 ܗܠܝܢ ܫܒܥ ܢܩ̈ܘܬܐ ܕܥܢܐ (MT: /*ševa' kvāśōt hā'ēlle*/) "these seven lambs"; Aphr. I 48.11 ܗܢܘܢ ܬܪ̈ܝܢ ܦܘܩܕ̈ܢܝܢ "those two commandments"; Mt 10.5S ܗܠܝܢ ܬܪܥܣܪ ܬܠܡܝ̈ܕܘܗܝ "these twelve disciples of his".

§82 Where the nucleus noun or noun phrase is expanded by both a numeral and a demonstrative, the noun appears to display closer cohesion with the numeral, and in such a syntagm the demonstrative comes first: Ac 11.12 ܗܠܝܢ ܫܬܐ ܐܚ̈ܝܢ (ἕξ ἀδελφοὶ οὗτοι); Rev 9.18 ܗܠܝܢ ܬܠܬ ܡܚ̈ܘܢ (τῶν τριῶν πληγῶν τούτων). Cf. also 1 Sm 7.9 ܐܡܪܐ ܚܕ ܕܚܠܒܐ "a sucking lamb" (MT: /*ṭlē ḥālāv 'eḥād*/).

§83 If a noun qualified by a numeral is considered determined, the latter may optionally be suffixed: Mt 26.37 ܬܪ̈ܝܗܘܢ ܒܢ̈ܝ ܙܒܕܝ "the two sons of Zebedee"; Mk 13.27 ܐܪܒܥܬܝܗܘܢ ܪ̈ܘܚܐ "the four winds (= directions)"[98].

§84 Like the quantifier ܣܓܝ (§76), the relative position of ܩܠܝܠ "little, few" is also free, but, unlike the former, it is indeclinable: Aphr. I 532.19 ܗܠܝܢ ܡ̈ܠܐ ܩܠܝܠ "these few words"; ib. I 757.12 ܗܠܝܢ ܩܠܝܠ ܥܘܗ̈ܕܢܐ "these few memories"[99]. In contrast, ܣܓܝ may be declined or not declined: ܣܓܝ̈ܐܢ ܙܒ̈ܢܝܢ "many times"; ܣܓܝ ܩܪ̈ܒܐ "many battles". Cf. Nöldeke, §211, 214.

§85 Two (or more) nouns one of which modifies the other may be joined synthetically by means of the traditional *status constructus* or by fusion with

98 On the forms of these suffixed numerals, see Nöldeke, §149. The diphthong /*ay*/ of ܐܪܒܥܬܝܗܘܢ and the like is due to the analogy of ܬܪ̈ܝܗܘܢ with its genuine (and original) dual ending, whilst the *quššaya* of the Taw is due to the analogy of ܬܠܬܝܗܘܢ "they three", where its gemination in turn has resulted from assimilation: */*tlātatayhon*/ > /*tlāttayhon*/, in which the construct form was used where the nucleus noun was determined.

99 It is fully declined where it means "swift" or "light": Aphr. I 664.16 ܩܠܝܠܐ ܗܝ ܡܚܫܒܬܗ ܡܢ ܫܡܫܐ "his thought is swifter than the sun"; Acta Thomae 195.6 ܡܘܒܠܐ ܩܠܝܠܬܐ "the light burden".

the nucleus noun, where the modifier is a pronoun: e.g., ܡܠܟ ܒܒܠ "the king of Babylon"; ܪܘܚ ܩܘܕܫܐ "the Holy Spirit"; ܡܠܟܗܘܢ "their king". Cf. Nöldeke, § 205 A, B.

§ 86 However, the analytical structure with the particle – ܕ is far more common and idiomatic, where the modifying noun is not pronominal: ܡܠܟܐ ܕܒܒܠ. Note a fluctuation: 1 Sm 6.8 ܡܐ̈ܢܐ ܕܕܗܒܐ "golden vessels", but ib. 6.15 ܡܐ̈ܢܝ ܕܗܒܐ.

§ 87 Even when the modifier is pronominal, Syriac may resort to an analytical structure with –ܕܝܠ, often with some emphasis on the possessive pronoun: ܒܝܬܐ ܕܝܠܝ /baytā dil/ "*my* house"; ܥܘܕܪܢܐ ܕܝܠܢ. "*our* aid". The analytical structure lends itself to its positioning before the noun for emphasising the pronominal element: Aphr. I 269.23 ܕܝܠܗܘܢ ܠܒܘܫܝܗܘܢ ܠܐ ܒܠܝܢ "their garments, in contrast, do not wear out". Likewise its emphatic repetition: ib. 269.25 ܫܘܦܪܗܘܢ ܕܝܠܗܘܢ "their beauty, in contrast"[100]. But hardly emphatic in any sense in Mt 10.2 P ܕܝܠܗܘܢ ܕܬܪܥܣܪ ܫܠܝܚܝܢ ܫܡܗܐ "the names of the twelve apostles". Furthermore, a –ܕܝܠ form may be used substantivally like the English *mine*, *yours*, etc.: ܗܢܐ ܒܝܬܐ ܕܝܠܗ "this house is his". Cf. Nöldeke, § 225[101].

§ 88 The use of a *proleptic* pronoun with the nucleus noun is typically Aramaic: ܡܠܬܗ ܕܡܠܟܐ "the king's word". The pronoun "takes in advance" (πρόληψις) or anticipates the following noun. Usually the qualifying noun, ܡܠܟܐ in this instance, is determined in meaning: in other words, it is unidiomatic to say ܒܝܬܗ ܕܡܠܟܐ for "a royal residence". The same constraint applies to all other varieties of prolepsis. Cf. Nöldeke, § 205 C.

§ 89 As in Hebrew, the nucleus of the synthetic union is sometimes an adjective or its equivalent, or the modifier is a prepositional phrase: e.g., ܝܩܝܪܬ ܕܛܝܡܐ "expensive" (lit. "heavy of price"); ܢܣܝܒ ܗܘܢܐ "insane" (lit. "taken,

100 Like Ct 1.6 /*karmi šelli*/.

101 It is only rarely that the preposition Lamadh is used to break up a construct phrase: Gn 28.19 ܠܘܙ ܫܡܗ ܗܘܐ ܠܐܬܪܐ ܗܘ "the name of that place was Luz"; Ex 18.17 ܚܡܘܗܝ ܠܡܘܫܐ "Moses' father-in-law".

i.e. deprived of intellect"); ܪܓܡܬ ܠܐܝܠܝܢ ܕܫܠܝܚܝܢ ܠܘܬܗ "one who stones those who are sent to her"; ܐܢܬܬܐ ܫܦܝܪܬ ܚܙܘܐ "a good-looking woman". Cf. Nöldeke, §205 A, 206[102].

§90 Where an adjective qualifies one of the two nouns in analytical union, the former immediately follows the qualified noun as in Aphr. I 29.12 ܥܒܕܐ ܛܒܐ ܕܗܝܡܢܘܬܐ "the good works of faith", but only rarely is it removed as in ib. I 28.27 ܐܓܪܬܐ ܕܩܘܪܢܬܝܐ ܩܕܡܝܬܐ "the First Epistle to the Corinthians", where the strong cohesion of the noun phrase may be responsible, but this explanation is not valid in Ex 14.21 ܪܘܚܐ ܕܩܘܕܡܐ ܥܫܝܢܬܐ "a fierce wind of blight" or Ac 13.34 ܛܝܒܘܬܗ ܕܕܘܝܕ ܡܗܝܡܢܬܐ "the sure mercy of David"[103]. Compare further Gn 44.2 ܐܣܩܘܦܐ ܕܝܠܝ ܕܟܣܦܐ "my silver cup" with ib. 23.9 ܡܥܪܬܐ ܥܦܝܦܬܐ ܕܝܠܗ "his double cave".

§91 The word ܡܕܡ, apart from its use as an indefinite pronoun "something, anything", is highly versatile in its syntactic associations with nouns or adjectives or both: ܡܕܡ ܕܡܐܟܘܠܬܐ "something to eat"; ܡܕܡ ܒܝܫ "something evil"; ܡܕܡ ܪܒ "something large"; ܡܕܡ ܝܘܬܪܢ "some benefit"; ܡܘܗܒܬܐ ܡܕܡ "some gift"; ܡܕܡ ܦܬܓܡܐ "some word"; Aphr. I 272.21 ܗܠܝܢ ܡܕܡ ܕܝܐܝܢ ܠܝܚܝܕܝܐ "those things which are suitable to monks". Cf. Nöldeke, §219.

§92 Apart from its substantival use as in ܐܫܠܡ ܟܠ ܒܐܝܕܘܗܝ "he delivered everything into his hands" or ܒܫܠܡܐ ܬܠܐ ܟܘܠ "everything depends on peace", the ubiquitous ܟܠ (or ܟܘܠ) may form close union with a noun: ܟܠ ܝܘܡ "every day"; ܟܠ ܩܢܝܢܝܢ "all possessions". In such cases it usually takes the suffix pronoun matching the noun in gender and number, whether proleptically or resumptively: ܟܠܗ ܡܕܝܢܬܐ "the entire city";

102 Already Bar-Hebraeus (13th century) discusses this question in his grammar: A. Moberg (ed.), *Le livre des splendeurs* etc. (Lund, 1922), p. 61, lines 22-28. Cf. T. Muraoka, "The status constructus of adjectives in Biblical Hebrew", *Vetus Testamentum*, 27 (1977), 375-80; we do not entirely agree with this native Syriac grammarian. Cf. also S. D. Luzzatto, *Commentary to the Book of Isaiah* [in Heb.] (Tel Aviv, 1970), p. 8 ad Is 1.4.

103 Cf. Bar-Hebraeus, op. cit. (n. 102), p. 61, lines 10-16.

ܢܦܫܝ ܟܠܗ̇ "my whole soul"; ܟܠܗܘܢ ܚܛܗ̈ܐ "all the sins"; ܗܠܝܢ ܟܠܗܝܢ ܨܒܘ̈ܬܐ "all these things". Cf. Nöldeke, § 202D, 217-18.

The combination of a noun with a demonstrative pronoun and ܟܠ appears in a variety of patterns: Ex 18.18 ܟܠܗ ܥܡܐ ܗܢܐ "all this people"; ib. 11.8 ܥܡܐ ܗܢܐ ܟܠܗ; Gn 33.8 ܗܢܐ ܟܠܗ ܡܫܪܝܬܐ "all this encampment".

The situation in the Peshitta Pentateuch is discussed in I. Avinery, "The position of the declined *KL* in Syriac", *J. of the American Oriental Society*, 104 (1984), 333.

§ 93 *Relative clause* (Nöldeke, § 235-36)

A noun can be expanded by means of a complete clause, *relative clause*. Here Syriac possesses a great variety of possibilities[104]. The simplest type is a proclitic ܕ– introducing such a clause: ܡܠܟܐ ܕܫܡܥ ܗܕܐ "the king who heard this". The antecedent, in this case ܡܠܟܐ, may be wanting, and then the proclitic can be either personal or impersonal: ܕܫܡܥ ܗܕܐ "one who heard this"; ܕܫܡܥ ܡܠܟܐ "that which the king heard, what the king heard".

One often comes across demonstrative pronouns prefixed to the particle as in — ܗܘ ܕ "one who" or "that which". Likewise ܗܠܝܢ ܕ-, ܗ̇ܝ ܕ-, ܗܢܘܢ ܕ-, ܗܢܝܢ ܕ-. Also with interrogatives: ܐܝܕܐ ܕ-, ܐܝܢܐ ܕ-, ܐܝܠܝܢ ܕ-, ܡܢܘ ܕ-, ܡܢ ܕ-, all with indefinite reference. These can be further combined to produce forms such as ܗܘ ܡܢ ܕ-, ܗܘ ܐܝܢܐ ܕ-. Otherwise expressed, an interrogative not followed by the proclitic remains a pure interrogative, whilst one followed by such is a relative pronoun[105]. Thus ܝܕܥ ܗܘܐ ܡܢܐ ܗܘܐ "he knew what had happened", i.e. he did not need to ask "What happened?", but ܟܬܒ ܠܝ ܥܠ ܡܢܐ ܕܗܘܐ "he wrote to me about *what* (= things which) had happened".

Demonstratives or ܐܝܢܐ are often found in conjunction with the antecedent: ܗܠܝܢ ܡܠܟܐ ܕ- "those kings who (or: whom, whose)"; ܐܝܠܝܢ ܟܘܟܒܐ ܕ- "those stars which".

104 Pending a close study of the subject, it is easy to see the contrast between Acta Thomae 192.16 ܐܠܗܐ ܗܘ ܕܡܟܪܙ ܐܢܬ "that god whom you preach" and ib. 192.19 ܡܫܝܚܐ ܗܢܐ ܕܡܟܪܙ ܐܢܐ "this messiah whom I preach".

105 See above § 62.

§94 Where a prepositional phrase qualifies a noun, the former is regularly turned into a pseudo-relative clause with the addition of the particle ܕ- : Gn 3.3 ܦܐܪܐ ، ܕܐܝܠܢܐ ܕܒܡܨܥܬܗ ܕܦܪܕܝܣܐ "the fruits of the tree which (is) in the middle of the garden"; ib. 1.9 ܢܬܟܢܫܘܢ ܡܝܐ ܕܠܬܚܬ ܡܢ ܫܡܝܐ ܠܐܬܪܐ ܚܕ. "Let the waters that (are) under the sky come together to one place". In the latter example the absence of the proclitic may lead to a different interpretation: "... come together to one place under the sky"[106]. Note also a case like Mt 10.36P ܡܢ ܕܪܚܡ ܐܒܐ ܐܘ ܐܡܐ ܝܬܝܪ ܡܢ ܕܠܝ "one who loves (his) father or mother more than (he loves) me ...".

Attributive adjectives also occasionally display this same syntax: Gn 18.7 ܢܣܒ ܥܓܠܐ ܚܕ ܕܫܡܝܢ ܘܛܒ "he took a fat and good calf"; Ex 3.8 ܠܡܦܩܘܬܗ ܡܢ ܐܪܥܐ ܗܝ܂ ܠܐܪܥܐ ܕܪܘܝܚܐ ܘܛܒܐ "to bring them out of that land to a spacious and good land". The relativisation may have something to do with an underlying contrast: Abraham picked up out of the herd a calf which was fat and good, and not a lean, poor-quality one. So perhaps Gn 41.4 ܐܟܠ ܬܘܪ̈ܬܐ ܕܒܝ̈ܫܢ ܚܙܘܗܝܢ ܘܚܣܝ̈ܢ ܒܣܪܗܝܢ ܠܫܒܥ ܬܘܪ̈ܬܐ ܕܫܦܝ̈ܪܢ ܚܙܘܗܝܢ ܘܡܫܡ̈ܢܢ ܒܣܪܗܝܢ "the cows which (were) ugly in appearance and lean ate up the seven cows which (were) good-looking and fat". But ib. 41.20 ܐܟܠ ܬܘܪ̈ܬܐ ܚܣܝܟܬܐ ܘܒܝ̈ܫܬܐ ܠܫܒܥ ܬܘܪ̈ܬܐ ܩܕܡܝܬܐ ܫܡܝܢܬܐ must make one pause. See also Mt 5.30 ܐܝܕܟ ܕܝܡܝܢܐ "your right hand". Is the presence of an element further complementing the adjectives partly responsible? See also Ex 9.3 ܡܘܬܢܐ ܕܝܩܝܪ ܛܒ "a very formidable plague"; similarly ib. 9.18, 10.9, Mt 4.8.

§95 *Verb expanded*

A) Many verbs are complemented by a noun, noun phrase or pronoun, what is traditionally known as verbal rection or government. One must distinguish, however, between essential and non-essential complementation: whilst 'in the next room' in 'he lives in the next room' can be considered essential, the same phrase in 'someone is snoring in the next room' can hardly be so regarded.

106 Hebrew also uses /'*ăšer*/ in an analogous fashion, but not as regularly as Syriac; in the latter Gn passage it is missing in MT.

A verb which always requires an essential complement may be called transitive. Or a verb so used may be said to be transitively used. In contrast, a verb which does not require an essential complement or is not accompanied by such may be called intransitive.

Essential complementation may not be formally marked or may be mediated by the proclitic preposition – ܠ, in which case we call the complement a direct object: ܫܕܪ ܡܠܐܟܐ or ܫܕܪ ܠܡܠܐܟܐ "he sent a (or: the)[107] messenger". Some essential complements, however, are regularly mediated by some preposition or other[108]: e.g., ܒܣܐ "to despise" as in Mt 18.10S ܬܒܣܘܢ ܒܚܕ. ܡܢ ܗܠܝܢ ܙܥܘܪܐ "you despise one of those little ones". The fact that the ܠ can mark both direct and indirect object may sometimes lead to grammatical ambiguity, which is true of rarely used verbs in particular. Only those verbs which, in their non-construct participial form, can take an object unaccompanied by any preposition can be confidently declared transitive[109]. Cf. Nöldeke, § 278-92.

B) Where the direct object is a pronoun, it is normally attached directly to the verb as in ܫܕܪܟ "he sent you" = /*šaddar*/ + /*āḵ*/ "you (m. sg.)". However, the form for the 3 pl. "them" is enclitic, ܐܢܘܢ m. or ܐܢܝܢ f., which immediately follows the verb.

In the case of a participle, the direct pronominal object is always mediated by ܠ: ܡܫܕܪ ܐܢܐ ܠܟ "I am going to send you"; ܡܫܕܪ ܠܗܘܢ ܡܪܐ "the master is sending them".

107 *Pace* Nöldeke (§ 288 ad init.), the preposition ܠ prefixed to a direct object does not necessarily imply that the latter is definite, as can be seen, for example, in Ex 2.11 ܚܙܐ ܠܓܒܪܐ ܡܨܪܝܐ ܕܡܚܐ ܠܗ ܠܓܒܪܐ ܥܒܪܝܐ "he saw an Egyptian striking a Hebrew". This recognition could take care of most types of the seemingly puzzling use of ܠ discussed by Nöldeke (§ 288C).

108 True, there are verbs which allow both types of complementation (e.g., ܒܣܐ "to despise"). Nonetheless the two ought to be kept apart. That some verbs may be followed by more than one preposition with similar meaning or that some other verbs may require different prepositions for their different senses is another question.

109 Though dictionaries such as Brockelmann's *Lexicon* are informative in these matters, the information contained in them is not always full nor incontrovertible. So under ܒܣܐ Pa "despise", ܒ ought to be listed alongside ܥܠ as a linking particle. Also the entry in *Lexicon* for ܥܕܪ Pa. "help" (*c. acc. pers.*) is objectionable, as some of Brockelmann's references are cases of a pronoun suffix attached directly to the verb; on this question, see T. Muraoka, "On verb complementation in Biblical Hebrew", *Vetus Testamentum*, 29 (1979), 425-35. Cf. also G. A. Khan, "Object markers and agreement pronouns in Semitic languages", *Bulletin of the School of Oriental and African Studies*, 47 (1984), 468-500, in which an attempt is made to determine under what conditions the object is marked or left unmarked.

C) In the following cases a pronominal direct object may be detached from its verb and prefixed by ܠ [110]:

i. Emphatic or contrastive fronting as in Gn 41.13 ܠܝ ܐܗܦܟ ܥܠ ܬܫܡܫܬܝ، ܘܠܗ ܙܩܦ "*me* he restored to my office, whilst *him* he hanged",

ii. With another co-ordinate object as in Gn 41.10 ܐܪܡܝ ܒܒܝܬ ܐܣܝܪܐ... ܠܝ ܘܠܪܒ ܢܚܬܘܡܐ "he jailed us... me and the chief baker",

iii. With some particles as in Gn 38.10 ܐܡܝܬܗ ܐܦ ܠܗ "he also killed him"; 1 Sm 7.3 ܦܠܘܚܘܗܝ، ܠܗ ܒܠܚܘܕܘܗܝ، "Serve him alone"; Gn 39.9 ܠܐ ܚܣܟ ܡܢܝ ܡܕܡ ܐܠܐ ܐܢ ܠܟܝ "he did not withhold from me anything but you".

iv. Where two objects of a verb are both pronominal as in Acta Thomae 173.7 ܚܘܝܗ ܠܗ ܡܢ ܪܘܚܩܐ ܠܬܐܘܡܐ "he showed to him him, i.e. Thomas, from a distance"; 2 Sm 15.25 ܢܚܘܝܢܝ ܠܗ "to show me it".

D) The proleptic use of object pronouns is quite common: ܫܕܪܗ ܠܒܪܐ "he sent him (i.e.), the son" or, rarely without the preposition, ܫܕܪܗ ܒܪܐ.

E) With infinitives their pronominal object may enter a construct relationship as in Mt 8.2P ܠܡܕܟܝܘܬܝ، "to cleanse me" alongside ib. C ܠܡܕܟܝܘܬܝܢ, and ܠܡܘܩܕܘܬܗܘܢ "to burn them" instead of ܠܡܘܩܕܘ ܐܢܘܢ. See Nöldeke, §294.

§96 *Infinitive absolute*

A bare infinitive, namely without ܠ, is frequently used in the manner of the Hebrew infinitive absolute to colour the verbal notion in a variety of ways [111]. Whatever its historical origin, the usage is by no means confined to the Syriac Old Testament where one might justifiably suspect Hebrew influence. For example, Aphr. I 465.11 ܕܢܒܢܐ ܒܢܝܐ "so that he can build (and not destroy)". Such an infinitive may follow the main verb as in Dan 9.21 ܦܪܚ ܡܦܪܚ "it did fly away" or it may be separated from the latter as in Aphr. I 637.3 ܡܚܛܐ ܠܡܢܐ ܚܛܝܬ "why did you indeed sin?"

Where an infinitive absolute is to be expanded with the addition of an attributive adjective, numeral, relative clause and the like, a verbal noun whose form varies is used instead. Examples: ܡܝܬ ܡܘܬܐ ܒܝܫܐ "he died a terrible death"; ܚܪܒܬ ܚܘܪܒܗ ܐܚܪܝܐ "it was destroyed for the last

110 Cf. I. Avinery, "Pronominal objects in the Peshitta version" [in Heb.], *Leshonenu*, 38 (1974), 220-24.

111 See G. Goldenberg, "Tautological infinitive", *Israel Oriental Studies*, I (1971), 36-85.

time"; ܟܡܐ ܙܒܢ̈ܐ ܒܪܟܬܟ "I blessed you many times"; ܚܕ ܙܒܢܐ ܒܠܚܘܕ ܢܬܩܛܠ ܗܢܐ "this one shall be killed once only". Cf. Nöldeke, §298.

§97 Verbs, especially those of wishing, beginning, being able and the like may be complemented by another verb, which latter may appear in a variety of forms.

1) Infinitive as in ܛܠܝܐ ܨܒܐ ܠܡܐܟܠ "the boy wants to eat"; Gn 17.22 ܫܠܡ ܠܡܡܠܠܘ "he finished speaking",

2) Participle as in Ac 3.2 ܡܝܬܝܢ ܗܘܘ ܡܝܬܝܢ ܘܣܝܡܝܢ ܠܗ "they were in the habit of bringing and placing him ..."; Mk 5.17P ܫܪܝܘ ܒܥܝܢ ܡܢܗ ܕܢܐܙܠ ܠܗ "they began to beg him to go away"; Mt 8.22S ܫܒܘܩ ܡܝܬܐ ܩܒܪܝܢ ܡܝܬܝܗܘܢ "Leave the dead to bury their own dead",

3) Imperfect in a ܕ -clause as in Gn 19.22 ܠܐ ܡܫܟܚ ܐܢܐ ܕܐܥܒܕ ܡܕܡ "I cannot do anything"; Judg 3.28 ܠܐ ܫܒܩܘ ܠܐܢܫ ܕܢܥܒܪ "they did not allow anybody to get across",

4) Bare Imperfect as in Lk 18.13P ܠܐ ܨܒܐ ܗܘܐ ܐܦ ܠܐ ܥܝܢܘܗܝ ܢܪܝܡ ܠܫܡܝܐ "he did not want even to lift his eyes to heaven"; Josh Styl., 3.12 ܠܝ ܬܒܥܬܘܢ ܐܟܬܘܒ ܠܟܘܢ "you demanded me to write to you". More examples may be found in Nöldeke, §267, 2nd para.

At least with some of these verbs the four constructions are apparently freely interchangeable[112]. See Aphr. I 88.10-12 ܐܢ ܟܠ ܒܟܠܙܒܢ ܩܪܝܢ

112 There does not appear to be any meaningful correlation between the inflectional category (Pf., Impf., etc.) of the main verb and that of the complementing verb. See the following statistics for ܫܪܝ in the Peshitta New Testament.

Main Verb	Complementing verb	
Pf.	Inf.	38
	Ptc.	20
	ܕ + Impf.	10
Impf.	Inf.	7
Ptc.	Impf.	1

The figures for Aphrahat, and those for ܐܫܟܚ "be able" are not markedly different. The statistics for ܐܫܟܚ in the Peshitta New Testament are:

Pf.	Inf.	9
	ܕ + Impf.	6
Ptc.	Inf.	75
	ܕ + Impf.	58
	Impf.	3
	Ptc.	4

ܠܣܢܐܝܢ ܘܥܠ ܦܩܕܢ ܕܢܪܚܡ... "if he commanded us about our enemies that we should love them and about our enemies that we should pray about them ..."; ib. I 460.16-18 ܡܢ ܕܠܐ ܨܗܐ ܠܐ ܡܫܟܚ ܕܢܫܬܐ ܘܡܢ ܕܠܐ ܟܦܢ ܠܐ ܡܫܟܚ ܠܡܐܟܠ "one who is not thirsty cannot drink, and one who is not hungry cannot eat"; Mt 26.54S ܗܟܢܐ ܘܠܐ ܠܡܗܘܐ "thus it ought to be" as against ib. P ܗܟܢܐ ܘܠܐ ܕܢܗܘܐ. Cf. Nöldeke, § 272, 368. See also Nöldeke, § 337B for examples of the rare combination such as ܐܫܬܘܝ + another Perfect.

If the subjects of the two verbs differ, the complementing verb can appear only as Imperfect: Jn 21.22P ܐܢ ܨܒܐ ܐܢܐ ܕܢܩܘܐ ܗܢܐ ܥܕܡܐ ܕܐܬܐ ܐܢܐ "if I wish this one to remain until I come". We have not come across an instance of a bare Imperfect.

§ 98 As in some of the examples cited in § 97, the *asyndetic* construction is also found (a) where two actions follow in quick succession or (b) one of them is subordinate to the other, somewhat like in examples given in § 97. Usually the two verbs match in respect of inflectional category, and only little, if any, mainly the subject, is allowed to intervene between the two.

a) Especially common where the first verb denotes a physical movement from place to place as in Gn 27.14 ܐܙܠ ܢܣܒ "he went (and) took" (MT: */wayyēlek̠ wayyiqaḥ/*); Ex 4.19 ܗܦܘܟ ܙܠ "Go back" (MT: */lēk̠ šuv/*); ib. 10.6 ܗܦܟܘ ܢܦܩܘ "they turned and went out" (MT: */wayyifen wayyēṣē'/*); ib. 17.9 ܦܘܩ ܐܬܟܬܫ ܥܡ ܥܡܠܩ "Go out, fight" (MT: */ṣē' hillāḥēm/*)[113]; Gn 25.34 ܩܡ ܐܙܠ "he got up and went away" (MT: */wayyāqom wayyēlak̠/*); Acta Thomae 184.11 ܐܙܠܘ ܡܬܟܪܟܝܢ ܗܘܘ ܒܥܝܢ ܠܗ "they went, were going round, seeking him".

b) Mt 24.45 ܩܕܡܬ ܐܡܪܬ "I have told beforehand"; Aphr. I 52.14 ܡܩܕܡ ܗܘܐ ܡܠܝܟ ܗܘܐ (Pa. ptc. pass.) "which was promised beforehand"[114]); Gn 45.13 ܣܪܗܒܘ ܐܚܬܘ ܠܐܒܝ "Bring my father down quickly" (MT: */mihartem whōradtem 'et 'āvi/*)[115]. Cf. Nöldeke, § 337A.

Impf.	ܕ + Impf.	5
	Impf.	8
	Inf.	6

113 There is a variant reading: ܠܡܬܟܬܫ (inf.).
114 On the repeated enclitic, cf. Lk 13.7P ܐܬܐ ܐܢܐ ܒܥܐ ܐܢܐ, but the enclitic need not be repeated as in ib. S ܐܬܐ ܒܥܐ ܐܢܐ.
115 Cf. Gn 18.7 ܣܪܗܒ ܕܢܥܒܕܝܘܗܝ "he cooked it quickly"; ib. 41.32 ܡܣܪܗܒ ܐܠܗܐ ܠܡܥܒܕܗ "God hastens to do it".

The addition of the conjunction Waw indicates a different nuance of the verb: Gn 20.8 ܩܕܡ ܐܒܝܡܠܟ ܒܨܦܪܐ ܘܩܪܐ ... "Abimelech rose early in the morning and summoned ...".

In some cases one may speak of hendiadys: Lk 13.31 ܦܘܩ ܙܠ "Go out"; ib. 14.5 ܕܠܐ ܡܚܕܐ "pulls up".

§99 *Verbs of perception* (seeing, hearing, etc.) often take two complements, the one referring to a person or a thing being perceived and the other describing in what state he or it is or was found or what action he or it is or was found performing. This syntagm may take one of the following three forms. The second complement is normally non-preterital in form.

1) Verb + 1st Complement + ܕ + 2nd Complement

Gn 1.3 ܚܙܐ ܐܠܗܐ ܠܢܘܗܪܐ ܕܫܦܝܪ "God saw the light that (it was) good"; ib. 6.2 ܘܚܙܘ ܒܢܝ ܐܠܗܝܡ ܠܒܢܬܗ ܕܐܢܫܐ ܕܫܦܝܪܢ ܐܢܝܢ "the sons of gods saw the daughters of men that they were beautiful"; Ex 32.22 ܐܢܬ ܝܕܥ ܐܢܬ ܠܗ ܠܥܡܐ ܗܢܐ ܕܒܝܫ ܗܘ "you know this nation that it [= they] (are) evil"; ib. 33.10 ܚܙܐ ܟܠܗ ܥܡܐ ܥܡܘܕܐ ܕܥܢܢܐ ܕܩܐܡ ܒܬܪܥܐ "the whole people saw the pillar of cloud that (it) stood at the gate, standing at the gate"; Mt 20.6 ܐܫܟܚ ܐܚܪܢܐ ܕܩܝܡܝܢ ܘܒܛܝܠܝܢ "he found others standing and idling away"; Ephrem, *Comm. on Exodus* (ed. R.-M. Tonneau, CSCO 152), sec. 27.1 ܚܙܐ ܠܪܚܝܠ... ܕܒܚܦܝܘܬܗ "he saw Rachel barefoot [lit. in her barefootedness]". Analogously with a verb of saying: Mk 8.27 ܡܢܐ ܐܡܪܝܢ ܐܢܫܐ ܕܐܝܬܝ، "what are people saying that I am?".

2) Verb + 1st Compl. + ܟܕ + 2nd Compl.

Gn 26.8 ܚܙܝܗ، ܠܐܝܣܚܩ ܟܕ ܡܓܚܟ ܥܡ ܪܦܩܐ "he saw Isaac playing [lit., as he plays] with Rebecca"; Ex 2.11 ܚܙܐ ܠܓܒܪܐ ܡܨܪܝܐ ܟܕ ܡܚܐ ܠܓܒܪܐ ܥܒܪܝܐ "he saw an Egyptian striking a Hebrew"; Mt 26.40 ܐܫܟܚ ܐܢܘܢ ܟܕ ܕܡܟܝܢ "he found them asleep".

3) Verb + 1st Compl. + 2nd Compl. (a rare construction)

Gn 21.9 ܚܙܬ ܣܪܐ ܠܒܪܗ ܕܗܓܪ... ܡܓܚܟ "Sarah saw Hagar's son ... playing"; ib. 42.27 ܚܙܐ ܟܣܦܗ ܣܝܡ. (v. l. ܕܣܝܡ) ܒܦܘܡ ܛܥܢܗ "he saw his silver placed in the mouth of his pack"; Jdg 3.25 ܚܙܘ ܡܪܗܘܢ ܪܡܐ ܥܠ ܐܪܥܐ ܘܡܝܬ "they saw their master lying [lit., thrown] on the ground and dead".

Note the important distinction between (ptc.) ܫܡܥܬ ܠܓܒܪܐ ܕܡܡܠܠ ܥܠ ܡܫܝܚܐ "I heard the man speaking about the messiah" and ܫܡܥܬ ܠܓܒܪܐ ܕܡܠܠ (pf.) ܥܠ ܡܫ' "I heard [= was told] that the man had spoken about the messiah"[116].

§ 100 Clauses introducing *direct speech* are often prefixed with ܕ- in the manner of ὅτι *recitativum* in Greek: Mt 2.4P ܡܫܐܠ ܗܘܐ ܠܗܘܢ ܕܐܝܟܐ ܡܬܝܠܕ ܡܫܝܚܐ "he kept asking them, 'where is the Messiah going to be born?' ". Cases such as the following may be similarly interpreted: Mt 22.15S ܢܣܒܘ ܡܠܟܐ ܕܐܝܟܢܐ ܢܨܕܘܢܗ ܒܡܠܬܐ "they took counsel (asking themselves) how to entangle him in his talk".

Clause structure

§ 101 A clause may be conveniently classified as either nominal or verbal. A *verbal clause* contains a finite verb (Perfect, Imperfect or Imperative), which may include within itself the subject as in ܟܬܒܬ ܟܬܒܐ "I wrote a book" or the subject may be extraposed[117] either before or after the verb (e.g., ܫܠܚ ܡܠܐܟܐ "*he* sent a messenger"; ܫܠܝܚܐ ܟܬܒܘ ܟܬܒܐ "the apostles wrote the book"). A nominal clause, in contrast, has as its predicate a participle or some other part of speech such as noun, adjective, prepositional phrase and the like.

§ 102 It is the *nominal clause* that displays the greatest variety of forms and structures[118]. Apart from clauses with ܐܝܬ and those signifying existence and location, which will be treated later (§ 107), the standard Syriac nominal clause may be classified according to the number of its major components:

116 Apart from the choice of ܐܡܪ to render the Heb. /*dibber*/, the Peshitta in Gn 27.5f. is therefore far from satisfactory: ܪܦܩܐ ܫܡܥܬ ܟܕ ܐܡܪ ... ܫܡܥܬ ܠܥܣܘ ܕܐܡܪ .. "Rebecca heard when Isaac said [i.e., from a third party, or: after Isaac had said] to Esau ... I have heard that your father said [hardly = I heard your father, who said ...]."

117 That is to say, placed outside of the nominal clause framework.

118 The classic treatment by Nöldeke (§ 309-14) of this complex subject has been both substantially and substantively refined and modified by the following recent studies, although some issues are still outstanding: G. Goldenberg, "On Syriac sentence structure", in M. Sokoloff (ed.), *Arameans, Aramaic and the Aramaic Literary Tradition* (Ramat Gan, 1983), pp. 97-140; T. Muraoka, "On the nominal clause in the Old Syriac Gospels", *J. of Semitic Studies*, 20 (1975), 28-37; idem, "On the Syriac particle *'iṯ*", *Bibliotheca Orientalis*, 34 (1977), 21-22.

mostly two or three, but sometimes four. Furthermore, one can identify three structural meanings which can be expressed by them: descriptive, identificatory, and contrastive.

§ 103 *Formally* speaking, bipartite nominal clauses consisting of a subject and a predicate may be grouped into those with a personal pronoun (*I*, *you* etc.) as one component and those which do not contain such: Lk 22.26S ܐܢ̄ܬܘܢ ܠܐ ܗܟܢܐ "you are not like that"; Gn 27.22 ܩܠܐ ܕܝܥܩܘܒ ܘܓܫܬܐ ܕܐܝ̈ܕܝܐ ܕܥܣܘ "the voice is that of Jacob and the feel of the hands is that of Esau"; ib. 33.13 ܛܠܝ̈ܐ ܛܠܝܢ "the children are young"; Dt 3.5 ܟܠܗܝܢ ܗܠܝܢ ܩܘܪ̈ܝܐ ܕܚܣܝܢܢ ܫܘܪ̈ܝܗܝܢ "all these are cities whose walls are fortified"; Ec 1.17 ܐܦ ܗܢܐ ܛܘܪܦܐ ܕܪܘܚܐ "this is also a mind-tormenting exercise" [119].

However, by far the most common pattern is a tripartite one, which is particularly true where neither subject nor predicate is a personal pronoun. The third component is provided by an enclitic personal pronoun. The interpretation of the nature of this enclitic presents a difficult problem: it may represent the subject of the clause nucleus [120] as an extension of the normal "non-emphatic" bipartite clause of the type ܛܒ ܐܢܐ "I am good", ܫܦܝܪܐ ܗܝ "she is beautiful", or it may be an enclitic whose basic function is to extrapose or underline the immediately preceding clause component mostly in the manner of a cleft sentence. This latter type of extraposing enclitic may follow any part of speech, even an adverb or verb [121]. It usually

119 *Pace* Goldenberg (art. cit., p. 132) I do not consider it unsound to state that a nominal predicate may form a sentence by just being juxtaposed with any nominal subject. Goldenberg suggests that all these cases and many such others — including those classified by him as exceptional — are basically elliptical clauses wanting an enclitic pronominal subject; this is, in my view, forcing data into a theoretical strait-jacket. I for one would not run the risk of adjudging the *propriety* (see Goldenberg, art. cit., p. 133 [4]) of the last-quoted example (Ec 1.17) vis-à-vis ib. 2.15 et passim in Ec ܐܦ ܗܢܐ ܗܒܠܐ ܗܘ "this is also vanity". Frequency count is, of course, an entirely different issue.

120 Symbolised by Goldenberg (art. cit., p. 103, n. 10), following Jespersen, with a lower case *s*.

121 Of the examples quoted by Nöldeke (§ 221), see, for instance, ܠܚܕ ܗܘ ܐܠܗܐ ܣܓܕܝܢܢ "we worship only one God"; ܐܢ ܠܡܐܠܦ ܗܘ ܨܒܐ ܐܢܬ "if you wish to *learn*". Even after a feminine noun: Jdg 7.2 ܐܝܕܝ ܗܘ ܦܪܩܬܢܝ "it is my hand that won me victory"; Aphr. I 140.27 ܢܘܪܐ ܗܘ ܡܠܚܟܐ ܗܘܬ ܠܗܘܢ "fire was licking them". Whilst for Goldenberg (art. cit., § 6) cases of the lack of grammatical agreement or concord between the subject and the enclitic are careless blunders — e.g., Ex

takes the form of the third person m. sg. ܗܘ, which however may be varied by attraction or analogy of ܗܘܝܘ (< *ܗܘ ܗܘ) as in Mt 24.5 ܐܢܐ ܐܢܐ ܡܫܝܚܐ "I am the messiah" [122].

Schematically presented, 'David is my master' [123] may be rendered in Syriac by four tripartite structures:

16.26 ܝܘܡܐ ܫܒܝܥܝܐ ܫܒܬܐ ܗܝ "the seventh day is a sabbath" — our twofold perspective confers some respectability on such cases, suggesting that there is something fundamental about them. Would it be fair to the Peshitta translator, who in a verse consisting of two neat parallel hemistichs has written, in Is 9.14(15) [discussed by Goldenberg, art. cit., p. 107]. ܣܒܐ ܘܗܕܝܪ ܐܦܐ ܗܘܝܘ ܪܝܫܐ ܘܢܒܝܐ ܕܡܠܦ ܫܘܩܪܐ ܗܘܝܘ ܕܘܢܒܬܐ "the head is (= symbolises) an elder and honoured man, whilst the tail is a prophet who teaches lies", to criticise his carelessness? How about Gn 40.12 ܬܠܬ ܫܒܫܝܢ ܬܠܬܐ ܐܢܝܢ ܝܘܡܝܢ "the three branches are three days" and Mt 12.50S ܟܠ ܡܢ ܕܥܒܕ ܨܒܝܢܗ ܕܐܒܝ ܕܒܫܡܝܐ ܗܘܝܘ ܐܚܝ ܘܚܬܝ (sic!) ܘܐܡܝ "anyone that does the will of my heavenly father is my brother, sister and mother"? In all these cases of apparent discord we can perhaps see a weakened extraposing enclitic attracted in form to the preceding component in respect of gender and number. Something of the complexity of the issue can be observed in the following cases where the relative orders of the symbol (= subject) and its referent (= predicate) are reversed with Goldenberg's unit *p-s* intact in the middle: Mt 13.20 ܗܘ ܕܐܙܕܪܥ ܥܠ ܫܘܥܐ ܗܘܝܘ ܕܫܡܥ ܡܠܬܐ ܘܒܚܕܘܬܐ ܡܩܒܠ ܠܗ "one which was sown on a rock is he who hears the word and accepts it gladly..." versus ib. 19 ܟܠ ܐܢܫ ܕܫܡܥ ܡܠܬܐ ܕܡܠܟܘܬܐ ܘܠܐ ܡܣܬܟܠ ... ܗܘܝܘ ܕܐܙܕܪܥ ܥܠ ܝܕ ܐܘܪܚܐ "every man who hears the word of the kingdom and does not comprehend (it) ... is the one which was sown by the roadside": Goldenberg has no alternative pattern other than his D (*P-p-s-S*). See also Mt 13.39S.

122 Goldenberg (art. cit., § 8) and I ("Nominal clause", § 5) are in agreement in rejecting the common notion of pronominal copula as applied by Nöldeke and others to Syriac.

That ܐܢܐ ܐܢܐ ܡܫܝܚܐ and ܐܢܐ ܗܘ ܡܫܝܚܐ are interchangeable variants is suggested by examples such as Aphr. I 748.2 ܚܢܢ ܐܢܚܢ ܥܡܗ ܕܐܠܗܐ ܘܒܢܝ ܐܒܪܗܡ "we are God's people and Abraham's sons" // ib. 4 ܚܢܢ ܚܢܢ ܒܢܝ ܐܒܪܗܡ // ib. 17 ܚܢܢ ܐܢܚܢ ܒܢܝ ܐܒܪܗܡ ܘܚܢܢ ܐܢܚܢ ܥܡܗ ܕܐܠܗܐ on one hand, and Ac 9.5 ܐܢܐ ܐܢܐ ܝܫܘܥ (ἐγώ εἰμι Ἰησοῦς) // ib. 22.8, 26.15 (Paul reporting the same incident on twc other occasions) ܐܢܐ ܗܘ ܝܫܘܥ (Gk: ditto) on the other.

123 Goldenberg (op. cit., n. 14) reports that he has found no instance of a clause like ܐܒܪܗܡ ܐܢܐ "I am Abraham" as a reply to the question "What's your name?" and goes as far as to suggest that my choice of a proper noun to be included in the model was

a) ܡܪܝ ܗܘ ܕܘܝܕ P — s[124] — S (Goldenberg's pattern C)

b) ܕܘܝܕ ܗܘ ܡܪܝ P — s — S (pattern C)

c) ܕܘܝܕ ܡܪܝ ܗܘ S — P — s (pattern B)

d) ܡܪܝ ܕܘܝܕ ܗܘ P — S — s

The last pattern is rather rare: ܟܠ ܦܓܪܝܢ ܫܠܝܛ ܐܢܬ ܗܘ "you are master of our bodies"; ܩܕܝܫ ܐܢܬ ܗܘ "thou art holy"; ܝܠܝܕ ܐܢܬ ܗܘ ܪܘܚܢܐܝܬ "thou art spiritually born"; ܐܪܙܗ ܕܐܠܗܐ ܡܫܝܚܐ ܗܘ "Christ is a mystery of God"[125]; Mt 12.8S ܡܪܗ ܕܫܒܬܐ ܒܪܗ ܗܘ ܕܐܢܫܐ "The son of man is lord of the sabbath"[126]; Odes of Solomon (ed. J.H. Charlesworth), 5.2 ܣܒܪܝ ܐܢܬ ܗܘ "you are my hope"; Jn 9.9S ܗܘ ܗܢܘ[127] "this is him".

§104 *Ellipsis*

A pronominal subject of bipartite clauses may be deleted in a relative clause, a clause complementing verbs of knowing, believing, seeing etc. or a circumstantial clause. Whether there exists any rule governing deletion or retention of such enclitic is not known, except that the deletion is extremely rare with the first and second persons.

Acta Thomae 194.15 ܕܪܚܝܩܝܢ ܡܢܗ "(things) which are far from it"; Lk 21.21P ܐܝܠܝܢ ܕܒܝܗܘܕ ܐܢܘܢ.. ܘܐܝܠܝܢ ܕܒܓܘܗ ܐܢܘܢ.. ܘܕܒܩܘܪܝܐ "those who are in Judea... and those who are in it... and those who are in villages..."; Mt 15.31P ܚܙܝܢ ܚܪܫܐ ܕܡܡܠܠܝܢ

not only infelicitous, but even a mistake. But is it at all conceivable that no Syriac speaker ever made such an utterance otherwise than elliptically (ܐܒܪܗܡ) or circuitously (say, ܐܒܪܗܡ ܥܒܕܝ)?

124 Goldenberg uses a lower cases for our E, which stands for Enclitic. S = subject; P = predicate.

125 References: F.C. Burkitt (ed.), *Euphemia and the Goth* etc. (London & Oxford, 1913), Syr. text, p. 13; P. Bedjan (ed.), *Mar Jacobi Sarugensis homiliae selectae* (Paris/Leipzig, 1905-10), I, pp. 222, 225; L. Leloir, Saint Ephrem: *Commentaire de l'Évangile concordant* (Dublin, 1963), p. 2.

126 That this hardly represents the identificatory pattern — "it is the son of man that is lord of the sabbath" — is shown by a parallel passage, Lk 6.5P ܡܪܗ ܗܘ ܕܫܒܬܐ ܒܪܗ ܕܐܢܫܐ and Mt 12.8P ܡܪܗ ܕܫܒܬܐ ܐܝܬܘܗܝ ܒܪܗ ܕܐܢܫܐ; cf. also Mk 2.28P, and Ephrem's commentary on the Diatessaron (ed. Leloir [see n. 125]), XIV, 4.

127 Perhaps to be read */haw/* rather than */hu/*. In Colloquial English one might paraphrase: 'This is that bloke alright'.

ܘܓܕܝܡ̈ܐ ܕܡܬܚܠܡܝܢ "...saw the dumb speaking, the maimed recovering"; Ex 14.3 ܐܡܪ . . . ܕܢܘܟܪ̈ܝܢ ܐܢܘܢ "he said... that they were foreigners"[128]; Acta Thomae 200.4 ܠܗ ܐܩܝܡ ܟܕ ܚܝ "to raise him up alive".

The enclitic is normally retained in causal clauses: Ex 5.8 ܡܛܠ ܕܒܛܠܢܐ ܐܢܘܢ "because they are idle".

Where there are two or more co-ordinate predicates, the identical enclitic subject need not be repeated: Ac 1.11 ܡܢܐ ܩܝܡܝܢ ܐܢܬܘܢ ܘܚܝܪܝܢ ܠܫܡܝܐ "why are you standing and looking at the sky?" but ib. 2.33 ܚܙܝܢ ܐܢܬܘܢ ܘܫܡܥܝܢ ܐܢܬܘܢ "you see and hear" (ὑμεῖς καὶ βλέπετε καὶ ἀκούετε).

§ 105 *Structural meaning*

Where 'David is my master' is, or can be construed as, a reply to the question 'What is David?', the clause may be said to be descriptive in meaning. If it is, or can be construed as, a reply to the question 'Who (or: Which) among you (or: them) is David?', its structural meaning is that of identification[129]. Finally, 'David is my master' may be contrasted, whether explicitly or implicitly, with, say, 'John is my servant'.

Of the four patterns mentioned above (§ 102), *a* and *d* are usually descriptive, *b* identificatory, and *c* contrastive.

Since the subject has not been fully researched from the point of view of structural meaning, many of the following illustrative cases are those with a personal pronoun as either their subject or predicate.

(*a*) *Descriptive*: Acta Thomae 173.14 ܡܪܟ ܗܘ ܗܢܐ "Is this your master?"; Aphr. I 116.9f. ܣܓܝܐܝܢ ܐܢܘܢ ܥܒܘܕܘܗܝ "its makers are many"; Mt 16.13S ܡܢܘ ܠܡ ܗܢܐ ܒܪܗ ܕܐܢܫܐ "Who is this son of man?".

128 This the most likely interpretation of Mt 14.30 ܚܙܐ ܠܪܘܚܐ ܕܥܫܝܢܐ "he saw the wind being strong" rather than "the wind which was strong". The anarthrous adjective ἰσχυρόν is wanting in some Greek manuscripts. Cf. the Curetonian version with ܕܥܫܝܢܐ ܗܝ and our discussion above (§ 94).

129 Ascriptive and equative respectively according to J. Lyons, *Semantics*, vol. 2 (Cambridge, 1977), pp. 471-73. He is aware of the grammatical ambiguity inherent in the morphologically defined equative structure, but we like to point out that the ambiguity is non-existent at a prosodic level. This prosodic distinction dismisses as irrelevant the scepticism expressed by P. H. Matthews, *Syntax* (Cambridge, 1981), p. 120: "is this [i.e., the ambiguous distinction between ascriptive and equative] syntactic in English?".

For examples of (*d*), see above § 102 end.

Where the subject is a personal pronoun, the bipartite construction is the norm: Mt 8.26S ܠܡܢܐ ܕܚܝܠܬܢܝܢ ܐܢܬܘܢ "Why are you fearful?; ib. 19.6S ܚܕ ܐܢܘܢ ܒܣܪ "they are one flesh" [130].

(*b*) *Identificatory*: Mt 27.11 ܐܢܬ ܗܘ ܡܠܟܐ ܕܝܗܘܕܝܐ "are *you* the king of the Jews?; Lk 7.19P ܐܢܬ ܗܘ ܗܘ ܕܐܬܐ "are *you* the one to come?"; Aphr. I 20.17 ܗܢܐ ܗܘ ܦܘܩܕܢܝ "*this* is my commandment".

* ܗܘ ܗܘ appears as ܗܘܝܘ: Jn 4.29 ܗܘܝܘ ܡܫܝܚܐ "*he* is the messiah".

As remarked above (§ 103: p. 61 and n. 122), the enclitic may be replaced by the same form as the preceding pronominal predicate as in Mt 24.5 ܐܢܐ ܐܢܐ ܡܫܝܚܐ "*I* am the messiah". However, with the second person, ܐܢܬ ܗܘ, for instance, seems to be favoured rather than ܐܢܬ ܐܢܬ, perhaps for the sake of euphony.

This structure is quite common with interrogatives: ܡܢܘ "Who is it that ...?"; ܐܝܟܘ "Where?, Where is it that ...?", etc.

(*c*) *Contrastive*: Mt 20.15 ܥܝܢܟ ܒܝܫܐ ܘܐܢܐ ܛܒ ܐܢܐ "your eye is evil, but I am good"; Jn 8.23P ܐܢܬܘܢ ܡܢ ܕܠܬܚܬ ܐܢܬܘܢ ܘܐܢܐ ܡܢ ܕܠܥܠ ܐܢܐ "ye are from below, but I am from above"; Bardaisan 540.20-22 ܗܝܡܢ ܠܡ ܗܝܡܢܘܬܐ ܘܟܠ ܡܕܡ ܡܫܟܚ ܐܢܬ ܘܐܢܐ ܠܐ ܡܫܟܚ ܐܢܐ ܠܡܗܝܡܢܘ ܐܠܐ ܐܢ ܐܬܦܝܣܬ "Just believe, and then you will be capable of anything, but I cannot believe unless I am convinced".

The same structural meaning can also be expressed in a bipartite form as well: Jn 15.5S ܐܢܐ ܓܦܬܐ ܘܐܢܬܘܢ ܫܒܛܬܐ "I am the vine, whilst you are branches" [131]. See also Mt 20.15 cited above.

Where the subject is not a personal pronoun, the contrast in structural meaning may become blurred: Mt 5.12S ܐܓܪܟܘܢ ܣܓܝ ܗܘ ܒܫܡܝܐ "your reward is great in heaven" (Descriptive); ib. 23.10S ܡܠܦܢܟܘܢ ܡܫܝܚܐ ܗܘ "the Messiah is your teacher" (Identificatory) [132].

130 Where the element preceding the enclitic consists of more than one word, it is idiomatic for the enclitic to be placed immediately after the first component. On this question, see I. Avinery, "On the nominal clause in the Peshitta", *J. of Semitic Studies*, 22 (1977), pp. 48 f., and Goldenberg, art. cit., § 2 (pp. 100-102).

131 See our "Nominal clause", pp. 30-33.

132 That the translator exercised a measure of independence from the Greek is exemplified by Mt 27.54S ܗܢܐ ܒܪܗ ܗܘ ܕܐܠܗܐ for θεοῦ υἱὸς ἦν. Incidentally, the last example (Mt 23.10), though seemingly of Goldenberg's pattern B, reinforces our view on the twofold nature of the enclitic, for here the enclitic is hardly an *s*.

A problematic example may be found in Acta Thomae 187.7 where the apostle, in response to the king's query as to the progress of the commissioned building work, says ܦܠܛܪܝܢ ܐܝܬ ܓܡܝܪ ܗܘ܂ ܘܬܛܠܝܠܐ ܗܘ ܚܣܝܪ ܠܗ "the palace is complete, but the roof is wanting to it". This hardly represents Goldenberg's Pattern C (*P—s—S*); for it is a kind of afterthought: "there is, though, the roof which is yet to be added"[133].

§ 106 There are found on occasion clauses with *four components* as an extension of the pattern P—E—S or S—E—P used apparently in order to avoid clumsiness or misunderstanding: Dt 7.9 ܡܪܝܐ ܐܠܗܟ ܗܘ ܗܘ ܐܠܗܐ "the Lord your God is the God". Goldenberg symbolises the pattern as *P—p—s—S*[134]. The *p* is originally a resumptive element, just as in a verbal clause like Mt 24.13 ܡܢ ܕܡܣܝܒܪ ܠܚܪܬܐ ܗܢܐ ܗܘ ܢܚܐ "one who endures till the end shall be saved". An example as an extension of S—E—P is Mt 13.39S ܙܪܘܥܗܘܢ ܗܘ ܗܘ ܒܝܫܐ "their sower is the evil one" (a parable interpreted). The resumptive pronoun may be ܗܢܘ (e.g. Mt 13.19S) or ܗܘ (Mt 15.11P).

§ 107 *Existence, location and* ܐܝܬ

That some object exists ("existential" clause) or is to be found at a specific location ("locative") is normally expressed with the mediation of the particle ܐܝܬ, though the latter may be absent as in Mt 1.23S ܐܠܗܐ ܥܡܢ "God is with us"; ib 13.56S ܐܚܘܬܗ ܟܠܗܝܢ ܠܘܬܢ "all his sisters are with us"; Gn 41.12 ܘܬܡܢ ܥܡܢ ܛܠܝܐ ܥܒܪܝܐ "and there was there with us a Hebrew lad" (circumstantial clause). Compare Lk 1.66S ܐܝܕܗ ܕܡܪܝܐ ܥܡܗ "the hand of the Lord (was) with him" and ib. P ܐܝܕܗ ܕܡܪܝܐ ܐܝܬ ܗܘܬ ܥܡܗ.

133 The roof was not mentioned nor hinted at in the king's query. It is perfectly legitimate to claim that, in utterances such as 'Listen. A possum is moving about in the loft' or 'Look! A dog is chasing our neighbour's kitten', the entire clauses excluding the initial attention-catching words are predicates in the sense that they can be transformed into 'there is a possum moving about ...' and 'there is a dog chasing ...'. Or, since one can only predicate of something specific as subject, one should rather say that utterances like these do not lend themselves to such a logico-grammatical dichotomy. I am not particularly happy with the notion of locative subject canvassed by Lyons, op. cit. (n. 129), pp. 480 f.

134 Op. cit., pp. 106 f.

135 See Nöldeke, § 301-303, T. Muraoka, "On the Syriac particle *'iṯ*", *Bibliotheca Orientalis*, 34 (1977), 21-22, and especially Goldenberg, art. cit., pp. 117-31.

With very few exceptions[136] — the last-quoted being one of them — the unsuffixed ܐܝܬ has an indeterminate object whose existence or non-existence (ܠܝܬ) is indicated.

Conversely, when the subject is determinate, the particle, if used, is suffixed[137]: e.g., Jn 4.37 ܒܗܕܐ ܐܝܬܝܗ ܡܠܬܐ ܕܫܪܪܐ "herein is the word of truth".

In addition to "existential" and "locative" uses, the particle is also found as a substitute for a pronominal enclitic of tripartite nominal clauses[138]. Such a use of ܐܝܬ, however, is rare in identificatory clauses. No doubt the exposure to the Greek culture has a great deal to do with the development of the copulaic ܐܝܬ, as is suggested by its relative infrequency in the Old Syriac Gospels (esp. S) compared with the Peshitta version: e.g., Mt 12.8S ܡܪܗ ܕܫܒܬܐ ܒܪܗ ܗܘ ܕܐܢܫܐ // P ܡܪܗ ܕܫܒܬܐ ܐܝܬܘܗܝ ܒܪܗ ܕܐܢܫܐ "the son of man is the lord of the sabbath". Also ib. 13.38, 39 16.13; Lk 19.46.

Applied to the past, ܐܝܬ ܗܘܐ is occasionally treated as indeclinable: Lk 1.7P ܠܝܬ ܗܘܐ ܠܗܘܢ ܕܘܟܬܐ // S ... ܠܝܬ ܗܘܬ "they had no place" or ib. 4.40P ܕܟܠܗܘܢ ܐܢܫܝܢ ܐܝܬ ܗܘܐ ܠܗܘܢ ܟܪܝܗܐ // S ܟܠܗܘܢ ܐܢܫܝܢ ܕܐܝܬ ܗܘܘ ܠܗܘܢ .. "all those who had sick people".

Note a subtle distinction between 1 Sm 1.2 ܗܘܘ ܠܦܢܢܐ ܒܢܝܐ "Peninnah had children, i.e. she gave birth to children" and ib. ܐܝܬ ܗܘܐ ܠܗ ܬܪܬܝܢ ܢܫܝܢ "he had two wives, i.e. he was leading a polygamous life"; ܐܝܬ ܗܘܬ ܠܗ ܒܢܝܐ would probably mean "she was a mother of children", thus ܗܘܐ indicating a process (*werden*) and ܐܝܬ ܗܘܐ a state (*sein*)[139].

136 Goldenberg (art. cit., p. 124), whose study seems to be based on a considerable number of early Syriac documents, adduces a total of seven examples, which I suspect is pretty much a complete list.

137 Goldenberg (art. cit., p. 124) again adduces a small number of apparent exceptions, all from a single passage: e.g., ܐܝܬܝܗܘܢ ܒܢܝܢܫܐ ܐܝܠܝܢ "there are people who ...", which reminds one of similar prolepsis in Modern Hebrew /*yešnam 'anašim še* .../. For another exception (in Mt 8.28S), see our article (n. 135), p. 21b.

138 For examples of apparent interchange between the two structures, see our study (cited in n. 135), § 7.2.

139 Cp. Addai 7.11 ܦܕܓܪܐ ܐܝܬ ܗܘܐ ܠܗ ܒܪܓܠܘܗܝ "he had a gout in his legs" with ib. 7.13 ܘܬܘܒ ܠܐ ܗܘܬ ܠܗ ܦܕܓܪܐ "he did not suffer a relapse of the gout".

The combination of ܐܝܬ with the Imperfect of ܗܘܐ is infrequent: Overbeck, *S. Ephraemi Syri* etc., p. 160: ܐܝܟ ܕܢܗܘܐ ܐܝܬܘܗܝ ܠܗ ܘܠܟܠ ܕܪ̈ܝܢ ܢܣܐ ܡܟܢܫܢܐ "so that he would be a rallying banner for all generations".

Compared with Hebrew, Syriac thus offers a rich variety of structures, as far as the nominal clause is concerned: in addition to the *simple juxtaposition* of the two nuclei as in Mt 13.56S ܐܚܘܬܗ ܟܠܗܝܢ ܠܘܬܢ "all his sisters are with us" and the addition of the enclitic as in ib. P ܐܚܘܬܗ ܟܠܗܝܢ ܠܐ ܗܐ ܠܘܬܢ ܐܝܬܝܢ the same message could be conveyed by ܐܚܘܬܢ ܟܠܗܝܢ ܠܘܬܢ ܐܝܬܝܗܝܢ.

§ 108 Although one occasionally meets with examples of the classic *circumstantial clause* as in Gn 14.12 ܘܗܘ ܝܬܒ ܒܣܕܘܡ "and he was dwelling in Sodom", it is more often than not transformed into a variety of constructions: often introduced by ܟܕ as in Lk 16.23P ܘܟܕ ܡܫܬܢܩ ܒܫܝܘܠ ܐܪܝܡ ܥܝܢܘܗܝ ܡܢ ܪܘܚܩܐ "whilst he was being tormented in Hades, he raised his eyes from a distance"; Gn 11.4 ܢܒܢܐ ܠܢ ܡܕܝܢܬܐ ܘܡܓܕܠܐ ܕܪܫܗ ܒܫܡܝܐ "Let's build a city and a tower with its top reaching the sky" (MT: */wrō'šō vaššāmayim/*); ib. 16.1 ܘܐܝܬ ܗܘܬ ܠܗ ܐܡܬܐ ܡܨܪܝܬܐ "and she had an Egyptian maid-servant" (MT: */wlāh šifḥā miṣrit/*).

§ 109 *Prolepsis* [140]

Where a person or a thing is considered definite, Syriac, like many other Aramaic idioms, is fond of referring to it with the appropriate pronoun first, and later specifying it by using the noun itself. This taking-in-advance, *prolepsis*, may be applied to various syntactic relations.

a) Simple prepositional adverbial adjuncts
ܡܠܦ ܗܘܐ ܒܗ ܒܣܦܝܢܬܐ "he was teaching in the boat"
ܒܗ ܒܠܠܝܐ "on that same night"

b) Indirect (prepositional) verb complements
ܐܡܪܬ ܠܗ ܠܡܠܟܐ "she said to the king"

c) Direct verb complements [141]
ܩܒܠܗ ܠܡܠܬܐ or ܩܒܠܗ ܡܠܬܐ "he accepted the word"
ܩܒܠ ܐܢܝܢ ܠܡ̈ܠܐ "he accepted the words"

140 Cf. G. A. Khan, art. cit. (n. 109), 482-84.
141 See § 95D and Nöldeke, § 288.

d) ܕ -mediated analytical substitute for construct phrases[142]
ܒܢܘ̈ܗܝ ܕܐܠܗܐ "the sons of God"

e) ܕ -mediated prepositional adjuncts[143]
ܥܡܗ ܕܒܢ̈ܬܗ "with his daughters"

f) With ܟܠ "all, every" (§ 92)
ܟܠܗܘܢ ܥܡ̈ܡܐ "all the nations"

g) With numerals (§ 83)
ܬܪ̈ܬܝܗܝܢ ܡܕ̈ܝܢܬܐ "the two cities"

h) With possessive pronouns ܕܝܠ (§ 87 and Nöldeke, § 225)
ܕܝܠܢ ܐܬܪܐ "our place"

i) Third person pronouns (Nöldeke, § 227)
ܐܡܪ ܗܘ ܐܪܡܝܐ "Jeremiah said"
ܗܝ ܕܗܕܐ ܠܡܥܒܕ "to do this".

A proleptic pronoun may not be immediately followed by the noun referred to by it as in Mt 13.56S ܡܢ ܐܝܟܐ ܠܗ ܗܠܝܢ ܟܠܗܝܢ ܠܗܢܐ "whence did this one get all this?" and Ac 8.10 ܗܢܘ ܚܝܠܗ ܪܒܐ ܕܐܠܗܐ "this is the great power of God".

§ 110 *Negation* (Nöldeke, § 328-30)

A verb, including a participle, is generally negated by ܠܐ placed immediately before the verb, saving short particles like ܓܝܪ, ܕܝܢ, which may intervene between the two: ܠܐ ܐܙܠ ܐܢܐ "I am not going"; ܠܐ ܓܝܪ ܐܙܠܬ "for I did not go".

Although Syriac lacks a distinct negative of prohibition (like Heb. /'al/), ܠܐ with an Imperfect in independent (i.e. not subordinate) clauses is usually prohibitive: ܠܐ ܬܫܬܐ "Don't drink" or "You shall not drink".

Even an adjectival predicate may be negated by ܠܐ: ܠܐ ܫܦܝܪ ܗܢܐ ܐܝܟ ܗܘ "this is not as beautiful as that".

A negative nominal sentence, however, normally shows ܠܝܬ, ܠܐ ܗܘܐ or ܠܘ (< ܠܐ ܗܘ): ܠܝܬ ܗܪܟܐ ܠܚܡܐ "there is no bread here"; ܡܘܬܐ ܗܢܐ ܠܐ ܡܘܬܐ "this death is no death"; ܐܢܐ ܕܝܢ ܠܐ ܗܘܐ ܡܢ ܒܪܢܫܐ ܢܣܒ ܐܢܐ ܣܗܕܘܬܐ "I do not receive the testimony from man".

142 See § 88 and Nöldeke, § 205C.
143 See Nöldeke, § 222.

The latter two are placed immediately before the word or phrase which is being negated. In particular, the last containing the extraposing enclitic often retains such a function: ܠܘ ܡܛܠ ܕܪ̈ܚܝܩܝܢ ... "it is not because they are distant".

ܕܠܐ followed by a noun means "without", signifying the want or absence of something, and frequently mirrors the α-*privativum* of Greek: ܕܠܐ ܐܠܗ "godless" (ἄθεος); ܕܠܐ ܚܝܠܐ "without strength, powerless".

Emphatic double negation, which does *not* amount to affirmation, is common: Ex 9.6 ܠܐ ܡܝܬ ܐܦ ܠܐ ܚܕ "not even one (of them) died"; ܠܐ ܡܫܟܐ ܗܘܐ ܒܐܝ̈ܕܘܗܝ ܠܐ ܡܫܬܟܚܐ ܘܠܐ ܒܣܪܐ "neither skin nor flesh was remaining on his hands".

"Nobody" is ܠܐ ܐܢܫ: Mt 6.24C ܠܐ ܐܢܫ ܡܫܟܚ ܦܠܚ ܬܪܝܢ ܡܪ̈ܘܢ "nobody can serve two masters"; the negative may be separated as in Mk 16.8P ܠܐܢܫ ܡܕܡ ܠܐ ܐܡܪ̈ܝܢ "they said nothing to nobody". The separation is the rule with ܡܕܡ "nothing"; Jn 3.27P ܠܐ ܡܫܟܚ ܒܪ ܐܢܫܐ ܠܡܣܒ ܡܕܡ "man can receive nothing". Cf. Am 6.13 ܚܕܝܢ ܥܠ ܠܐ ܡܕܡ "they rejoice over what amounts to nothing".

§ 111 *Compound sentences*[144] are as common as in Hebrew. In this sentence type the topic of an utterance, usually a noun or pronoun, is extraposed, being placed first, followed by the comment part, which constitutes a complete clause by itself and contains a pronominal element referring back to the topic: Ps 125.2 ܐܘܪܫܠܡ ܛܘܪ̈ܐ ܚܕܪܝܢ ܠܗ (MT: /*yrušālayim hārim sāviv lāh*/); Aphr. I 33.9 ܗܒܝܠ ܓܝܪ ܡܛܠ ܗܝܡܢܘܬܗ ܐܬܩܒܠ ܩܘܪܒܢܗ "for in the case of Abel his offering was accepted because of his faith".

144 On this clause type in Hebrew, cf. S. R. Driver, *A Treatise on the Use of the Tenses in Hebrew and Some Other Syntactical Questions* (Oxford, [3]1892), Appendix I, pp. 195-211.

CHRESTOMATHY

Text no. 1

Genesis 39: 7-23 (Peshitta version)

The Peshitta (ܦܫܝܛܬܐ "simple") is the oldest complete Syriac Bible. The earliest attempt to produce a Syriac translation of the Bible must date to the late first or early second century A.D. The Peshitta is in general a literal version.

Editions: *The Old Testament in Syriac according to the Peshitta Version. Edited by the Peshitta Institute, Leiden* (Leiden, 1966-); ܟܬܒܐ ܩܕ. ܝܫܐ : ܕ. ܕܝܬܩܐ ܥܬܝܩܬܐ (Urmia, 1852 [repr.: London: Trinitarian Bible Society, 1913]); *Biblia Sacra juxta versionem simplicem quae dicitur Pschitta* (Mosul, 1887-92 [repr.: Beirut, 1951]).

Bibliography: E. Nestle, "Syriac versions", in J. Hastings (ed.), *A Dictionary of the Bible* (Edinburgh, 1902), vol. IV, pp. 645-52; C. van Puyvelde, "Orientales de la Bible (Versions): syriaques", in L. Pirot et al. (eds.), *Dictionnaire de la Bible. Supplément. Tom. VI* (Paris, 1960), cols. 834-84; A. Vööbus, "Syriac versions", in K. Crim (ed.), *The Interpreter's Dictionary of the Bible. Supplementary Volume* (Abingdon, 1976), pp. 848-54.

7) ܘܗܘܐ ܡܢ ܒܬܪ ܦܬܓܡܐ ܗܠܝܢ: ܐܪܡܝܬ ܐܢܬܬ ܡܪܗ ܥܝܢܗ
ܥܠ ܝܘܣܦ: ܘܐܡܪܬ ܠܗ: ܕܡܟ ܥܡܝ.

/wahwā men bātar petgāme hāllen 'armyat 'attat māreh 'aynāh 'al yawsef wemrat leh dmak 'am/

ܡܢ ܒܬܪ: "after" of time.

ܗܠܝܢ: pl. of ܗܢܐ (§ 13a).

ܐܪܡܝܬ: Af. 3 f. sg. of ܪܡܐ "to throw, cast".

ܐܢܬܬ: cst. sg. of ܐܢܬܬܐ /'attā/.

ܕܡܟ: impv. m. sg. of ܕܡܟ Pe. /e-a/. Used like the Engl. *sleep* in both the literal and figurative (sexual) senses.

ܥܡܝ: note the silent Yodh, /'am/ (§ 11), and the vowel /a/ as against the /i/ of the Hebrew equivalent.

8) ܘܠܐ ܨܒܐ. ܘܐܡܪ ܠܐܢܬܬ ܡܪܗ: ܗܐ ܡܪܝ ܠܐ ܝܕܥ ܥܡ
ܡܢܐ ܐܝܬ ܒܒܝܬܗ: ܘܟܠ ܕܐܝܬ ܠܗ ܐܫܠܛ ܒܐܝܕܝ.

/wlā ṣvā wemar lattaṯ māreh. hā mār lā yāḏāʿ ʿam mānā ʾiṯ bvayteh wḵul diṯ leh ʾašleṭ biḏay/

ܗܐ: like Heb. */hinnē/* this particle draws the hearer's attention.

ܠܐ ܝܕܥ : the participle is usually negated by ܠܐ (§ 110).

ܐܫܠܛ: Af. Perf. 3 m. sg.

ܒܐܝܕܝ: lit. "in my hands". On the secondary Alaf of ܐܝܕܐ, see § 7F.

9) ܘܠܝܬ ܕܪܒ ܒܒܝܬܐ ܗܢܐ ܡܢܝ: ܘܠܐ ܚܣܟ ܡܢܝ ܡܕܡ: ܐܠܐ
ܐܢ ܠܟܝ ܕܐܢܬܬܗ ܐܢܬܝ. ܘܐܝܟܢܐ ܐܥܒܕ ܒܝܫܬܐ ܗܕܐ
ܪܒܬܐ: ܘܐܚܛܐ ܠܐܠܗܐ.

/wlayt drab bvaytā hānā men wlā ḥsak men meddem ʾellā ʾen leḵ datteh ʾat. waykannā ʾeʿbeḏ bištā hāḏe rabbṯā weḥṭe lalāhā/

ܠܝܬ: contracted from ܠܐ ܐܝܬ "there is not".

ܕܪܒ ...: the antecedent, "one who ...", is understood.

ܪܒ: being a predicate, it stands in the abs. st.

ܡܢܝ: the Yodh is again (see under vs. 7) silent.

ܡܕܡ: "something, anything".

ܐܠܐ ܐܢ: "except" (lit. "but if").

ܠܟܝ: the Lamadh is the marker of direct object. On the syntax, see § 95A.

ܐܥܒܕ: Pe. impf. 1 sg. of ܥܒܕ */a-e/*.

ܒܝܫܬܐ ܗܕܐ ܪܒܬܐ: ܒܝܫܬܐ f. sg. emph., is used as a noun, "evil thing". On the position of the demonstrative pronoun, see § 80.

ܪܒܬܐ: Heb. */rav/* emphasises the quantity, "much", its Aramaic equivalent the quality, "great".

10) ܘܟܕ ܐܡܪܐ ܗܘܬ ܠܗ ܟܠܝܘܡ: ܘܠܐ ܫܡܥ ܗܘܐ ܠܗ:
ܠܡܕܡܟ ܠܘܬܗ ܘܠܡܗܘܐ ܥܡܗ.

/wḵaḏ ʾāmrā wāṯ leh kulyom wlā šāmaʿ wā lāh lmeḏmaḵ lwāṯāh walmehwā ʿammāh/

ܟܕ: composed of ܕ (relative pron.) and ܟ like Heb. *ka'ăšer*.

ܐܡܪܐ ܗܘܬ : a compound past tense to indicate a continuous or repeated action in the past. See § 71. Also ܫܡܥ ܗܘܐ.

ܟܠܝܘܡ: this common idiom is not usually written as two separate words. Note the use of the st. abs. (§ 58B).

ܫܡܥ: Pe. ptc. for */šāmeʿ/ (§ 7B).

ܠܡܕܡܟ : Pe. inf.

ܠܘܬܗ: ܠܘܬ + 3 f. sg. suf.

ܠܡܗܘܐ: Pe. inf. of ܗܘܐ.

(11 ܘܗܘܐ ܒܚܕ ܡܢ ܝܘܡܬܐ: ܘܥܠ ܝܘܣܦ ܠܒܝܬܐ ܠܡܥܒܕ ܥܒܕܐ: ܘܠܝܬ ܐ̱ܢܫ ܡܢ ܐ̱ܢܫܝ ܒܝܬܐ ܬܡܢ ܒܒܝܬܐ.

/wahwā bḥad men yawmāṯā wʿal yawsef lvaytā lmeʿbad ʿvāḏā wlayt nāš men nāšay baytā tammān bvaytā/

ܝܘܡܬܐ: though the noun is masculine in gender, in its pl. emph. this form is more common than ܝܘܡ̈ܐ, which latter, in contrast, is more common in the abs. (ܝܘܡܝܢ and with a pron. suf. like ܝܘܡ̈ܘܗܝ "his days".

ܥܠ: of a geminate root ܥܠܠ.

ܠܝܬ: a circumstantial clause, hence a nominal clause without ܗܘܐ.

ܐ̱ܢܫ: the sg. abs. of the noun is used with a negator in the sense of "nobody".

ܬܡܢ: Heb. /šām/ with the ending /ān/ typical of Late Aramaic.

(12 ܘܐܚܕܬܗ ܒܠܒܫܗ: ܘܐܡܪܬ ܠܗ: ܕܡܟ ܥܡܝ: ܘܫܒܩܗ ܠܠܒܫܗ ܒܐܝ̈ܕܝܗ: ܘܥܪܩ ܢܦܩ ܠܗ ܠܫܘܩܐ.

/weḥatteh balvāšeh wemraṯ leh. dmaḵ ʿam. wšavqeh lvāšeh biḏeh waʿraq nfaq leh lšuqā/

ܐܚܕܬܗ: ܐܚܕܬ Pe. Pf. 3 f. sg. (Syr. /d/ = Heb. /z/) with the 3 m. sg. suf. The alveolar /ḏ/ was assimilated to the following /ṯ/ in pronunciation.

ܫܒܩܗ : ܫܒܩ Pe. Pf. + 3 m. sg. suf., which is proleptic (§ 109c).

ܐܝ̈ܕܝܗ: Apart from the *seyame* (pl. sign), the Yodh before the He marks the noun as pl.: ܐܝܕܗ = "his hand".

ܥܪܩ ܢܦܩ: asyndesis (§ 98a).

ܢܦܩ ܠܗ: the Lamad is centripetal in force, on which see our study, "On the so-called *dativus ethicus* in Hebrew", *J. of Theological Studies* NS 29 (1978), 495-98.

(13 ܘܗܘܐ ܕܟܕ ܚܙܬ ܕܫܒܩܗ ܠܠܒܫܗ ܒܐܝ̈ܕܝܗ: ܘܥܪܩ ܠܫܘܩܐ.

/wahwā dḵaḏ ḥzāṯ dšavqeh lvāšeh biḏeh waʿraq lšuqā/

ܘܗܘܐ ܕ: like "it came to pass that" of the King James Version, it is a stereotyped translation of Heb. /*wayhi ka'ăšer*/ or the like.

(14 ܩܪܬ ܠܐܢܫܝ ܒܝܬܗ ܘܐܡܪܬ ܠܗܘܢ: ܚܙܘ ܕܐܝܬܝ ܠܢ ܥܒܕܐ ܥܒܪܝܐ ܠܡܓܚܟ ܥܠܝܢ. ܥܠ ܥܠܝ ܠܡܕܡܟ ܥܡܝ: ܘܩܥܝܬ ܒܩܠܐ ܪܡܐ.

/*qrāt̲ lnāšay baytāh wemrat̲ lhon. ḥzaw dayti lan ʿavdā ʿevrāyā lmeg̲ḥak̲ ʿlayn. ʿal ʿlay lmed̲mak̲ ʿam waqʿēt̲ bqālā rāmā*/

ܩܪܬ: Pe. pf. 3 f.sg. of ܩܪܐ, which is conjugated like a Lamadh Yodh verb.
ܚܙܘ: Pe. impv. m. pl. of ܚܙܐ "to see".
ܐܝܬܝ: Af. pf. 3 m. sg. of ܐܬܐ "to come". A highly irregular verb (§ 55B).
ܥܠܝܢ: ܥܠ "on" + 1 pl. suf.

(15 ܘܟܕ ܫܡܥ ܕܐܪܝܡܬ ܩܠܝ ܘܩܥܝܬ: ܫܒܩܗ ܠܠܒܘܫܗ ܠܘܬܝ: ܘܥܪܩ ܢܦܩ ܠܗ ܠܫܘܩܐ.

/*wk̲ad̲ šmaʿ darimet̲ qāl waqʿēt̲ šavqeh lvāšeh lwāt̲ waʿraq nfaq leh lšuqā*/

ܐܪܝܡܬ: Af. pf. 1 sg. of ܪܡ (rt: R-W-M).

(16 ܘܣܡܬܗ ܠܠܒܘܫܗ ܠܘܬܗ: ܥܕܡܐ ܕܥܠ ܡܪܗ ܠܒܝܬܐ.

/*wsāmt̲eh lvāšeh lwāt̲āh ʿd̲ammā dʿal mārāh lvaytā*/

ܥܕܡܐ: "until", which as a conjunction must be followed by the relative ܕ-, whilst as a preposition it is usual to say ܥܕܡܐ ܠ-.

(17 ܘܐܡܪܬ ܠܗ ܐܝܟ ܡܠܐ ܗܠܝܢ: ܥܠ ܥܠܝ ܥܒܕܐ ܥܒܪܝܐ ܕܐܝܬܝܬ ܠܢ ܠܡܓܚܟܘ ܒܢ.

/*wemrat̲ leh 'ak̲ melle hāllen. ʿal ʿlay ʿavdā ʿevrāyā daytit lan lamgaḥḥāk̲u ban*/

ܐܝܟ ܡܠܐ ܗܠܝܢ: lit. "like these words". Note the pronunciation of ܐܝܟ.
ܠܡܓܚܟܘ: Pa. inf.

(18 ܘܟܕ ܐܪܝܡܬ ܩܠܝ ܘܩܥܝܬ: ܫܒܩܗ ܠܠܒܘܫܗ ܒܐܝܕܝ: ܘܥܪܩ ܢܦܩ ܠܗ ܠܫܘܩܐ.

/*wk̲ad̲ 'arimet̲ qāl waqʿēt̲ šavqeh lvāšeh bid̲ay waʿraq nfaq leh lšuqā*/

(19 ܘܟܕ ܫܡܥ ܡܪܗ ܡܠܘܗܝ ܕܐܢܬܬܗ ܕܐܡܪܬ ܠܗ: ܕܐܝܟ ܡܠܐ ܗܠܝܢ ܥܒܕ ܠܝ ܥܒܕܟ: ܐܬܚܡܬ ܪܘܓܙܗ.

/*wk̲ad̲ šmaʿ mārāh melleh datteh demrat̲ leh dak̲ melle hāllen ʿvad̲ li ʿavdāk̲ 'et̲ḥammat̲ rug̲zeh*/

ܡ̈ܠܝܗ̇ ܕܐܢܬܬܗ̇: lit. "her words of his wife", with a proleptic pronoun (§ 88).

ܕܐܟܢ : the conjunction ‒ ܕ often introduces direct speech (like the Greek ὅτι *recitativum*).

ܐܟܢ ܡ̈ܠܐ ܗܠܝܢ : lit. "like these words".

ܐܬܬܚܡܬ: Ethpa. pf. 3 m. sg. of ܚܡܬ.

(20 ܘܕܒܪܗ ܡܪܗ ܘܐܪܡܝܗ ܒܝܬ ܐܣܝܪܐ : ܐܬܪ ܕܐܣܝܪ̈ܝ ܡܠܟܐ ܐܣܝܪܝܢ ܗܘܘ : ܘܗܘܐ ܬܡܢ ܒܝܬ ܐܣܝܪܐ.

|wdavreh māreh warmyeh bēṯ 'asire 'aṯar dasiray malkā 'asirin waw. wahwā tammān beṯ 'asire|

ܕܒܪܗ: Pe. pf. 3 m. sg. of ܕܒܪ + 3 m. sg. suf.

ܐܪܡܝܗ: Af. pf. 3 m. sg. of ܪܡܐ + 3 m. sg. suf.

ܒܝܬ: for ܒܝܬ.

ܒܝܬ ܐܣܝܪܐ: lit. "house of the bound". ܐܣܝܪ is a Pe. pass. ptc., used here as a noun.

ܐܬܪ: possibly cst. of ܐܬܪܐ, cst. followed by a clause instead of a noun, like Heb. *|mqōm 'ăšer|*. See Nöldeke, § 359.

ܗܘܘ: Pe. pf. 3 m. pl. of ܗܘܐ used enclitically.

(21 ܘܗܘܐ ܡܪܝܐ ܥܡ ܝܘܣܦ : ܘܐܪܡܝ ܥܠܘܗܝ ܚܣܕܐ : ܘܝܗܒܗ ܠܪ̈ܚܡܐ ܒܥ̈ܝܢܝ ܪܒ ܒܝܬ ܐܣܝܪܐ.

|wahwā māryā 'am yawsef warmi 'law ḥesdā wyahbeh lraḥme b'aynay rab beṯ 'asire|

ܡܪܝܐ : exclusively of the God of Israel or the Lord Jesus Christ, as distinct from ܡܪܐ "human master".

ܐܪܡܝ: Af. pf. 3 m. sg. of ܪܡܐ "cast, put".

ܥܠܘܗܝ : lit. "on him".

ܝܗܒܗ : lit. "he gave him".

(22 ܘܐܫܠܡ ܪܒ ܐܣܝܪܐ ܒܝܕ ܝܘܣܦ ܟܠܗܘܢ ܐܣܝܪܐ ܕܒܒܝܬ ܐܣܝܪܐ. ܘܟܠ ܕܥܒܕܝܢ ܗܘܘ ܬܡܢ : ܗܘ ܥܒܕ ܗܘܐ.

|wašlem rab 'asire byaḏ yawsef kullhon 'asire davveṯ 'asire wḵul d'āvdin waw tammān hu 'āveḏ wā|

ܐܫܠܡ: Af. pf. 3 m. sg.

ܪܒ ܐܣܝܪܐ: lit. "chief of prisoners". Some MSS have *|rab beṯ 'asire|*.

ܟܠ ܕܥܒܕܝܢ ...: lit. "all they did he did it", i.e. whatever they did was regarded as his doing, he was in control of all their doings. Note the compound tense twice.

(23 ܘܪܒ ܐܣܝܪܐ ܠܐ ܚܙܐ ܗܘܐ ܡܕܡ ܒܐܝܕܗ: ܡܛܠ ܕܡܪܝܐ
ܥܡܗ. ܘܟܠ ܡܕܡ ܕܥܒܕ ܗܘܐ: ܡܪܝܐ ܡܨܠܚ.

/wrab 'asire lā ḥāze wā meddem bideh meṭṭul dmāryā 'ammeh wkul meddem d'āved wā māryā maṣlaḥ/

ܡܨܠܚ: Af. ptc. act. < */maṣleḥ/ (§7 B).

Text no. 2

Deuteronomy 4: 1-14 (Peshitta version)

(1 ܡܟܝܠ ܐܝܣܪܝܠ: ܫܡܥܘ ܢܡܘܣܐ ܘܕܝܢܐ ܕܡܠܦ ܐܢܐ ܠܟܘܢ
ܝܘܡܢܐ ܠܡܥܒܕ: ܕܬܚܘܢ: ܘܬܥܠܘܢ ܘܬܐܪܬܘܢ ܐܪܥܐ ܕܝܗܒ
ܠܟܘܢ ܡܪܝܐ ܐܠܗܐ ܕܐܒܗܝܟܘܢ.

ܐܝܣܪܝܠ: also spelled often with an Alaf, ܐܝܣܪܐܝܠ.

ܢܡܘܣܐ: Gk. νόμος.

ܡܠܦ = *ܡܐܠܦ, Pa. ptc. See §71.

ܝܘܡܢܐ: contracted from /yawmā hānā/ "this day".

ܬܚܘܢ: irregular verb (Pe.) ܚܝܐ. See §55 F.

ܬܥܠܘܢ Pe. impf. of ܥܠܠ. The simple ܕ- followed by an imperfect frequently introduces a final (purpose) clause.

ܬܐܪܬܘܢ: the Alaf is a vowel letter. Pe. impf. of ܝܪܬ (= Heb. יָרַשׁ), an /e-a/ verb: ܝܪܬ, ܐܪܬ.

ܕܐܒܗܝܟܘܢ: the elision of the glottal stop, /'/, is not consistently carried out in printed editions (§7,I). The noun is the irregular pl. of ܐܒܐ with the added secondary /h/. See §30.

(2 ܠܐ ܬܘܣܦܘܢ ܥܠ ܦܬܓܡܐ ܕܡܦܩܕ ܐܢܐ ܠܟܘܢ: ܘܠܐ
ܬܒܨܘܢ ܡܢܗ ܐܠܐ ܛܪܘ ܦܘܩܕܢܘܗܝ ܕܡܪܝܐ ܐܠܗܟܘܢ ܕܡܦܩܕ
ܐܢܐ ܠܟܘܢ:

ܬܘܣܦܘܢ: Af. impf. 2 m. pl. of ܝܣܦ.

ܡܦܩܕ: Pa. ptc., "command".

ܬܒܨܪܘܢ: Pa impf. 2 m. pl.

ܐܠܐ: = ܐܢ ܠܐ "if not", "but", often after a negative.

ܛܪܘ: Pe. impv. of ܢܛܪ "to observe" with the elision of the Nun (§ 48). Cf. Heb. נצר, and Aramaising נטר in Biblical Hebrew.

ܦܘܩܕܢܘܗܝ: with a proleptic pronoun (§ 88).

3) ܥܝܢܝܟܘܢ ܚܙܝ ܟܠܡܕܡ ܕܥܒܕ ܡܪܝܐ ܠܒܥܠܦܥܘܪ: ܡܛܠ ܕܟܠ ܓܒܪܐ ܕܐܙܠ ܒܬܪ ܒܥܠ ܦܥܘܪ: ܐܘܒܕܗ ܡܪܝܐ ܐܠܗܟܘܢ ܡܢ ܒܝܢܬܟܘܢ.

ܚܙܝ: Pe. pf. 3 f. pl. of ܚܙܐ.

ܟܠܡܕܡ: may be spelled separately ܟܠ ܡܕܡ.

ܐܘܒܕܗ: Af. pf. 3 m. s. of ܐܒܕ + 3 m. s. object suf. resuming the preceding /*kol gavrā*/.

4) ܘܐܢܬܘܢ ܕܐܬܢܩܦܬܘܢ ܠܡܪܝܐ ܐܠܗܟܘܢ: ܗܐ ܚܝܝܢ ܐܢܬܘܢ ܟܠܟܘܢ ܥܕܡܐ ܠܝܘܡܢܐ.

ܐܬܢܩܦܬܘܢ: Ethpe. pf. 2 m. pl. of ܢܩܦ.

ܥܕܡܐ ܠ: cp. Heb. /*ʿad l-*/.

5) ܚܙܘ ܕܐܠܦܬܟܘܢ ܢܡܘܣܐ ܘܕܝܢܐ: ܐܝܟܢܐ ܕܦܩܕܢܝ ܡܪܝܐ ܐܠܗܝ: ܕܬܥܒܕܘܢ ܐܢܘܢ ܒܐܪܥܐ ܕܐܙܠܝܢ ܐܢܬܘܢ ܠܗ ܠܡܐܪܬܗ.

ܚܙܘ: Pe. impv. m. pl. of ܚܙܐ.

ܐܠܦܬܟܘܢ: Pa. pf. 1 sg. + 2 m. pl. object suffix.

ܦܩܕܢܝ: Pa. pf. 3 m. sg. + 1 sg. object suffix.

ܐܢܘܢ: 3 m. pl. object "them", which cannot be attached directly to the verb (§ 95 B).

ܐܙܠܝܢ: Pe. ptc. m. pl. of ܐܙܠ. The form can also be spelled without the Alaf, and is here joined to the enclitic pronoun /*'atton*/.

ܠܡܐܪܬܗ: Pe. inf. /*lmēraṯ*/ (from ܝܪܬ) + 3 f. sg. object suf. referring to /*'arʿāʿ*/.

6) ܘܬܛܪܘܢ ܘܬܥܒܕܘܢ ܐܢܘܢ: ܕܗܝ ܗܝ ܚܟܡܬܟܘܢ ܘܣܘܟܠܟܘܢ ܠܥܝܢ ܥܡܡܐ: ܕܢܫܡܥܘܢ ܗܠܝܢ ܟܠܗܘܢ ܢܡܘܣܐ: ܘܢܐܡܪܘܢ ܚܟܝܡ ܗܘ ܘܣܟܘܠܬܢ ܥܡܐ ܗܢܐ ܪܒܐ.

ܬܛܪܘܢ: Pe. impf. 2 m. pl. of ܢܛܪ with the assimilation of the Nun (§ 48).

ܗܝ ܗܝ: the second pronoun is enclitic. See § 105b. Read: /hiyi/.

ܥܡܡܝܐ: a spelling probably reflecting a stage in which a vowel separated the two identical consonants. Cf. Nöldeke, § 21D.

ܚܟܝܡ ܗܘ: ܗܘ is enclitic. The prefixed /d-/ often introduces direct speech.

ܥܡܐ ܗܢܐ ܪܒܐ: on the word-order, see § 80. Cf. Heb. /haggōy haggādōl hazze/.

7) ܐܝܢܘ ܓܝܪ ܥܡܐ ܪܒܐ ܕܩܪܝܒ ܠܗ ܐܠܗܗ: ܐܝܟ ܡܪܝܐ ܐܠܗܢ
ܒܟܠ ܕܩܪܝܢܢ ܠܗ.

ܐܝܢܘ: ܐܝܢܐ "which?, what?" with the enclitic.

ܓܝܪ: like the similar-sounding γάρ, this particle is never placed at the beginning of a clause.

ܪܒܐ: see above on Gn 39.9.

ܩܪܝܒ: a common Aramaic adjective formation. Also /ḥakkim/ (vs. 6), /šappir/ "beautiful", /saggi/ "much, many", /ʿammiq/ "deep", etc.

ܐܠܗܗ: the suffix "his" agrees with the singular /ʿammā/.

ܐܝܟ: note the silent Yodh.

ܩܪܝܢܢ: Pe. m. ptc. pl. of ܩܪܐ + the enclitic /an/ "we".

8) ܘܐܝܢܘ ܥܡܐ ܪܒܐ ܕܐܝܬ ܠܗ ܢܡܘܣܐ: ܘܕܝܢܐ ܙܕܝܩܐ:
ܐܝܟ ܟܠܗ ܢܡܘܣܐ ܗܢܐ ܕܝܗܒ ܐܢܐ ܩܕܡܝܟܘܢ ܝܘܡܢܐ.

ܐܝܬ: like Heb. /yēš/, it often indicates, in addition to existence, possession with the Lamad for the possessor.

ܙܕܝܩܐ: pl. m. emph. of /zaddiq/, a form dissimilated from */ṣaddiq/.

ܟܠܗ: on the proleptic pronoun, see § 109 f.

ܝܗܒ ܐܢܐ: ܐܢܐ is enclitic.

ܩܕܡܝܟܘܢ: ܩܕܡ "before" is a preposition, which, like ܥܠ and others, requires the masculine plural set of suffixes. See § 32.

9) ܠܚܘܕ ܐܙܕܗܪܘ ܘܛܪܘ ܢܦܫܟܘܢ ܛܒ ܕܠܐ ܬܛܥܘܢ ܟܠ
ܦܬܓܡܐ ܕܚܙܝ ܥܝܢܝܟܘܢ: ܘܠܐ ܢܥܒܪܘܢ ܡܢ ܠܒܟܘܢ ܟܠܗܘܢ
ܝܘܡܝ ܚܝܝܟܘܢ: ܘܐܘܕܥܘ ܐܢܘܢ ܠܒܢܝܟܘܢ: ܘܠܒܢܝ ܒܢܝܟܘܢ.

ܐܙܕܗܪܘ: Ethpe. impv. m. pl. The imperative of Ethpe. is distinct from the pf.: ܐܬܩܛܠ /'etqaṭl/ vs. ܐܬܩܛܠ /'etqṭel/. Here we also have a case of metathesis and partial assimilation: */'etzahr/ > */'ezthar/ > /'ezdahr/.

ܛܒ: most likely an adverb, "very much". The Heb. has */m'ōd/*.

ܢܦܫܬܟܘܢ: pronounced in ES */naβšāṯkon/*, indicated with a semi-circle underneath the Pe. */nafšā/* is used like its Heb. equivalent for a reflexive pronoun.

ܕ ܠܐ: */d-/* followed by an impf. indicating a purpose.

ܟܠܗܘܢ: with a proleptic pronoun.

ܐܘܕܥܘܢ: Af. impv. m. pl. of ܝܕܥ.

(10 ܝܘܡܐ ܕܩܡܬܘܢ ܩܕܡ ܡܪܝܐ ܐܠܗܟܘܢ ܒܚܘܪܒ܂ ܟܕ ܐܡܪ
ܠܝ ܡܪܝܐ܂ ܟܢܫ ܩܕܡܝ ܠܥܡܐ ܘܐܫܡܥ ܐܢܘܢ ܦܬܓܡܝ܂ ܘܢܐܠܦܘܢ
ܠܡܕܚܠ ܡܢ ܩܕܡܝ܂ ܟܠܗܘܢ ܝܘܡܬܐ ܕܚܝܝܢ ܥܠ ܐܪܥܐ܂ ܘܠܒܢܝܗܘܢ
ܢܠܦܘܢ܀

ܟܢܫ: Pa. impv. Cf. Heb. כנס.

ܠܥܡܐ: The Lamadh is the direct object marker.

ܐܫܡܥ: Af. impf. 1 sg., which, without the Heb. (*/'ašmi'ēm/*), could be taken as impv. Being the causative of a transitive verb, it may take double objects as here.

ܢܐܠܦܘܢ: Pe. impf. of ܝܠܦ (originally ܐܠܦ).

ܩܕܡܝ: lit. "before me".

ܝܘܡܬܐ : a variant pl. of ܝܘܡܐ. Cf. n. on Gn 39.11 and Heb. cst. pl. */ymōt/*.

ܚܝܝܢ: m. pl. of the adjective ܚܝ.

ܢܠܦܘܢ: Pa. impf. of ܐܠܦ. See § 49B.

(11 ܘܩܪܒܬܘܢ ܘܩܡܬܘܢ ܒܥܩܒܝ ܛܘܪܐ܂ ܘܛܘܪܐ ܡܬܒܥܪ ܗܘܐ
ܒܢܘܪܐ܂ ܥܕܡܐ ܠܠܒܗ ܕܫܡܝܐ܂ ܘܚܫܘܟܐ܂ ܘܥܢܢܐ܂ ܘܥܪܦܠܐ܀

ܘܩܪܒܬܘܢ: it is doubtful that the conjunction Waw here, unlike the Waw consecutive in the Heb. (*/wattiqrvun/*), is used in the manner of the Arb. */fa-/* "then", but it is rather a mechanical translation.

ܥܩܒܝ: pl. cst. of ܥܩܒܐ "bottom, base".

ܛܘܪܐ: etymologically corresponding to Heb. */ṣur/* "rock".

ܡܬܒܥܪ ܗܘܐ: a quadriliteral ptc. followed by the enclitic */wā/* (§ 33D).

(12 ܘܡܠܠ ܡܪܝܐ ܥܡܟܘܢ ܡܢ ܓܘ ܢܘܪܐ܂ ܩܠܗ ܕܡܡܠܠܐ
ܫܡܥܝܢ ܗܘܝܬܘܢ܂ ܘܕܡܘܬܐ ܠܐ ܚܙܝܢ ܗܘܝܬܘܢ܂ ܐܠܐ
ܩܠܗ ܒܠܚܘܕ܀

ܡܡܠܠܐ: a verbal noun, "speaking, speech".

ܫܡܥܝܢ ܗܘܝܬܘܢ: a compound past like ܚܙܝܢ ܗܘܝܬܘܢ, hence the enclitic /*wayton*/.

13) ܘܚܘܝܟܘܢ ܩܝܡܗ: ܘܦܩܕܟܘܢ ܕܬܥܒܕܘܢ ܥܣܪܐ ܦܬܓܡܝܢ: ܘܟܬܒ ܐܢܘܢ ܥܠ ܬܪܬܝܢ ܠܘ̈ܚܝܢ ܕܟܐܦܐ.

ܘܚܘܝܟܘܢ: Pa. pf. ܚܘܝ + 2 m. pl. object suffix. The Syriac verb can also mean here "he showed you..."

14) ܘܠܝ ܦܩܕܢܝ ܡܪܝܐ ܒܙܒܢܐ ܗܘ: ܕܐܠܦܟܘܢ ܢܡܘ̈ܣܐ ܘܕܝ̈ܢܐ: ܕܬܥܒܕܘܢ ܐܢܘܢ ܒܐܪܥܐ ܕܥܒܪܝܢ ܐܢ̄ܬܘܢ ܠܬܡܢ ܠܡܐܪܬܗ:

ܠܝ: the fronted emphatic /*'ōti*/ in the Heb. is expressed twice, /*li*/ and /*n(y)*/ of /*faqqdan*/ (from Pa. pf. /*paqqed*/). See § 95C.

ܕܐܠܦܟܘܢ: Pa. impf. 1 sg. ܐܠܦ (= *ܐܐܠܦ) + 2 m. pl. object suffix. See Nöldeke, § 174D.

ܥܒܪܝܢ ܐܢ̄ܬܘܢ: enclisis from */*'āvrin 'atton*/.

Text no. 3

Matthew 6: 5-15 (Peshitta version)

On the Peshitta in general, see the introduction to Text no. 1 (p. 71). The Syriac New Testament, particularly the Gospels, has come down to us in a rich variety of forms, the earliest being the famed *Diatessaron* attributed by tradition to Tatian. The Peshitta, the *textus receptus* of the Syrian church, in comparison with the earlier versions known as Vetus Syra, displays a greater degree of conformity to the Greek text, though its Syriac is not unduly Grecised.

Editions: Ph. E. Pusey and G. H. Gwilliam, *Tetraeuangelium Sanctum juxta simplicem Syrorym versionem...* (Oxford, 1901); *The New Testament in Syriac* (London: The British and Foreign Bible Society, 1905-20; repr. 1950), still readily available.

Bibliography: in addition to the works mentioned under Text no. 1, see also S. P. Brock, "The Syriac versions", in Bruce M. Metzger (ed.), *The Early Versions of the New Testament: Their Origin, Transmission and Limitations* (Oxford, 1977), pp. 3-98.

5) ܘܡܐ ܕܡܨܠܝܢ ܐܢ̄ܬܘܢ: ܠܐ ܬܗܘܘܢ ܐܝܟ ܢܣܒ̈ܝ ܒܐܦ̈ܐ: ܕܪܚܡܝܢ
ܠܡܩܡ ܒܟ̈ܢܘܫܬܐ ܘܒܙܘܝ̈ܬܐ ܕܫܘ̈ܩܐ ܠܡܨܠܝܘ: ܕܢܬܚܙܘܢ ܠܒܢ̈ܝ
ܐ̱ܢܫܐ. ܘܐܡܝܢ ܐܡܪ ܐ̱ܢܐ ܠܟܘܢ: ܕܩܒܠܘ ܐܓܪܗܘܢ.

ܡܐ ܕ-: "when", usually with reference to future. It can also be followed by a perfect.

ܡܨܠܐ: Pa. ptc. of ܨܠܐ "pray".

ܢܣܒܝ ܒܐܦܐ: /nāsbay/, Pe. ptc. m. pl. cst. of ܢܣܒ "take" + prep. ܒ and ܐܦ̈ܐ pl. emph. "face", used always in the pl. like Heb. dual /'appayim/. The phrase as a whole mirrors Gk πρόσωπον λαμβάνειν, "hypocrite". As in Heb., a cst. may be followed by a preposition; Nöldeke, § 206.

ܪܚܡܝܢ: Pe. ptc. m. pl. of ܪܚܡ "to love".

ܠܡܩܡ Pe. inf. of ܩܡ "to rise, stand".

ܙܘ̈ܝܬܐ pl. of ܙܘܝܬܐ "corner". Nouns whose singular ending is /uṯa/, /oṯa/ or /iṯa/ recover the consonantal /w/ or /y/ in their plural forms. So ܕܡܘܬܐ "form" — ܕܡܘ̈ܝܬܐ ; ܨܒܘܬܐ "thing" — ܨܒ̈ܘܬܐ ; ܨܠܘܬܐ "prayer" — ܨܠ̈ܘܬܐ.

ܠܡܨܠܝܘ: Pa. inf. of ܨܠܐ.

ܒܢܝ̈ ܐܢܫܐ: pl. of ܒܪ ܐܢܫܐ (also spelled ܒܪ ܢܫܐ) "man", lit. "son of man".

ܐܡܪ: Pe. ptc. for *ܐܡܪ (§ 7B).

(6 ܐܢܬ ܕܝܢ ܐܡܬܝ ܕܡܨܠܐ ܐܢܬ܂ ܥܘܠ ܠܬܘܢܟ܂ ܘܐܚܘܕ ܬܪܥܟ܂ ܘܨܠܝ ܠܐܒܘܟ ܕܒܟܣܝܐ܂ ܘܐܒܘܟ ܕܚܙܐ ܒܟܣܝܐ ܢܦܪܘܥܟ ܒܓܠܝܐ܂

ܐܡܬܝ ܕ-: = ܡܐ ܕ-. Cf. Heb. /māṯay/.

ܥܘܠ: Pe. impv. m. sg. of ܥܠܠ "enter".

ܐܚܘܕ: the Aramaic verb — cf. Heb. /'āḥaz/ — means "shut" as well as "grasp, seize".

ܬܪܥܟ: ܬܪܥܐ = Heb. /ša'ar/ with metathesis.

ܨܠܝ: Pa. impv. m. sg.

ܐܒܘܟ: on this irregular noun, see § 30.

(7 ܘܟܕ ܡܨܠܝܢ ܐܢܬܘܢ܂ ܠܐ ܗܘܝܬܘܢ ܡܦܩܩܝܢ ܐܝܟ ܚܢܦܐ܂ ܣܒܪܝܢ ܓܝܪ ܕܒܡܡܠܠܐ ܣܓܝܐܐ ܡܫܬܡܥܝܢ܂

ܗܘܝܬܘܢ ܡܦܩܩܝܢ: not to be confused with the continuous past /mfaqqin wayton/ (ܡܦܩܩܝܢ ܗܘܝܬܘܢ). This compound form is used with the force of the optative: "You shall never ..." See § 72. ܦܩܩ Pa. "to chatter".

ܣܓܝܐܐ: < *ܣܓܝܐܐ /saggi'ā/.

ܡܫܬܡܥܝܢ: Ethpe. ptc. with metathesis for *ܡܬܫܡܥܝܢ

8) ܠܐ ܗܟܝܠ ܬܬܕܡܘܢ ܠܗܘܢ. ܐܒܘܟܘܢ ܓܝܪ ܝܕܥ ܡܢܐ ܡܬܒܥܐ
ܠܟܘܢ ܥܕ ܠܐ ܬܫܐܠܘܢܝܗܝ܀

ܬܬܕܡܘܢ: Ethpa. 2 m. pl. of ܕܡܐ, */teddammon/* with the assimilated */t̠/* < */tet̠dammon/*.

ܝܕܥ: Pe. ptc. < */yāḏeʿ/*.

ܥܕ ܠܐ: "before". Cf. Mishnaic Heb. */ʿad šello/*.

ܬܫܐܠܘܢܝܗܝ: Pe. impf. 2 m. pl. ܬܫܐܠܘܢ (< */tešʾelun/* — § 7,I) plus 3 m. sg. obj. suf. See § 56 D,E.

9) ܗܟܢܐ ܗܟܝܠ ܨܠܘ ܐܢܬܘܢ. ܐܒܘܢ ܕܒܫܡܝܐ. ܢܬܩܕܫ ܫܡܟ.

ܨܠܘ: Pa. impv. m. pl.

10) ܬܐܬܐ ܡܠܟܘܬܟ. ܢܗܘܐ ܨܒܝܢܟ܆ ܐܝܟܢܐ ܕܒܫܡܝܐ ܐܦ ܒܐܪܥܐ.

ܬܐܬܐ: Pe. impf. 3 f. sg. of ܐܬܐ.

ܐܝܟܢܐ ܕ-: the particle of comparison as well as its non-expanded form ܐܝܟ */ʾak̠/* is followed by */d-/*, if the latter is in turn followed by a prepositional phrase, an adverb or a complete clause rather than by a noun or noun phrase. See § 64, p. 42.

11) ܗܒ ܠܢ ܠܚܡܐ ܕܣܘܢܩܢܢ ܝܘܡܢܐ.

ܗܒ: Impv. m. sg. of ܝܗܒ. See § 55E.

ܣܘܢܩܢܢ: lit. "our need".

12) ܘܫܒܘܩ ܠܢ ܚܘܒܝܢ܆ ܐܝܟܢܐ ܕܐܦ ܚܢܢ ܫܒܩܢ ܠܚܝܒܝܢ.

ܚܝܒܝܢ: "our debtors". ܚܝܒ is a common formation (*qaṭṭāl*) like Heb. */gannāv/* "thief".

13) ܘܠܐ ܬܥܠܢ ܠܢܣܝܘܢܐ. ܐܠܐ ܦܨܢ ܡܢ ܒܝܫܐ. ܡܛܠ
ܕܕܝܠܟ ܗܝ ܡܠܟܘܬܐ ܘܚܝܠܐ ܘܬܫܒܘܚܬܐ܆ ܠܥܠܡ ܥܠܡܝܢ܀

ܬܥܠܢ: ܬܥܠ (Af. impf. 2 m. sg. of ܥܠܠ) + 1 pl. obj. suf.

ܦܨܢ: ܦܨܐ (Pa. impv. m. sg. of ܦܨܝ) + 1 pl. obj. suf.

ܡܛܠ ܕ-: "because" (as conj.) vs. ܡܛܠ "because of" (as prep.) (§ 63).

ܕܝܠܟ: "yours". On the syntax of the clause, see § 105b.

14) ܐܢ ܓܝܪ ܬܫܒܩܘܢ ܠܒܢܝܢܫܐ ܣܟܠܘܬܗܘܢ܆ ܢܫܒܘܩ ܐܦ
ܠܟܘܢ ܐܒܘܟܘܢ ܕܒܫܡܝܐ.

ܒܢܝܢܫܐ: see on vs. 6 above.

ܣܟܠܘ̈ܬܗܘܢ: pl. of ܣܟܠܘܬܐ "sin" + 3 m. pl. suf. On the consonantal Waw, see above on v. 6.

(15 ܐܢ ܕܝܢ ܠܐ ܬܫܒܩܘܢ ܠܒܢܝ̈ܢܫܐ܆ ܐܦܠܐ ܐܒܘܟܘܢ ܫܒܩ ܠܟܘܢ ܣܟܠܘܬܟܘܢ܀

Text no. 4

Aphrahat: On Love, § 15.

A fourth-century ascetic and Syrian Christian writer, Aphrahat (also Aphraates and nick-named Persian sage), penned to so-called *Homilies* ܬܚܘܝ̈ܬܐ "demonstrations") consisting of twenty-three parts expounding various aspects of Christian doctrine and life.

Editions: W. Wright, *The Homilies of Aphraates the Persian Sage. Edited from Syriac Manuscripts of the Fifth and Sixth Centuries in the British Museum* (London, 1869); J. Parisot, *Aphraatis Demonstrationes* in Patrologia Syriaca, Pars prima, 1-2 (Paris, 1894-1907) with an extensive introduction, a useful Index verborum, and a Latin translation. The following extract from the second homily is quoted from Parisot's edition, the section-numbering of which differs from that in Wright's edition.

Bibliography: German translation by G. Bert, *Aphrahat's des persischen Weisen Homilien aus dem Syrischen übersetzt und erläutert.* TU Bd. III, Heft 3 und 4 (Leipzig, 1888); partial English translation (of eight homilies) in *A Select Library of Nicene and Post-nicene Fathers of the Christian Church.* Second Series, vol. 13, part II (Oxford, 1898), pp. 343-412; J. Neusner, *Aphrahat and Judaism. The Christian-Jewish Argument in Fourth-Century Iran.* Studia Post-Biblica 19 (Leiden, 1971).

ܬܘܒ ܟܕ ܐܠܦ ܡܪܢ ܠܨܠܘܬܐ ܠܬܠܡܝܕܘ̈ܗܝ ܐܡܪ ܠܗܘܢ:
ܕܗܟܢܐ[1] ܗܘܘ ܡܨܠܝܢ:[2] ܕܫܒܘܩ[3] ܠܢ ܚܘܒܝܢ ܘܐܦ
ܚܢܢ ܢܫܒܘܩ ܠܚܝܒܝܢ[4] ܘܬܘܒ ܐܡܪ: ܕܟܕ ܩܘܪܒܢܐ[5] ܕܟܝܐ

[1] "that thus ...", the ܕ- introducing a direct speech.
[2] Optative ܗܘܐ + Pa. ptc. m. pl. of ܨܠܐ (§ 72; Nöldeke, § 260).
[3] The proclitic particle again introduces a direct speech.
[4] Mt 6.12, but the text quoted here differs from the Peshitta form; see above, p. 82. The same text appears later in "On Prayer", 1.165.
[5] Cf. Jewish Aram. קָרְבָּן and New Testament Gk κορβᾶν (Mk 7.11).

ܐܢܬ ܕܬܩܪܒ [6] ܘܬܬܥܗܕ ܕܥܠ ܐܚܘܟ ܐܚܝܕ [7] ܐܢܬ ܐܟܬܐ [8]
ܦܘܩ: ܫܒܘܩ ܩܘܪܒܢܟ ܩܕܡ ܡܕܒܚܐ ܘܙܠ [9] ܘܐܬܪܥܐ [10] ܥܡ
ܐܚܘܟ ܘܗܝܕܝܢ ܬܐ [11] ܩܪܒ ܩܘܪܒܢܟ: [12] ܕܠܐ [13] ܟܕ ܢܨܠܐ
ܢܐܡܪ ܕܫܒܘܩ ܠܢ ܚܘܒܝܢ ܘܐܦ ܚܢܢ ܢܫܒܘܩ ܠܚܝܒܝܢ:
ܢܬܬܨܝܕ [14] ܒܗ [15] ܡܢ ܦܘܡܗ [16] ܘܢܬܐܡܪ ܠܗ ܡܢ [17] ܡܩܒܠ
ܨܠܘܬܐ: [18] ܕܐܢܬ ܠܐ ܫܒܩ ܐܢܬ [19] ܠܚܝܒܝܟ ܠܟ [20] ܐܝܟܢܐ
ܫܒܩܝܢ ܠܟ: ܘܬܬܟܪܙ ܠܗ [21] ܠܘܬܟ ܟܠ ܐܪܥܐ. ܘܬܘܒ ܚܘܝ [22]
ܡܪܢ ܬܚܘܝܬܐ [23] ܕܗܘ ܡܪܐ ܕܫܪܝ ܠܡܣܒ [24] ܚܘܫܒܢܐ ܡܢ
ܥܒܕܘܗܝ: ܘܚܕ ܩܪܒ ܥܒܕܗ ܩܕܡܘܗܝ [25] ܕܚܝܒ ܗܘܐ ܠܗ ܪܒܘ

[6] A clausal verb complement (§ 97,3).

[7] Pe. passive ptc., resultative in force: "having seized" > "holding" (§ 69, c).

[8] /'akkṯā/, f. sg. emph., pl. ܐܟ̈ܬܐ, like ܫܒܬܐ /šabbṯā/ "sabbath". Cf. Eth. /'ekkuy/.

[9] Irregular Pe. impv. of ܐܙܠ (§ 55C).

[10] /'eṯra''ā/, Ethpa. impv. m.sg. of ܪܥܐ. Cf. Heb. רצה.

[11] /tā/, irregular Pe. impv. m. sg. of ܐܬܐ "to come" (§ 55B). Cf. 1 Cor 16.22 μαρανaθα "our Lord, come!" or "our Lord has come".

[12] Mt 5.23 f., where the Peshitta reads: */'enhu hāḵēl damqarrev 'at qurbānāḵ 'al maḏbḥā wṯammān teddakkar daḥiḏ 'layk 'aḥuḵ 'akkṯā meddem [24] švoq tammān qurbānāḵ 'al maḏbḥā wzel luqḏām 'eṯra''ā 'am 'aḥuḵ whāyden tā qarrev qurbānāḵ/.* Note that it is your brother that holds something against you, and that the passages quoted elsewhere (ed. Parisot, 1.168) are in a form closer to the Peshitta.

[13] The particle /d-/ followed by an imperfect often indicates a purpose.

[14] /nettṣiḏ/, impf. Ettaf. 3 m.sg. of ܨܕ "to catch".

[15] Lamadh of disadvantage.

[16] "from his mouth", i.e. on account of what he is saying in prayer.

[17] The preposition indicates the agent ("by") in a passive construction.

[18] "Receiver of prayers" referring to the angel Gabriel. See Aphrahat, "On Fasting", § 14 and "On Prayer", § 13, where Gabriel is described as passing on prayers to God.

[19] A contrastive nominal clause (§ 105c).

[20] /lāḵ/ fronted for emphasis (§ 95C) and resumed later.

[21] A centripetal Lamadh; see n. on Gn 39.12 above, p. 73.

[22] /ḥawwyan/ = /ḥawwi/ "he showed", Pa. pf. of ܚܘܝ + /an/ "us".

[23] /taḥwiṯā/ "an example to demonstrate a case", a noun derived from the verb /ḥawwi/.

[24] /lmessav/ "to take", Pe. inf. of ܢܣܒ.

[25] /qḏāmaw/ "before him", prep. /qḏām/ + 3 m. sg. suf. (§ 32).

ܟܒܝܢ ܘܟܕ ܐܠܨܗ[26] ܡܪܗ ܕܢܬܠ[27] ܠܗ ܡܐ ܕܚܝܒ ܠܗ ܘܟܕ.
ܠܐ ܐܫܟܚ ܠܡܦܪܥ ܫܘܒܩܢܗ ܠܡܪܗ ܫܐܠ. ܡܪܗ ܘܫܪܝܗܝ[28] ܘܟܕ
ܕܚܝܒ ܥܡܗ ܠܗ. ܗܘ ܕܝܢ ܟܪܝܐ ܒܥܝܢܘܗܝ ܠܐ ܝܗܒ. ܫܘܒܩܢܐ
ܕܡܪܗ ܕܟܡܐ[29] ܐܣܓܝ[30] ܠܘܬܗ ܫܘܒܩܢܐ: ܘܗܘ ܠܐ.
ܢܦܩ ܐܫܟܚ[31] ܠܚܕ.[32] ܡܢ ܟܢܘܬܗ[33] ܕܚܝܒ ܗܘܐ ܠܗ ܕ̈ܝܢܪܐ
ܡܐܐ ܘܐܚܕܗ[34] ܘܚܢܩܗ ܗܘܐ ܠܗ ܘܐܡܪ ܠܗ: ܗܒ[35] ܠܝ ܡܕܡ
ܕܚܝܒ ܐܢܬ ܠܝ: ܘܠܐ ܩܒܠ ܒܥܘܬܐ ܕܟܢܘܬܗ ܕܒܥܐ ܡܢܗ ܐܠܐ
ܐܙܠ ܚܒܫܗ[36] ܒܝܬ[37] ܐܣܝܪܐ. ܘܡܛܠ ܕܠܐ ܥܒܕ ܠܚܢܬܗ
ܦܠܚܐ ܕܠܗ[38] ܦܩܕ ܐܫܬܒܩ ܠܗ ܗܘ ܠܕܢܓܕܐ ܕܢܢܓܕܘܢܗ[39]
ܒܢ̈ܝܐ ܕܢܦܠ ܡܐ ܕܚܝܒ. ܘܐܡܪ ܠܗܘܢ: ܕܗܟܢܐ ܢܚܒܢ. ܠܟܘܢ
ܐܒܝ ܕܒܫܡܝܐ[40] ܐܠܐ ܬܫܒܩܘܢ ܐܢܫ ܠܐܚܘܗܝ[41] ܀

[26] /'alṣeh/ "he urged him, pressed him".
[27] /nettel/ "he will give", irregular Pe. verb (§ 55E).
[28] /šrāy/ "he let him off", /šrā/ Pe. pf. + object suffix.
[29] /dakmā/: the particle is epexegetical.
[30] /'asgi/ "he multiplied, was generous in", Af. pf. of ܣܓܝ.
[31] /'eškaḥ/, a highly common, but slightly irregular — note the first vowel — verb meaning either "to find" or "can, to be able to".
[32] The preposition Lamadh here indicates the direct object; see § 95 (p. 54) and Nöldeke, § 288C.
[33] /knawāṯeh/: "his colleagues", pl. of /knāṯā/, which reappears below.
[34] /'aḥdeh/: "he caught him, grabbed him".
[35] /hav/: "Give", irreg. impv. of /y-h-b/ (§ 55E).
[36] /'ezal ḥavšeh/: "he went away (and) tied him up", an asyndetic construction (§ 98a), as in /tā qarrev/ above at n. 11.
[37] /beṯ/: the preposition /b-/ "into (the jail)" is understood, as often in Hebrew when the noun begins with a labial, esp. /b/ or /p/.
[38] /leh/ is emphatic; see n. 20 above. The preceding particle /d-/ is concessive in force.
[39] /dannaggḏuneh/: "so that they would flog him", /d-/ introducing the purpose clause.
[40] See § 94.
[41] /nāš laḥuy/ "a man to his brother", an expression of reciprocity "each other, one another" (like Heb. /'iš … 'āḥiw/), the choice of the intervening preposition depending on what preposition is required by the verb.

Text no. 5

Aphrahat: On Fasting, Third homily, § 10

ܬܘܒ ܫܡܥ ܚܒܝܒܝ: ܐܚܘܝܟ[1] ܕܨܘܡܐ ܡܩܒܠܐ[2] ܕܨܡܘ ܡܪܕܟܝ
ܘܐܣܬܝܪ: ܘܗܘܐ ܨܘܡܗܘܢ ܦܪܘܩܐ ܕܦܘܪܩܢܐ ܠܟܠܗܘܢ[3] ܒܢ̈ܝ
ܥܡܗܘܢ: ܘܒܛܠܗ ܥܒܕܗ ܢܟܝܬܗ ܕܗܡܢ ܡܕܠܚܢܗܘܢ[4]: ܘܗܦܟ
ܥܘܠܗ ܒܪܝܫܗ: ܘܐܬܦܪܥ ܒܠܗܘܢ, ܢܟܝܠܘܬܗ ܕܢܟܠ: ܘܒܪܢܫܐ
ܕܒܥܐ ܠܡܕܢ[5] ܐܬܬܕܝܢ: ܘܒܟܝܠܐ ܕܟܝܠ ܠܡܟܠܘ[6] ܐܬܬܟܝܠ[7]
ܠܗ: ܘܐܝܟ ܕܐܬܥܒܕ ܠܡܥܒܕ. ܐܬܥܒܕ. ܠܗ: ܘܐܬܦܢܝ ܒܫܒܠܐ
ܕܥܘܬܪܗ, : ܘܕܐܫܬܒܗܪ[8] ܒܥܘܬܪܗ ܠܐ ܠܘܝܗ,[9]: ܘܫܒܚܘܬܗ
ܠܐ ܦܪܩܬܗ: ܘܕܐܬܚܟܡ[10] ܠܒܝܫܬܐ[11] ܥܠ ܢܦܫܗ ܐܬܬܗܦܟܬ:
ܘܐܝܩܪܗ[12] ܚܪܐ ܢܣܒܗ: ܘܫܘܠܛܢܗ ܐܬܫܩܠ: ܘܓܢܒܪܘܬܗ[13]
ܐܬܡܟܟܬ: ܘܡܪܕܟܝ ܐܬܥܠܝ ܐܝܟ ܠܡܪܝܢܐ ܐܬܡܫܚ ܘܡܩܛܠܐ ܕܒܗ

[1] /'ehhawwek/ "I will demonstrate to you", Pa. impf. of /ḥ-w-y/ + obj. suf.

[2] /mqabblā/ "acceptable", Pa. pass. ptc. m. sg. The vowel deletion rule has obliterated the distinction between /*mqabbelā/ (act.) and /*mqabbalā/ (pass.)

[3] "to all of them" with a prolepsis (§ 109 f).

[4] /mdallḥānhon/ "one who perturbed them", a nomen agentis derived from Pa. /dallaḥ/ "to perturb, trouble" (§ 38).

[5] /lamdān/: "to judge", Pe. inf. of /d-w-n/.

[6] /lamkālu/: "to measure, mete out", Af. inf. of /k-y-l/. For the general thought, see Mt 7.1 f.

[7] An impersonal passive (§ 65). So the following /'et'ved/.

[8] /'eštavhar/ "he gloried", a quadriliteral (Šafel) Ethpa.

[9] /lwāy/: "it accompanied him", ܠܘܐ Pe. + obj. suf. The sentence could be improved to read: /'utreh deštavhar beh lā lwāy/ "his wealth in which he gloried did not accompany him, was not with him to support". Hardly = "the fact that he was glorified on account of his wealth was of no avail to him" (Bert).

[10] /dethakkam/: the particle /d-/ is more or less causal.

[11] /bištā/, an adjective used as a noun, "an evil, wicked thing".

[12] /wiqāreh/: on the spelling with an Alaf, see § 7F.

[13] /gabbāruteh/: ܓܢܒܪܐ /gabbārā/ "a hero, warrior" as well as its derivatives are spelled with a Nun, as against ܓܒܪܐ /gavrā/ "a man".

ܠܩܛܠ ܐܬܩܛܠ: ܡܛܠ ܕܒܥܐ ܕܢܘܒܕ [14] ܠܟܠܗܘܢ ܝܗܘ̈ܕܝܐ
ܕܐܝܬ ܒܫܘܠܛܢܗ ܕܐܚܫܝܪܫ ܡܠܟܐ. ܘܗܘܐ ܨܘܡܗܘܢ [15]
ܕܡܘܪܕܟܝ ܘܕܐܣܬܪ [16] ܣܒܪܐ ܘܦܘܪܩܢܐ ܠܝܗܘ̈ܕܝܐ، ܕܗܡܢ. ܘܗܡܢ
ܒܚܒܠܗ ܐܬܬܚܕ [17]: ܘܒܣܝܦܗ ܡܣܝܦܢܐ [18] ܥܠ [19] ܒܠܒܗ: ܘܩܫܬܗ
ܕܡܠܝܐ [20] ܗܘܬ ܠܥܘܠܐ ܐܬܬܒܪܬ: ܐܝܟ ܕܟܬܝܒ ܥܠ ܪܫܝܥܐ:
ܕܣܝܦܗܘܢ ܬܥܘܠ ܒܠܒܗܘܢ ܘܩܫ̈ܬܬܗܘܢ ܢܬܬܒܪܢ [21]. ܗܕܐ
ܥܒܕܬ ܠܗܘܢ، ܕܗܡܢ: [22] ܕܟܕ ܬܩܢ ܙܩܝܦܐ ܠܡܘܪܕܟܝ ܘܠܒܢ̈ܘܗܝ،
ܐܬܬܠܝ [23] ܒܗ، ܗܘ ܘܒܢ̈ܘܗܝ: ܘܐܬܬܚܕ ܒܚܘܦܪܐ ܕܟܪܐ.
ܘܐܬܬܣܝܡ ܒܢܦܫܗ ܕܐܬܪܐ ܘܡܪܝܐ ܕܝܠܗ ܠܗܘܢ، ܢܬܦܪܥܘܢ ܘܢܦܠ
ܒܢ̈ܝܫܘܗܝ، ܕܝܗܒ ܠܗ ܘܗܘܐ ܦܘܩܗ ܠܟܠܗ ·:·

[14] /nawbeḏ/ "to destroy", Af. impf. of /'-b-d/.

[15] /ṣawmhon/: "their fasting", with a proleptic pronoun.

[16] /dester/: "of Esther". Unlike Biblical Hebrew and Aramaic, Syriac does not tire of meticulously repeating particles like /d-, b-, l-, 'al/ before each co-ordinate member.

[17] /'etthed/ "was caught", Ethpe. pf. of /'-ḥ-d/. For the spelling, see § 49F.

[18] /msifānā/: "destructive, deadly", Af. *nomen agentis* of /s-w-p/. Cf. § 38.

[19] /'al/: "entered", Pe. pf. of /'-l-l/.

[20] /malyā/: "full", f. of /mle/ < */male/. The following preposition Lamadh is apparently a result of confounding the two structures, namely /malyā 'awlā/ "full of iniquity" and /malli (or: *mlā*) 'awlā/ "filled (someone) with iniquity". Alternatively, this may be a case of the typically Aramaic syntax dealt with in § 69, 2nd paragraph. Then one should translate: "that the wickedness had filled".

[21] /nettavrān/ Ethpe. impf. 3 f. pl., or possibly /nettabbrān/, Ethpa. of the same root /t-b-r/ "to break, shatter".

[22] = /'al hāmān/. See § 109e.

[23] /'ettli/: "he was hanged", Ethpe. of /t-l-y/.

Text no. 6

Ephrem on Genesis 39. 7-23

The commentary on Genesis and Exodus is all that has survived in Syriac of the Old Testament exegetical output by St Ephrem, an extremely prolific fourth-century Syrian writer. His extensive exegetical, dogmatic, controversial and ascetical writings are mostly in verse.

Editions: R.-M. Tonneau (ed.), *Sancti Ephraem Syri in Genesim et in Exodum commentarii.* CSCO, vols. 152 (Syr. text), 153 (Lat. tr.) (Louvain, 1955). The series CSCO (= Corpus Scriptorum Christianorum Orientalium) has been steadily bringing out critical editions with translations of works by Ephrem.

Bibliography: S. Hidal, *Interpretatio Syriaca: Die Kommentare des heiligen Ephräm des Syrers zu Genesis und Exodus mit besonderer Berücksichtigung ihrer auslegungsgeschichtlichen Stellung* (Lund, 1974); R. Murray, *Symbols of Church and Kingdom. A Study in Early Syriac Tradition* (Cambridge, 1975).

The following extract is Sect. xxxv 1-3, p. 98 in CSCO, vol. 152.

[1] ܒܬܪ ܕܝܢ ܕܐܪܕܘܗܝ ܘܗܘܐ ܠܦܘܠܚܢܐ܆ ܘܐܬܚܒܪ ܘܐܦ ܗܝ
ܒܚܠܬܗ ܗܘܐ. ܐܝܟ ܠܒܝ ܒܒܥܠܬܗ[1] ܕܐܒܘܗܝ، ܕܝܘܣܦ. ܐܬܚܒܒܬܗ
ܡܢܬܗ ܘܐܡܪܐ[2] ܠܗ ܕܫܟܘܒ ܥܡܝ. ܟܕ ܕܝܢ ܠܐ ܠܝܬ[3] ܡܢ ܕܡܨܛܢܥܐ[4]
ܠܗ ܘܠܐ ܡܬܛܦܝܣ[5] ܠܗ. ܐܥܠܬܗ[6] ܒܚܟܡܬܐ[7] ܠܩܝܛܘܢܐ
ܕܬܬܚܣܢܝܘܗܝ.[8] ܒܬܪ ܕܝܢ ܕܐܚܕܬܗ ܒܠܒܘܫܗ܆ ܘܐܪܦܝܗ.[9]

[1] */bʿellṯeh/* with a proleptic pronoun.

[2] */ʾāmrā/*: as in Bibl. Aram., the participle of this verb is often used to introduce what was said in the past.

[3] */leyaṯ/*, Pe. pf. 3 f. sg. of ܠܐܝ */li/* < */*lʾi/*, a stative Third Yodh verb meaning "to be tired".

[4] */meṣṭannʿā/*, Ethpa. ptc. f. sg. of */ṣ-n-ʿ/*, "to act artfully".

[5] */meṭṭpis/*, Ettaf. ptc. m. sg. of */p-y-s/*, from Gk πεῖσαι "to persuade".

[6] */ʾaʿʿelṯeh/*: "she led him (into)", Af. pf. */ʾaʿʿlaṯ/* of */ʿ-l-l/* + "him".

[7] */bḥeḵmā/*: "with wisdom". But something like "cunningly, slyly" is expected: either a scribal error for ܚܘܟܡܐ (= */ḥukkāmā/*) or a defective spelling?

[8] */dṯeḥsniw/*: "in order to overpower him, rape (!) him". Cf. Pesh. 2 Sm 13.14.

[9] */warpyeh/*: "and he left it", Af. ܐܪܦܝ */ʾarpi/* + an obj. suf. Is the conjunction */w-/* used here in the manner of Arb */fa/*, so-called */ḥarfu tartībin/* "then"? Otherwise we would have here a rather involved sentence: "After she seized ... and he left, because she thought ..., she shouted ..."

ܟܐܪܝܗ ܘܥܒܪܒ ܠܥܡܘܕܐ. ܡܛܠ ܕܣܥܪܬ ܕܗܘܬ ܠܗ ܓܘܚܟܐ[10]
ܒܟܝܢ ܚ̈ܒܪܝܗ. ܒܪܬ ܩܠܐ ܙܢܝܐ. ܘܐܬܟܢܫܘ ܒܥܒܪܝܗ ܥܡ̈ܘܪܝܗ[11]
ܠܡܗܘܐ ܠܗ̇ ܣܗ̈ܕܐ.[12] ܠܐ ܠܗ̇ܝ[13] ܕܠܡܥܒܕ. ܨܒܝܐ ܗܘܬ. ܐܠܐ
ܠܗ̇ܝ ܕܠܡܐܡܪ[14] ܡܛܝܒܐ ܗܘܬ܀

[2] ܢܫܟܚ ܕܝܢ ܗܘ ܕܠܡܥܪܩ.[15] ܘܒܗܕܐ ܟܠܒܐ ܠܡܐܬܐ
ܠܡܐܬ ܐܒܘܗ̄ܝ. ܡܫܟܚ ܗܘܐ. ܗܢܐ ܒܪܘܡܐ ܕܚܣܟ ܗܘܐ[16] ܠܗ
ܡܢ ܕܝܢܐ. ܘܚܡܣܢ[17] ܥܕ[18] ܚܝܐ ܕܠܐ ܡܚܐ ܦܢܝܡ[19] ܕܠܝܟܐ
ܕܚܝܐ ܗܘܐ. ܐܬܐ ܕܝܢ ܡܪܗ ܘܥܒܕ ܬܚܠܦ ܡܪܬܗ ܘܕܗܘܕܐ ܒܠ
ܦܬܟܪܗ ܡܫܬܡܫ ܗܘܐ. ܚܙܐ ܬܘܒ ܠܠܒܘܫ ܢܫܟܚ ܕܠܡܩܒܠ
ܢܫܟܚ ܐܝܬܘܗ̄ܝ ܗܘܐ. ܘܐܪܡܝܗ ܕܠܐ[19a] ܠܒܘܫܗ ܒܝܬ ܐܣܝܪܐ.
ܐܝܟ ܕܫܕܐܘܗܝ[20] ܒܝܘܡܐ ܕܒܥܒܕܐ[21] ܕܠܐ ܒܘܣܢܐ܀

[10] /guḥkā/: "she had made a laughing-stock of herself". Is the preposition a Lamadh of disadvantage?

[11] /'āmoreh/: "the members of her household". /'āmorā/ is a Pe. *nomen agentis* of /'mar/ "to dwell".

[12] /sāhde/: "witnesses", a Pe. ptc. m. pl. used as a noun.

[13] /lhāy/: "(witnesses) not to that which she had desired to do, but to that which she was prepared to say". /mṭayyvā/ is a Pa. ptc. pass. f. sg.

[14] Note the seemingly pleonastic /d-/: an adverbial prepositional phrase, including infinitives invariably prefixed with a Lamadh, is regularly preceded by such /d-/ (§ 64, p. 42).

[15] /lme'raq/: "to flee" is, together with /lmēṯā/ "to come", to be construed with /meškaḥ wā/.

[16] /ḥāseḵ wā/, a kind of conditional clause: "which would spare him". Cf. § 71 end.

[17] /ḥamsen/, a quadriliteral, "he held on, dug in his heels".

[18] /'aḏ/, a conjunction: "while".

[19] The proclitic of /dlaykā/ may be said to introduce what is comparable with a direct speech.

[19a] /dlā/: "without".

[20] /'aḵ dašḏa'uy/: "as they had cast him", from /š-d-y/.

[21] See § 94.

Text no. 7

Ishodad of Merv on Genesis 39

A ninth-century Nestorian bishop of Hedetta, Ishodad wrote a large number of commentaries on parts of the Old Testament and the whole of the New, full of quotations from earlier commentators, thus providing a rich storehouse of exegetical traditions. His approach follows the lines of the Antiochean school, being largely historical and literal as opposed to allegorical.

Editions: J.-M. Vosté and C. van den Eynde, *Commentaire d'Išoʿdad de Merv sur l'Ancien Testament, I. Genèse*. CSCO, vols. 126 (Syr. text), 156 (French tr.) (Louvain, 1950-55). The following extract is from vol. 126, pp. 204 f.

Bibliography: More commentaries of Ishodad have been published in the series CSCO and Horae Semiticae.

ܗܝ [1] ܕܫܒܩ ܠܒܫܗ. [2] ܗܢܘ. ܠܚܠܨܘܬܗ ܐܘ ܠܡܥܦܪܗ. ܘܠܐ
ܐܠܐ ܥܪܛܠ [3] ܫܒܩܗ. ܐܝܟ ܕܐܡܪ ܡܦܫܩܢܐ. [4] ܕܙܢܝܬܐ ܚܕ ܡܢ ܕܠܐ
ܡܬܒܥܝܐ ܠܡܬܚܒܠܘ ܡܓܘܙܠܐ ܠܗ [5] ܘܠܦܘܠܠܐ ܡܟܫܦܬܐ. ܩܪܝ ܫܡܫܐ ܐܪܟܐ ܡܬܥܦܐ. [6]
ܕܒܕ ܠܐ ܝܘܡܐ ܒܫܠܝܐ: ܚܫܒܬܐ ܩܪܬܗ ܘܟܠܗ ܐܘܚܕܢܐ
ܘܐܡܪܐ ܠܗܘ ܕܐܘܚܕܬ ܠܗ. [6a] ܗܝ ܕܐܡܪ ܒܟܘܠܗܝ [v. 21] ܚܣܕܐ [7] :

[1] /hāy d-/ "that which" is a standing formula for introducing a biblical text being commented on.

[2] /švaq lvāšeh/, Gn 39.12. Ishodad attempts to specify what sort of garment Joseph's was.

[3] An obscure word. The editors' reference to Gk ζημία and their translation *nu* "naked" are hardly satisfactory. The Syr. for "naked" is /ʿarṭellāy/. But see an addition to the LXX in the Arabic and Bohairic versions: "and she caught him by his garment, stripping him of them".

[4] /mfaššqānā/, "interpreter" (Pa. *nomen agentis*), most likely referring to Theodor of Mopsuestia, though his commentary on this particular verse has not survived in Greek.

[5] /mgawzlā/, a quadriliteral Pa. ptc. f., "to inflame".

[6] /maʿʿfā/, "(she) duplicates, repeats (her tactics)", Af. ptc. f. sg. of /ʿ-p-p/.

[6a] Note the diacritical dot below the letter Heh, indicating /leh/ "to him" as against ܠܗ̇ /lāh/ "to her". See also ܐܡܪ (line 2) = /ʾemar/ (pf.) as against ܐܡܪ /ʾāmar/ (ptc.). See § 6, (6) [p. 9].

[7] /ḥesdā/ as distinct from /ḥesdā/ "ignominy" according to Bar-Hebraeus, *Ktava dṣemḥe* (cited above in n. 102), p. 212.7, 11-12. But the distinction seems to be an artificial one; so Th. Nöldeke, *Neue Beiträge zur semitischen Sprachwissenschaft* (Strassburg, 1910), p. 93.

ܒܬܪ̈ܝܢ ܙܢܝܐ[7a] ܡܬܐܡܪ. ܐܘ ܚܠܦ ܙܒܢܐ. ܐܝܟ ܗܝ ܕܚܫܒܐ
ܕܢܦܫܗܘܢ[8] ܘܕܫܪܟܐ.[9] ܐܘ ܚܠܦ ܬܫܥܐ ܘܬܫܥܝܢܘܬܐ. ܐܝܟ ܗܝ
ܕܢܬܪ ܚܫܒܗ ܕܡܢ ܚܟ.[10] ܘܚܫܒܐ ܗܝ ܡܘܬܒܗܬܐ ܕܟܬܝܒ ܒܟܠ
ܬܪܝܢܬܐ.[11] ܘܚܘܫܒܢܗ ܕܡܢ ܚܕ ܠܟ[12] ܘܕܫܪܟܐ. [v:11] ܗܝ
ܕܟܠ ܚܫܘ ܠܒܝܬܐ ܠܚܣܕܐ ܕܒܕܐ.[13] ܥܒܪ ܚܕ:[14] ܠܡܥܒܕܗ
ܒܟܬܒܐ ܕܚܘܫܒܢܗ.

[7a] /*znayyā*/ "ways, modes", one of those few nouns showing the archaic m. pl. emph. ending (§ 21).

[8] Ps 79.12.

[9] /*wadšarkā*/ "etc., and the like": /*šarkā*/ = "remainder".

[10] Ps. 107.43.

[11] Ecclesiasticus 7.37.

[12] Lam 3.22.

[13] Commenting on vs. 11.

[14] /*ʿevrāyā*/, "Hebrew", i.e. the Hebrew text, which (/*mlaʾḵtō*/) by itself does not seem to support Ishodad's interpretation nor does the Syrohexapla, which reads /*ʿvāḏā*/. But cf. Targum Onkelos with its /*lmivdaq bikṯāve ḥušbāneh*/, and A. Baumstark, "Griechische und hebräische Bibelzitate in der Pentateucherklärung Isoʿdad's von Merw", *Oriens Christianus*, 2ᵉ série, t. I (1911), and a brief discussion of Ishodad's use of the term /*ʿevrāyā*/ in CSCO, vol. 156, pp. xxiv-xxv.

Text no. 8

Syro-Hexapla: Genesis 39. 7-12

In the first quarter of the seventh century Paul, Bishop of Tella, produced the most important of versions based on the Greek Old Testament. It is a Syriac version of the fifth column (Septuagint) of Origen's Hexapla, hence the name of Syro-Hexapla (Syh). The highly literary character of the translation, the fact that only tiny portions of the original Hexapla of Origin have survived, and the retention in the Syro-Hexapla of Origenic text-critical symbols (asterisk and obelus) as well as copious variant readings of "the Three" (Aquila, Symmachus and Theodotion) in the margins are features which render this version a text-critical tool of inestimable value for Biblical scholars, especially for the task of recovering Origen's fifth column.

Editions: The following extract is taken from the most recently recovered fragment of the Syro-Hexapla, an 11th or 12th cent. MS published by A. Vööbus, *The Pentateuch in the Version of the Syro-Hexapla. A Fac-simile Edition of a Midyat MS. Discovered 1964*. CSCO vol. 369 (Louvain, 1975), fol. 7a. Two other collections of a significant number of fragments were published by Ceriani and Lagarde.

Bibliography: S. Rørdam, "Dissertatio de regulis grammaticis quas secutus est Paulus Tellensis in Veteri Testamento ex graeco syriacae vertendo", pp. 1-59 of his *Libri Judicum et Ruth secundum versionem syriaco-hexaplarem* (Copenhagen, 1859-61).

(vii) ܘܗܘܐ ܒܬܪ ܡ̈ܠܐ ܗܠܝܢ ܘܐܪܡܝܬ[1] ܐܢܬܬܐ ܕܡܪܐ[2]
ܕܝܠܗ[3] ܥܝ̈ܢܐ ܕܝܠܗ̇ ܥܠ ܝܘܣܦ ܘܐܡܪܬ܂ ܕܡܟ ܥܡܝ܆ (viii) ܗܘ
ܕܝܢ ܠܐ ܨܒܐ ܗܘܐ.[4] ܐܡܪ ܕܝܢ ܠܐܢܬܬܐ ܕܡܪܐ ※ ܕܝܠܗ↙[5]
ܐܢ[6] ܡܪܐ ܕܝܠܝ ܠܐ ܝܕܥ[6a] ܡܛܠܬܝ[7] ܘܠܐ ܡܕܡ[8] ܕܒܒܝܬܐ ܕܝܠܗ.
ܘܟܠܗܝܢ ܗܠܝܢ ܕܐܝܬ ܠܗ ܝܗܒ ܒܐܝ̈ܕܝ̈ ܕܝܠܝ. (ix) ܘܠܐ
ܐܝܬ ܕܪܒ ܡܕܡ[9] ܕܒܒܝܬܐ ܕܝܠܝ[10] ܠܒ ܡ̇ܢܝ.[11] ܘܠܐ

[1] /warmyaṯ/ "and she cast", Af. of /r-m-y/. The conjunction Waw is a literal rendition of the underlying Gk καί, which in turn reflects the Hebrew syntax.

[2] The construct chain is extremely rare in the Syro-Hexapla (Syh), and instead the analytical structure dominates.

[3] The Gk possessive pronoun is usually rendered in Syh by means of the independent possessive pronoun of the /dil-/ series.

[4] /ṣāve wā/, a continuous, repeated action corresponding to the Gk impf. οὐκ ἤθελεν as against MT /waymā'ēn/: "he would not agree, kept refusing".

[5] The asterisk is an Origenic symbol to say that the Gk word or words so marked is wanting in the Hebrew text. The symbol has been mechanically transferred to the Syh version. In this case, the absence of the possessive suffix in the Heb. (MT: /'ădōnāw/) is rather unlikely.

[6] /'en/ "if" representing the Aramaising interpretation, as in the Gk εἰ, of MT /hēn/.

[6a] Note the diacritical dot above the Yodh, indicating /yāḏa'/, ptc. as against ܝܕܥ = /yiḏa'/ (pf.). See n. 6a) on p. 90.

[7] /meṭṭulāṯ/ from /meṭṭul/. See § 64 (p. 42).

[8] /wlā meddem/: a rendition reflecting an interpretation which derives the Gk οὐδέν from οὐδέ "nor" (= "and not"). Likewise οὐδείς is rendered in Syh by /wlā nāš/ with the otiose Waw, although the non-separation of /lā/ and /nāš/ is standard Syriac (§ 110, p. 69). Cf. Mish.Heb. /wlō klum/.

[9] In the light of the preceding note, one would expect /wlā meddem/. Something seems to be amiss with the first half of the verse.

[10] /bvaytā dil/ "in my house", for which there is no place in this context. Scribal error for /bvaytā hāḏe/ "in this house"? Lagarde's edition has /dileh/ for /dil/.

[11] The whole sentence is somewhat awkward. Possibly we have here two different

ܫܒ̈ܩܢ[12] ܡܢܝ ܘܠܐ ܡܕܡ. ܣܛܪ ܡܢ̈ܟܝ. ܡܛܠ ܕܐܢܬܝ ܐܢܬܬܐ
ܕܝܠܗ ܐܝ̈ܬܝܟܝ.[13] ܘܐܝܟܢܐ ܐܥܒܕ ܒܝܫܬܐ[14] ܗܕܐ[15] ܪܒܬܐ.
ܘܐܚܛܐ ܩܕܡ ܐܠܗܐ܀ (x) ÷ܘܗܘܐ ܕܟܕ[16]↙ ܡܡܠܠܐ ܗܘܬ. ܠܝܘܣܦ
ܝܘܡܐ ܡܢ ܝܘܡܐ.[17] ܘܠܐ ܡܫܬܡܥ ܗܘܐ ܠܗ̇، ܠܡܕܡܟ ܥܡܗ̇.
ܠܡܗܘܐ ܥܡܗ̇، (xi) ܗܘܐ ܕܝܢ ܝܘܡܐ ܕܐܝܟ ܗܢܝ، ܡܕܡ.[18] ܥܠ
ܝܘܣܦ ܠܒܝܬܐ ܠܡܥܒܕ ܥܒܕ̈ܐ ܕܝܠܗ. ܘܠܐ ܐܢܫ[19] ܡܢ ܗܠܝܢ
ܕܒܒܝܬܐ ܐܝܬ ܗܘܐ ܠܓܘ܀ (xii) **ܘܐܬܬܠܝܬ**.[20] ܒܠܒܘ̈ܫܐ ܕܝܠܗ
ܟܕ ܐܡܪܐ.[21] ܕܡܟ ܥܡܝ. ܘܫܒܩ ܡܐ̈ܢܐ[22] ܕܝܠܗ ܒܐܝ̈ܕܝܗ̇܀
ܕܝܠܗ.↙ ܥܪܩ ܘܢܦܩ[23] **ܠܒܪ**.

renderings clumsily put together, one corresponding to ὑπερέχει "to be above someone else's authority" and the other to a variant reading ὑπάρχῃ or ὑπάρχει "there exists".

[12] In the margin of Syh, we see two variant readings, /*wlā 'ašrek̠*/ and /*wlā mvaṣṣar*/, which correspond to the Greek variants καὶ οὐχ ὑπελίπετο and καὶ οὐκ ἀφαιρεῖ respectively; see F. Field, *Origenis Hexaplorum quae supersunt* etc. (Oxford, 1875), vol. I, ad loc.

[13] See § 107.

[14] Wevers' edition of the Göttingen Septuagint records no Gk MS which reads ῥῆμα. But Syh has /*mellṯā bištā*/ in the margin.

[15] Note the idiomatic position of the pronoun. See § 80, but cf. Jer 16.10, 32(39).42 Syh /*kullhen bišāṯā rawrvāṯā hāllen*/.

[16] καὶ ἐγένετο ἡνίκα are wanting in most Origenic (Hexaplaric) LXX manuscripts and the Armenian version affiliated thereto.

[17] Though the phrase is a verbatim rendering of Gk ἡμέραν ἐξ ἡμέρας, it appears that it is a genuine Syriac idiom meaning "day in day out". See Brockelmann, *Lex. Syr.*, s.v. /*yawmā*/.

[18] /*meddem*/ = τις.

[19] /*wlā nāš*/ = οὐδείς; see n. 8 above.

[20] /*'ettalyaṯ*/ "she took hold of", Ethpe. of /*t-l-y*/ or Ethpa. /*'ettallyaṯ*/ of the same. The point to the right of the final Taw is diacritical: ≠ /*'ettalyiṯ*/.

[21] /*kaḏ 'āmrā*/ "as she said; saying", a circumstantial clause.

[22] /*māne*/ "garments". The noun also means "instrument". Cf. the use of Heb. /*kli*/. Etymologically the word is related to Heb. /*'ŏni, 'ŏniyyā*/ "vessel".

[23] The point below the Pe is diacritical to indicate that /*nfaq*/ (pf.) is intended, and not /*nāfeq*/ (ptc. = **ܢܦܩ**). So with **ܢܦܩ** a line above. In other words, it is not a *rukkak̠a* point.

Text no. 9

"The Prodigal Son" (Luke 15.11-32, Vetus Syra Sinaitica)

The Gospels at least are known to have had a version or versions earlier than the Peshitta; this earlier version is called Vetus Syra (Old Syriac Gospels), and has survived in two recensions, Curetonianus (C) so called after W. Cureton, who discovered it among the rich collection of Syriac manuscripts in the British Museum and published it in 1848 [F.C. Burkitt republished it in 1904 with an English translation, to which a number of critical studies were appended], and Sinaiticus (S), a fourth or fifth century palimpsest manuscript discovered in 1892 by Mrs Agnes Smith Lewis and her twin sister Mrs Margaret Dunlop Gibson in the celebrated monastery of St Catharine on Mt Sinai, a definitive edition of which appeared in 1910 (see below). Their relative antiquity, mutual relationship, relationship with the Diatessaron and the Peshitta have been discussed for decades, without a consensus opinion having emerged yet. According to Nöldeke (*Gram.*, p. xiii), the Synoptic Gospels "exhibit almost invariably an exceedingly flowing, idiomatic style of Syriac, which upon the whole reads better than the Semitic Greek of the original. This feature comes into still stronger relief in the more ancient form of the text as contained in C and S".

Editions: A.S. Lewis, *The Old Syriac Gospels or Evangelion da-Mepharreshê* etc. (London, 1910) [repr. Makor: Jerusalem, n.d.]; Arthur Hjelt, *Syrus Sinaiticus* (Helsingfors, 1930). Even the latter, a photographic facsimile of the manuscript, is often obscure as to the reading of the underwriting.

Bibliography: A. Vööbus, *Studies in the History of the Gospel Text in Syriac*. CSCO, vol. 128 (Louvain, 1951); S.P. Brock, art. cit. (under Text no. 3), pp. 36-48; T. Muraoka, "On the nominal clause in the Old Syriac Gospels", *J. of Semitic Studies*, 20 (1975), 28-37.

(xi) ܐܡܪ ܠܗܘܢ ܓܒܪܐ ܚܕ ܐܝܬ ܗܘܐ ܠܗ ܬܪܝܢ ܒܢܝܢ[1]
(xii) ܐܡܪ ܗܘ[2] ܙܥܘܪܐ ܠܐܒܘܗܝ. ܗܒ ܠܝ ܡܢܬܐ ܕܡܛܝܐ ܠܝ[3]
ܡܢ ܩܢܝܢܟ ܘܦܠܓ ܠܗܘܢ ܟܠܗ ܩܢܝܢܗ (xiii) ܘܒܬܪ ܝܘܡܬܐ
ܩܠܝܠ[4] ܟܢܫ ܗܘ[4a] ܒܪܗ ܙܥܘܪܐ ܟܠ ܡܕܡ ܕܡܛܝܗ، ܘܐܙܠ
ܠܐܬܪܐ ܪܚܝܩܐ ܘܬܡܢ ܒܕܪ ܩܢܝܢܗ ܟܠܗ ܕܚܝܐ ܗܘܐ ܦܪܚܐܝܬ[5]

[1] A compound sentence: */gavrā ḥad/* is topicalised. See § 111.
[2] A proleptic pronoun. See § 109i.
[3] Cf. Mod. Heb. */maggiaʿ l-/*.
[4] On the lack of concord, see § 84.
[4a] */hu/*: see § 109i.
[5] */parrāḥāʾiṯ/*, an adverb derived from */parrāḥā/* "a prodigal person". The verb Pa. */parraḥ/* means "to fly; dissipate".

ܥܡ ܙܢܝܬܐ. (xiv) ܘܟܕ ܓܡܪ ܟܠ ܡܕܡ ܕܐܝܬ ܠܗ. ܘܗܘܐ
ܟܦܢܐ ܒܐܬܪܐ ܗܘ (xv) ܐܙܠ ܢܩܦ ܠܗ ܠܚܕ. ܡܢ ܒܢܝ ܗܘ ܐܬܪܐ
ܘܫܕܪܗ ܠܩܪܝܬܐ[6] ܠܡܪܥܐ ܚܙܝܪܐ (xvi) ܘܡܬܪܓܪܓ[7] ܗܘܐ ܡܢ
ܗܢܘܢ ܩܪܛܐ[8] ܕܐܟܠܝܢ ܗܘܘ ܚܙܝܪܐ ܕܢܡܠܐ ܟܪܣܗ ܘܠܐ
ܐܢܫ[9] ܝܗܒ ܗܘܐ ܠܗ (xvii) ܟܕ ܐܬܐ ܠܘܬ ܢܦܫܗ[10] ܐܡܪ ܟܡܐ
ܐܓܝܪܝܢ ܐܝܬ ܗܪܟܐ ܒܒܝܬ ܐܒܝ ܕܣܒܥܝܢ ܠܗܘܢ ܠܚܡܐ ܘܐܢܐ
ܐܒܕܢܐ[11] ܗܪܟܐ ܡܢ ܟܦܢܝ.[12] (xviii) ܐܠܐ ܐܩܘܡ ܐܙܠ[13]
ܠܘܬ ܐܒܝ ܘܐܡܪ[14] ܠܗ ܐܒܝ ܚܛܝܬ ܒܫܡܝܐ ܘܩܕܡܝܟ
(xix) ܘܠܐ ܫܘܝܢܐ[15] ܡܟܝܠ ܕܒܪܟ ܐܬܩܪܐ[16] ܥܒܕܝܢܝ[17] ܐܝܟ
ܚܕ ܡܢ ܐܓܝܪܝܟ. (xx) ܘܩܡ ܐܬܐ[18] ܠܘܬ ܐܒܘܗܝ، ܘܟܕ ܗܘ
ܪܚܝܩ ܚܙܝܗܝ، ܐܒܘܗܝ، ܘܐܬܪܚܡ ܥܠܘܗܝ، ܘܪܗܛ[19] ܢܦܠ[20] ܥܠ
ܨܘܪܗ ܘܢܫܩܗ (xxi) ܘܐܡܪ ܠܗ ܒܪܗ ܐܒܝ ܚܛܝܬ ܒܫܡܝܐ
ܘܩܕܡܝܟ ܘܡܟܝܠ ܠܐ ܫܘܐ ܐܢܐ[21] ܕܒܪܟ ܐܬܩܪܐ (xxii) ܐܡܪ

[6] /*qritā*/: here "field", not "city".
[7] /*metragrag*/ "to yearn for, crave", an Ethpalpal from the root /*r-g-g*/.
[8] /*qerate*/ "carob pods" from Gk κεράτιον. The prepositional phrase is taken out of the following relative clause /*dnemle'*.../.
[9] /*lā nāš*/ "nobody". See § 110 (p. 69).
[10] /*'etā lwāt nafšeh*/ "he came to himself, i.e. came to his senses".
[11] /*'ävednā*/ < /*'äved 'enā*/ "I am languishing".
[12] /*kafn*/ "my hunger".
[13] /*'ēzal*/ "I will go", Pe. impf. of /*'ezal*/. See § 55C.
[14] /*'ēmar*/, also Pe. impf.: "I will say".
[15] /*šāwenā*/ = /*šāwe*/ "worthy" + enclitic /*nā*/ "I".
[16] /*'etqre*/: the conjunction /*d*-/ introduces a clause which complements /*šāwe*/.
[17] /*'vedayn*/ "Make me", Pe. impv. with a pron. suf.
[18] On asyndesis, see § 98a.
[19] The root is related to Heb. רוץ with a medial increment as in ܒܗܬ "to be ashamed" (Heb. בוש).
[20] See n. 18 above.
[21] An alternative spelling of the form referred to in n. 15.

ܐܒܘܗܝ ܠܥܒܕܘܗܝ · ܐܦܩܘ[22] ܥܓܠ[23] ܐܣܛܠܐ[24] ܪܫܝܬܐ ܐܠܒܫܘܗܝ[25]
ܘܣܝܡܘ ܥܙܩܬܐ ܒܐܝܕܗ ܘܐܣܢܘܗܝ[26] ܡܣܢܐ (xxiii) ܘܐܝܬܝܘ[27]
ܩܛܘܠܘ ܥܓܠܐ ܗܘ ܕܦܛܡܐ ܢܐܟܘܠ ܘܢܬܒܣܡ (xxiv) ܕܗܢܐ
ܒܪܝ ܡܝܬܐ ܗܘܐ ܘܚܝܐ. ܘܐܒܝܕܐ ܗܘܐ ܘܐܫܬܟܚ ܘܫܪܝܘ
ܠܡܬܒܣܡܘ (xxv) ܘܗܘ ܒܪܗ ܩܫܝܫܐ ܒܚܩܠܐ ܗܘܐ ܘܟܕ ܐܬܐ
ܩܪܒ ܠܘܬ ܒܝܬܐ ܫܡܥ ܩܠ ܙܡܪܐ ܘܨܦܘܢܝܐ[28] (xxvi) ܘܩܪܐ
ܠܚܕ ܡܢ ܛܠܝܐ[29] ܘܫܐܠܗ[30] ܡܢܘ 31) ܗܢܐ (xxvii) ܐܡܪ ܠܗ
ܐܚܘܟ ܐܬܐ ܘܢܟܣ ܐܒܘܟ ܥܓܠܐ ܕܦܛܡܐ ܕܟܕ ܚܠܝܡ ܐܩܒܠܗ.[32]
(xxviii) ܘܪܓܙ ܘܠܐ ܨܒܐ ܗܘܐ ܠܡܥܠ.[33] ܘܢܦܩ ܐܒܘܗܝ ܘܒܥܐ
ܗܘܐ ܡܢܗ (xxix) ܒܪܐ ܘܐܡܪ ܠܗ[34] ܠܐܒܘܗܝ ܗܐ ܟܡܐ ܫܢܝܢ
ܦܠܚܢܐ[35] ܠܟ ܥܒܕܘܬܐ ܘܠܐ ܥܒܪܬ ܥܠ ܦܘܩܕܢܝܟ ܘܡܡܬܘܡ
ܓܕܝܐ ܚܕ ܠܐ ܝܗܒܬ[36] ܠܝ ܕܐܬܒܣܡ ܥܡ ܪܚܡܝ. (xxx) ܘܗܢܐ
ܒܪܟ ܟܕ ܦܙܪ ܩܢܝܢܟ ܥܡ ܙܢܝܬܐ. ܢܟܣܬ ܠܗ ܥܓܠܐ ܗܘ

[22] /'appeq/ "Bring out", Af. impv. pl. m. of /nfaq/.
[23] /'gal/ "quickly", also /ba'gal/.
[24] /'estlā/ "robe", from Gk στολή with a prosthetic Alaf.
[25] /'albšuy/ "Clothe him", Af. impv. pl. m. with a pron. suf.
[26] /wasenuy/ "Put shoes on his (feet)". Af. impv. m. pl. + a pron. suf. of /sen/ (ܣܐܢ), from which the following noun, /msānā/, is derived.
[27] /waytiw/ "Bring", Af. impv. m. pl. of /'eṯā/ for the standard /'aytaw/. See § 55B.
[28] /ṣepponyā/ "symphony" from Gk συμφωνία.
[29] /ṭlayyā/ if it means "servants", but /ṭlāye/ if it means "boys" (Nöldeke, § 146). Note that a *seyyame* is wanting.
[30] /šalleh/ "he asked him". The verb /š-'-l/ is usually used in Pa. /ša'el/ in the sense of "ask a question", but in Pe. /šel/ (< */š'el/) it means "ask for, beg".
[31] /mānaw/, i.e. /mānā/ "what?" with a topicalising enclitic (§ 105b end).
[32] /'aqbleh/ "he received him", Af. of /q-b-l/. Note the circumstantial clause: /kaḏ ḥlim/ "as he was healthy, in a healthy condition".
[33] /lme''al/ "to enter", Pe. inf. of /'-l-l/.
[34] On prolepsis, see § 109b.
[35] /pālaḥnā/ "I have served", a Pe. ptc. with the enclitic /nā/. On the force of the tense, see § 68.
[36] /yavt/ "you (m. sg.) gave". See § 55E.

ܕܦܝܠܣܦܐ (xxxi) ܐܡܪ ܠܗ ܒܪܝ، ܒܟܠܙܒܢ[37] ܟܡܝܪ ܐܢ̄ܬ. ܘܒܟܠ
ܡܕܡ ܕܚܠܝ ܕܝܠܟ ܗܘ.[38] (xxxii) ܠܡܬܒܣܡܘ ܕܝܢ ܘܠܐ[39]
ܗܘ̇ܐ ܘܠܡܚܕܐ[40] ܕܗܢܐ ܐܝܟ ܡܫܬܝܬܐ ܗܘܐ ܘܚܝܢܐ ܘܐܟܪܐ
ܗܘܐ ܘܐܫܬܒܚ.

[37] /bkulzvan/ "always": /kulzvan/, though composed of /kul/ and /zvan/ "time", is in this sense, normally spelled as a single word.
[38] /dilāku/ with an enclitic. On the independent possessive, see § 16.
[39] /wāle/ "fitting, appropriate".
[40] /walmeḥdā/ "to rejoice", Pe. inf. of /ḥ-d-y/.

Text no. 10

Two oriental anecdotes

From: E. A. Wallis Budge (ed.), *The Laughable Stories Collected by Mar Gregory John Bar-Hebraeus the Maphrian of the East from A.D. 1264 to 1286. The Syriac Text Edited with an English Translation* (London, 1897), which is a collection of humorous tales of varied origins and provenances. Syriac title: ܟܬܒܐ ܕܬܘܢܝܐ ܡܓܚܟܢܐ.

(CLIX) ܐܚܪܢܐ[1] ܐܡܪ ܕܟܠܗܘܢ ܚܝܢ ܗܢܘܢ ܕܡܗܪܝܢ ܥܡ
ܚܕ̈ܕܐ[2] ܒܒܘܚܢܐ.[3] ܐܝܬܝܗܘ ܕܠܥܠܡܐ ܢܚܘܢ ܘܠܐ[4] ܐܦ ܡܝܬܝܢ.
ܒܗܝ[5] ܕܥܠܡܐ ܚܕ ܗܘ. ܘܠܗ ܬܪ̈ܝܢ ܗܢܘܢ ܥܠܡܝܢ. ܐܝܬܝܗܘ ܕܝܢ
ܕܠܗ ܠܥܠܡܐ ܢܚܘܢ ܘܠܐ ܢܒܘܬܐ. ܗܦܟܐ ܠܗܘܢ ܕܪܐ. ܒܗܝ
ܕܠܐ ܡܨܐ ܚܕ ܡܢܗܘܢ ܢܙܟܐ.[6] ܐܠܘܠܐ[7] ܗܘ ܐܚܪܢܐ ܢܬܚܝܒ܀

[1] /ḥrēnā/ "another (Jewish sage)".
[2] /ḥdāde/ "each other, one another", short for /ḥad ʿam ḥad/. See Nöldeke, § 242.
[3] /buḥḥānā/ "examination; argument", a noun modelled on the common Peal action noun pattern /quṭṭālā/.
[4] For the conjunction, see n. 9 on Text no. 6, though Nöldeke (§ 339) denies such use of the Waw in an apodosis.
[5] /bhāy d-/ = /bad/ "in that; because".
[6] /nezke/: in conjunction with /mṣe/ "to be able to", the prefixation of /d-/ (/dnezke/) would have been more idiomatic.
[7] /'ellulā/ "unless".

(CCXXXIV) ܐܚܪܢܐ ܚܕ ܡܢ ܒܢ̈ܝ ܡܠܟ̈ܐ[8] ܙܥܘܪܐ ܗܘܐ.[9]
ܘܐܬܒܥܝ ܡܢ ܐܒܘܗܝ ܟܦܪܐ ܕܢܝܬܘܢ ܠܘܬܗ. ܘܟܕ ܠܐ ܚܙܝܗ̇
ܙܒܢܐ. ܐܝܟ ܗܘ ܕܡܢ ܩܕܡ ܐܟܝܠ ܗܘܐ ܠܗ.[10] ܘܐܡܪ ܠܗ. ܕܗܟܢܐ
ܗܝ ܟܦܪܐ ܐܟܠܬ. ܘܗܘ ܒܥܐ. ܘܟܕ ܫܐܠ ܠܡܪܒܝܢܘܗܝ,[11]
ܐܘܕܝܘ[12] ܕܐܝܢ.[13] ܗܟܢܐ ܟܠ ܟܦܪܐ ܡܕܡ ܟܕܐ ܘܐܟܠ. ܘܦܩܕ
ܡܠܟܐ ܕܒܫܦܝܢܐ ܢܚܘܟܘܢ[14] ܥܒܕ̈ܘܗܝ, ܐܝܟ ܕܢܟܐܒ[15] ܠܗ.
ܘܟܕ ܣܒܘ ܠܬ̈ܓܪܐ ܒܠܬ̈ܝܐ. ܟܕܐ ܘܐܡܪ ܠܡܠܟܐ. ܕܠܗܠܝܢ
ܬܫܬ̈ܬܐ ܥܒܕܘ ܠܙܒܬܐ[16] ܐܚܪ̈ܢܝܬܐ ܟܕ ܬܬܫܝܬ. ܘܗܟܢܐ
ܐܬܒܣܡ ܡܠܟܐ ܘܫܒܩܗ܀

[8] Mohammedan kings.
[9] Taking the initial /ḥrēnā/ as extraposed (a compound sentence), one misses /leh/ "to him", i.e. "he had a young (prince)". Or should we read /malkā/ without the *seyyame*?
[10] "he had eaten". See § 69.
[11] /*mrabbyānaw*/ "those who rear him", from a Pa. *nomen agentis* /*mrabbyān*/.
[12] /*'awdiw*/ "they admitted", Af. of /*y-d-y*/. Cf. Heb. /*hōdu*/.
[13] /*den*/: /*d-*/ introduces direct speech, whilst /*'ēn*/—not to be confused with ܐܶܢ /*'en*/ "if"—signifies "Yes".
[14] /*nḥuḵun*/ "they rub down"; the geminate form /*neḥḥḵun*/ is far more common.
[15] /*neḵav leh*/ "so that it would hurt him". The verb is used impersonally.
[16] The noun has two forms: f. /*zvattā*/ (with the assimilation of the Nun) "time" (of frequency, occurrence) and m. /*zavnā*/ "time" (as against space).

Text no. 11

On Mutual Incompatibility of some Syriac Sounds

The following passage is from a Syriac grammar by Jacob of Edessa (c. 640-708), the first native Syriac grammarian and biblical scholar. Judging by the tiny fragments that have survived, his approach is influenced by that of Classical Greek grammarians, but he reveals insights of an independent and sharp mind. Jacob is credited with inventing a whole set of vowel notations to be incorporated into the consonantal text itself, not to be added above or below the consonants, and the fragments have some examples of these symbols.

Edition: W. Wright, *Fragments of the* ܬܘܪܨ ܡܡܠܠܐ ܢܗܪܝܐ *or Syriac Grammar of Jacob of Edessa Edited from Manuscripts in the British Museum and the Bodleian Library. Only Fifty Copies Printed for Private Circulation* (London, 1871). The fragment was republished — but not the Bodleian fragment — in vol. 3, pp. 1169-73 of Wright's *Catalogue of the Syriac Manuscripts in the British Museum*, 3 vols. (London, 1870-72). The whole fragment was republished by A. Merx in his *Historia artis grammaticae apud Syros* etc. (Leipzig, 1889) as Abhandlungen für die Kunde des Morgenlandes, IX. Band, No. 2.

Bibliography: J. P. P. Martin, "Jacques d'Edesse et les voyelles syriennes", *Journal Asiatique*, Sixième série, Tome XIII (1869), 447-82; some aspects of Jacob as grammarian are treated in Merx, op. cit., and J. B. Segal, *The Diacritical Point and the Accents in Syriac* (London, 1953).

... ܥܗܝܕ.[1] ܐܢܬ ܗܟܝܠ ܐܘ ܩܪܘܝܐ[2] (BM Add. 17,217, fol. 37a)
ܐܝܟ ܡ̈ܠܟܐ. ܕܒܐܡܪܐ ܗܘ ܡܕܡܐ ܐܡܪܬ. ܕܡܢܗܝܢ[3] ܕܐܬ̈ܘܬܐ.
ܗܦܩܕ̈ܠܢ ܠܬ̈ܢܕܐ.[4] ܘܠܐ ܡܩ̈ܒܠܢ ܐܘ ܕܢܣܬܬܣܝܡܢ[5] ܡܕܡ
ܬ̈ܢܕܐ. ܐܘ ܕܢ̈ܬܬܐܬܝܢ[6] ܒܬܪ ܬ̈ܢܕܐ. ܗܢܘ[7] ܕܝܢ ܥ̈ܒܝܬܐ[8]
ܠܡ̈ܨܥܝܬܐ ܘܠܢܩ̈ܕܬܐ. ܘܡ̈ܨܥܝܬܐ ܠܥ̈ܒܝܬܐ ܘܠܢܩ̈ܕܬܐ. ܘܢܩ̈ܕܬܐ
ܗܢ ܒܗ̇ ܒܕܡܘܬܐ[9] ܠܥ̈ܒܝܬܐ ܘܠܡ̈ܨܥܝܬܐ. ܘܐܢ[10] ܗܘ ܕܬܣܬܟܠ
ܐܬܘܬܐ ܕܥ̈ܒܝܬܐ ܡܕܡ ܡ̈ܨܥܝܬܐ ܐܘ ܡܕܡ ܢܩ̈ܕܬܐ. ܡܫܬܚܠܦܐ[11].

[1] /ʿhid/, pass. ptc., passive in form only and emphasising the state "you remember, have not forgotten".
[2] /qāroyā/, Pe. *nomen agentis*, "reader".
[3] /menhen dāṯwāṯā/ "some of the letters (of the alphabet)". On the particle /d-/, see § 109e, and on the partitive force of the preposition /men/, cf. Dan 2.33 /minnhēn di farzel/ "some of them were of iron". The /'āṯwāṯā/ is the pl. of /'āṯuṯā/ "letter", not of /'āṯā/ "sign".
[4] See n. 2 on Text no. 10.
[5] The standard spelling is ܢܬܬܣܝܡܢ /nettsimān/, Ettaf. of /sām/.
[6] /nettaytyān/ "they are brought, put", Ettaf. impf. 3 f. pl. of /'-t-y/.
[7] /hānaw/ "that is to say, i.e."
[8] Jacob classifies some of the Syriac consonants into three groups;
/ʿavyāṯā/ aspiratae = ܒ . ܓ . ܕ . ܪ . ܟ
/meṣʿāyāṯā/ mediae = ܦ . ܒ . ܬ . ܣ . ܫ . ܢ
/naqdāṯā/ tenues = ܦ . ܛ . ܓ . ܣ
For a discussion, see Merx, *Historia*, pp. 52-55.
[9] /bāh badmuṯā/ "in the like manner" with a proleptic pronoun (§ 109a).
[10] /'en hu d-/ = /'en/ "if".
[11] /meštaḥlfā/ "changes", Eštafal of /ḥ-l-p/.

ܐܦ ܗܝ. ܘܗܘܝܐ [12] ܐܘ ܡܚܠܦܬܐ ܐܘ ܢܘܗܪܬܐ: ܘܡܦܠܓ ܗܕܐ ܐܦ
ܒܫܡ̈ܗܐ [13] ܗܠܝܢ ܕܩܕܡ ܐܬܟܬܒܘ [14] ܗܟܢܐ: ܗܘ ܕܝܢ
ܪܘܓܙܬܢܐ ܒܣܘܬܢܐ. ܪܓܘܙܬܢܐ. ܐܝܟ ܕܬܒܥ ܗ̄ܘܐ [15] ܗܘ
ܡܦܩܗ ܕܩܠܬ ܠܐ ܟܬܒܬ. [16] ܟܕ ܫܠܚܬ ܐܢܝܢ [17] ܠܐܬܘܬܐ.
ܠܟܠܚܕܐ ܠܒܪܬ ܓܢܣܗ [18] : ܠܘܬ ܐܬܘܬܐ ܗܝ ܕܡܬܬܐܡܝܐ
ܗܘܬ ܟܕ ܚܕܐ ܚܕܐ ܡܢܗܝܢ. ܟܕ ܪܓܘܙܬܢܐ ܢܬܪ ܘܒܣܘܬܢܐ:
ܡܛܠ ܕܠܐ ܡܫܬܟܚܐ ܬ̄ ܕܬܬܐܡܬܐ ܟܕ ܪ̄ ܕܐܝܬܘܗ̇ [19] ܒܟܝܢܬܐ:
ܐܘ ܟܕ ܦ̄ ܕܐܝܬܘܗ̇ ܢܦܝܫܬܐ: ܟܕ ܐܝܬܘܗ̇ ܗ̇ܝ ܡܟܝܟܬܐ.
ܠܡܟܝܟܬܐ ܕܐܟܘܬܗ [20] ܟ̄ ܫܚܠܦܬ ܠܬܪ̈ܬܝܗܝܢ. ܟܕ ܪܓܘܙܬܢܐ ܕܝܢ
ܕܐܝܬܘܗܝ. ܡܢ ܥܒܕܐ ܕܙܘܓܐ: ܘܟܝܢܐܝܬ [21] ܐܝܬ ܗܘܐ ܠܗ ܒܗ
ܙ̄. ܟܕ ܠܐ ܩܒܠܬ [22] ܠܥܒܝܘܬܗ̇. ܠܘܬ ܦ̄ ܕܐܝܬܘܗ̇ ܐܦ ܗܝ
ܡܟܝܟܬܐ. ܫܚܠܦܬ ܠܗܕܐ. ܒܗ̇ ܒܕܘܟܬܐ ܠܗܠܝܢ. ܐܦ
ܒܕ̈ܘܟܝܬܐ [23] ܩܢܘܢܝܬܐ ܡܟܢܫ ܐܝܬ ܕܢܝܙ ܗ̣ܘ ܗܢܐ ܚܘܠܦܐ
ܕܐܬ̈ܘܬܐ. ܐܝܟܢܐ ܕܒܬ̈ܠܐ ܢܬܪܐܬ: ܐܝܟܢܐ ܕܐܦ ܕܠܝܢܐܬ
ܡܫܬܠܡܗ ܐܠܦܐ ܟܕ ܐܝܢܐ. ܫܠܡ.

[12] */hāwyā/*, "becomes", Pe. ptc. f. sg.

[13] */šmāhe/*, the irregular pl. of */šmā/* "noun". For the addition of */h/* in the pl., see also */'avāhāṯā/* from */'avā/* "father".

[14] */qaddem 'eṯkṯev/* "were written about (= mentioned) earlier". On the asyndesis, see § 98b.

[15] A quasi-conditional: "which the pronunciation of the sound would require". See § 71 end.

[16] But the actual manuscript reading contradicts Jacob's claim, for only */ragguz-tānā/* is spelled ܪܓܘܙܬܢܐ.

[17] A proleptic pronoun; see § 109c.

[18] */baṯ gensāh/* "its congener, homogeneous sound".

[19] */diṯeh/* "which is".

[20] */dakwāṯāh/* "like it". "I changed both to the *mediae* which are similar to it, (i.e.) */k/*". On the form of the preposition, see § 32 end.

[21] */kyānā'iṯ/*, an adverb derived from */kyānā/* "nature, essence", Germ. *Wesen*. "It (= the word) has a Zay essentially, a Zay is inherent in it, it contains a Zay etymologically".

[22] */kaḏ lā qabblaṯ l'avyuṯāh/* "when it (i.e. the sound */t/*) did not admit of its aspirate feature".

[23] */dukkyāṯā/*, irregular pl. of */dukkṯā/* "place".

PSALM 1. 1-3 IN THE THREE SYRIAC SCRIPTS

(1) ܛܘܒܘܗܝ ܠܓܒܪܐ ܕܒܡܠܟܐ ܕܪܫܝܥܐ ܠܐ ܗܠܟ. ܘܒܐܘܪܚܐ ܕܚܛܝܐ ܠܐ ܩܡ :

ܛܘܒܘܗܝ ܠܓܒܪܐ ܕܒܡܠܟܐ ܕܪܫܝܥܐ ܠܐ ܗܠܟ. ܘܒܐܘܪܚܐ ܕܚܛܝܐ ܠܐ ܩܡ :

ܛܘܒܘܗܝ ܠܓܒܪܐ ܕܒܡܠܟܐ ܕܪܫܝܥܐ ܠܐ ܗܠܟ : ܘܒܐܘܪܚܐ ܕܚܛܝܐ ܠܐ ܩܡ .

(2) ܘܥܠ ܡܘܬܒܐ ܕܡܡܝܩܢܐ ܠܐ ܝܬܒ. ܐܠܐ ܒܢܡܘܣܗ ܕܡܪܝܐ ܨܒܝܢܗ :

ܘܥܠ ܡܘܬܒܐ ܕܡܡܝܩܢܐ ܠܐ ܝܬܒ. ܐܠܐ ܒܢܡܘܣܗ ܕܡܪܝܐ ܨܒܝܢܗ :

ܘܥܠ ܡܘܬܒܐ ܕܡܡܝܩܢܐ ܠܐ ܝܬܒ : ܐܠܐ ܒܢܡܘܣܗ ܕܡܪܝܐ ܨܒܝܢܗ :

ܘܒܢܡܘܣܗ ܢܗܓܐ ܐܝܡܡܐ ܘܠܠܝܐ.

ܘܒܢܡܘܣܗ ܢܗܓܐ ܐܝܡܡܐ ܘܠܠܝܐ.

ܘܒܢܡܘܣܗ ܢܗܓܐ ܐܝܡܡܐ ܘܠܠܝܐ .

(3) ܢܗܘܐ ܐܝܟ ܐܝܠܢܐ ܕܢܨܝܒ ܥܠ ܬܦܩܝ ܡܝܐ : ܕܦܐܪܘܗܝ ܢܬܠ ܒܙܒܢܗ

ܢܗܘܐ ܐܝܟ ܐܝܠܢܐ ܕܢܨܝܒ ܥܠ ܬܦܩܝ ܡܝܐ : ܕܦܐܪܘܗܝ ܢܬܠ ܒܙܒܢܗ

ܢܗܘܐ ܐܝܟ ܐܝܠܢܐ ܕܢܨܝܒ ܥܠ ܬܦܩܝ ܡܝܐ : ܕܦܐܪܘܗܝ ܢܬܠ ܒܙܒܢܗ

ܘܛܪܦܘܗܝ ܠܐ ܢܬܪܘܢ. ܘܟܠ ܕܥܒܕ ܡܫܟܚ :

ܘܛܪܦܘܗܝ ܠܐ ܢܬܪܘܢ. ܘܟܠ ܕܥܒܕ ܡܫܟܚ :

ܘܛܪܦܘܗܝ ܠܐ ܢܬܪܘܢ : ܘܟܠ ܕܥܒܕ ܡܫܟܚ .

Note a peculiar ligature in the Nestorian script at the end of a word, as is met with in certain editions: e.g., ܩܝܢܬܐ = ܩܝܢܬܐ */qinātā/* "dirges"; ܡܠܬܐ = ܡܠܬܐ "word". The ligature occurs only when the penultimate Taw is joined to the preceding letter.

VERB PARADIGMS

[The typical forms only are given. For uncommon forms, refer to the appropriate paragraphs in the Morphology section. A degree of artificiality is unavoidable; the verb root chosen for Paradigm I, i.e. */k-t-b/* is not attested in Pael, Ethpaal and Ettafal.]

I. Regular Triliteral Verbs

	Peal	Ethpeel	Pael
Pf. sg. 3 m	ܟܬܰܒ	ܐܶܬ݂ܟܬ݂ܶܒ	ܟܰܬܶܒ
f	ܟܶܬܒܰܬ݂	ܐܶܬ݂ܟܰܬ݂ܒܰܬ݂	ܟܰܬ݁ܒܰܬ݂
2 m	ܟܬ݂ܰܒܬ݁	ܐܶܬ݂ܟܬ݂ܶܒܬ݁	ܟܰܬ݁ܒܬ݁
f	ܟܬ݂ܰܒܬ݁ܝ	ܐܶܬ݂ܟܬ݂ܶܒܬ݁ܝ	ܟܰܬ݁ܒܬ݁ܝ
1	ܟܶܬ݂ܒܶܬ݂	ܐܶܬ݂ܟܬ݂ܶܒܶܬ݂	ܟܰܬ݁ܒܶܬ݂
pl. 3 m	ܟܬ݂ܰܒܘ	ܐܶܬ݂ܟܬ݂ܶܒܘ	ܟܰܬ݁ܒܘ
f	ܟܬ݂ܰܒ	ܐܶܬ݂ܟܬ݂ܶܒ	ܟܰܬ݁ܒ
2 m	ܟܬ݂ܰܒܬ݁ܘܢ	ܐܶܬ݂ܟܬ݂ܶܒܬ݁ܘܢ	ܟܰܬ݁ܒܬ݁ܘܢ
f	ܟܬ݂ܰܒܬ݁ܶܝܢ	ܐܶܬ݂ܟܬ݂ܶܒܬ݁ܶܝܢ	ܟܰܬ݁ܒܬ݁ܶܝܢ
1	ܟܬ݂ܰܒܢ	ܐܶܬ݂ܟܬ݂ܶܒܢ	ܟܰܬ݁ܒܢ
Impf.			
sg. 3 m	ܢܶܟܬ݁ܘܒ	ܢܶܬ݂ܟܬ݂ܶܒ	ܢܟܰܬܶܒ
f	ܬܶܟܬ݁ܘܒ	ܬܶܬ݂ܟܬ݂ܶܒ	ܬܟܰܬܶܒ
2 m	ܬܶܟܬ݁ܘܒ	ܬܶܬ݂ܟܬ݂ܶܒ	ܬܟܰܬܶܒ
f	ܬܶܟܬ݁ܒܺܝܢ	ܬܶܬ݂ܟܰܬ݂ܒܺܝܢ	ܬܟܰܬ݁ܒܺܝܢ
1	ܐܶܟܬ݁ܘܒ	ܐܶܬ݂ܟܬ݂ܶܒ	ܐܶܟܰܬܶܒ
pl. 3 m	ܢܶܟܬ݁ܒܽܘܢ	ܢܶܬ݂ܟܰܬ݂ܒܽܘܢ	ܢܟܰܬ݁ܒܽܘܢ
f	ܢܶܟܬ݁ܒܳܢ	ܢܶܬ݂ܟܰܬ݂ܒܳܢ	ܢܟܰܬ݁ܒܳܢ
2 m	ܬܶܟܬ݁ܒܽܘܢ	ܬܶܬ݂ܟܰܬ݂ܒܽܘܢ	ܬܟܰܬ݁ܒܽܘܢ
f	ܬܶܟܬ݁ܒܳܢ	ܬܶܬ݂ܟܰܬ݂ܒܳܢ	ܬܟܰܬ݁ܒܳܢ
1	ܢܶܟܬ݁ܘܒ	ܢܶܬ݂ܟܬ݂ܶܒ	ܢܟܰܬܶܒ
Impv.			
sg. m	ܟܬ݂ܘܒ	ܐܶܬ݂ܟܬ݂ܶܒ	ܟܰܬܶܒ
f	ܟܬ݂ܘܒܝ	ܐܶܬ݂ܟܬ݂ܶܒܝ	ܟܰܬ݁ܒܝ
pl. m	ܟܬ݂ܘܒܘ	ܐܶܬ݂ܟܬ݂ܶܒܘ	ܟܰܬ݁ܒܘ
f	ܟܬ݂ܘܒܝ	ܐܶܬ݂ܟܬ݂ܶܒܶܝܢ	ܟܰܬ݁ܒܝ
	ܟܬ݂ܘܒܶܝܢ	ܐܶܬ݂ܟܬ݂ܶܒܶܝܢ	ܟܰܬ݁ܒܶܝܢ

(§ 33, 36, 41-43)

	Ethpaal	Afel	Ettafal
Pf. sg. 3 m	ܐܬܟܬܒ	ܐܟܬܒ	ܐܬܬܟܬܒ
f	ܐܬܟܬܒܬ	ܐܟܬܒܬ	ܐܬܬܟܬܒܬ
2 m	ܐܬܟܬܒܬ	ܐܟܬܒܬ	ܐܬܬܟܬܒܬ
f	ܐܬܟܬܒܬܝ	ܐܟܬܒܬܝ	ܐܬܬܟܬܒܬܝ
1	ܐܬܟܬܒܬ	ܐܟܬܒܬ	ܐܬܬܟܬܒܬ
pl. 3 m	ܐܬܟܬܒܘ	ܐܟܬܒܘ	ܐܬܬܟܬܒܘ
f	ܐܬܟܬܒ	ܐܟܬܒ	ܐܬܬܟܬܒ
2 m	ܐܬܟܬܒܬܘܢ	ܐܟܬܒܬܘܢ	ܐܬܬܟܬܒܬܘܢ
f	ܐܬܟܬܒܬܝܢ	ܐܟܬܒܬܝܢ	ܐܬܬܟܬܒܬܝܢ
1	ܐܬܟܬܒܢ	ܐܟܬܒܢ	ܐܬܬܟܬܒܢ
Impf.			
sg. 3 m	ܢܬܟܬܒ	ܢܟܬܒ	ܢܬܬܟܬܒ
f	ܬܬܟܬܒ	ܬܟܬܒ	ܬܬܬܟܬܒ
2 m	ܬܬܟܬܒ	ܬܟܬܒ	ܬܬܬܟܬܒ
f	ܬܬܟܬܒܝܢ	ܬܟܬܒܝܢ	ܬܬܬܟܬܒܝܢ
1	ܐܬܟܬܒ	ܐܟܬܒ	ܐܬܬܟܬܒ
pl. 3 m	ܢܬܟܬܒܘܢ	ܢܟܬܒܘܢ	ܢܬܬܟܬܒܘܢ
f	ܢܬܟܬܒܢ	ܢܟܬܒܢ	ܢܬܬܟܬܒܢ
2 m	ܬܬܟܬܒܘܢ	ܬܟܬܒܘܢ	ܬܬܬܟܬܒܘܢ
f	ܬܬܟܬܒܢ	ܬܟܬܒܢ	ܬܬܬܟܬܒܢ
1	ܢܬܟܬܒ	ܢܟܬܒ	ܢܬܬܟܬܒ
Impv.			
sg. m	ܐܬܟܬܒ	ܐܟܬܒ	ܐܬܬܟܬܒ
f	ܐܬܟܬܒܝ	ܐܟܬܒܝ	ܐܬܬܟܬܒܝ
pl. m	ܐܬܟܬܒܘ	ܐܟܬܒܘ	ܐܬܬܟܬܒܘ
f	ܐܬܟܬܒܝ	ܐܟܬܒܝ	ܐܬܬܟܬܒܝ
	ܐܬܟܬܒܝܢ	ܐܟܬܒܝܢ	ܐܬܬܟܬܒܝܢ

I. Regular Triliteral Verbs

	Peal	Ethpeel	Pael
Ptc. act. m	ܟ݂ܬ݂ܒ	ܡܬ݂ܟ݂ܬ݂ܒ	ܡܟ݂ܬ݂ܒ
f	ܟ݂ܬ݂ܒܐ	ܡܬ݂ܟ݂ܬ݂ܒܐ	ܡܟ݂ܬ݂ܒܐ
pass. m	ܟܬ݂ܝܒ		ܡܟ݂ܬ݂ܒ
f	ܟܬ݂ܝܒܐ		ܡܟ݂ܬ݂ܒܐ
Inf.	ܠܡܟ݂ܬ݂ܒ	ܠܡܬ݂ܟ݂ܬ݂ܒܘ	ܠܡܟ݂ܬ݂ܒܘ

II. Third-Yodh (§ 51)

	Peal		Ethpeel
Pf. sg. 3 m	ܒܟ݂ܐ	ܕܟ݂ܝ	ܐܬ݂ܒܟ݂ܝ
f	ܒܟ݂ܬ݂	ܐܕܟ݂ܝܬ݂	ܐܬ݂ܒܟ݂ܝܬ݂
2 m	ܒܟ݂ܝܬ݂	ܐܕܟ݂ܝܬ݂	ܐܬ݂ܒܟ݂ܝܬ݂
f	ܒܟ݂ܝܬ݁ܝ	ܐܕܟ݂ܝܬ݁ܝ	ܐܬ݂ܒܟ݂ܝܬ݁ܝ
1	ܒܟ݂ܝܬ݂	ܐܕܟ݂ܝܬ݂	ܐܬ݂ܒܟ݂ܝܬ݂
pl. 3 m	ܒܟ݂ܘ	ܐܕܟ݂ܝܘ	ܐܬ݂ܒܟ݂ܝܘ
f	ܒܟ݂ܝ	ܐܕܟ݂ܝ	ܐܬ݂ܒܟ݂ܝ
2 m	ܒܟ݂ܝܬ݁ܘܢ	ܐܕܟ݂ܝܬ݁ܘܢ	ܐܬ݂ܒܟ݂ܝܬ݁ܘܢ
f	ܒܟ݂ܝܬ݁ܝܢ	ܐܕܟ݂ܝܬ݁ܝܢ	ܐܬ݂ܒܟ݂ܝܬ݁ܝܢ
1	ܒܟ݂ܝܢ	ܐܕܟ݂ܝܢ	ܐܬ݂ܒܟ݂ܝܢ
Impf. sg. 3 m	ܢܒܟ݂ܐ		ܢܬ݂ܒܟ݂ܐ
f	ܬܒܟ݂ܐ		ܬܬ݂ܒܟ݂ܐ
2 m	ܬܒܟ݂ܐ		ܬܬ݂ܒܟ݂ܐ
f	ܬܒܟ݂ܝܢ		ܬܬ݂ܒܟ݂ܝܢ
1	ܐܒܟ݂ܐ		ܐܬ݂ܒܟ݂ܐ
pl. 3 m	ܢܒܟ݂ܘܢ		ܢܬ݂ܒܟ݂ܘܢ
f	ܢܒܟ݂ܝܢ		ܢܬ݂ܒܟ݂ܝܢ
2 m	ܬܒܟ݂ܘܢ		ܬܬ݂ܒܟ݂ܘܢ
f	ܬܒܟ݂ܝܢ		ܬܬ݂ܒܟ݂ܝܢ
1	ܢܒܟ݂ܐ		ܢܬ݂ܒܟ݂ܐ

[Hardly any Third-Yodh verb is known in Ettafal.
/bkā/ = "he wept"; /dki/ = "he was clean".]

(§ 33, 36, 41-43)

	Ethpaal	Afel	Ettafal
Ptc. act. m	ܡܬܟܬܒ	ܡܟܬܒ	ܡܬܬܟܬܒ
f	ܡܬܟܬܒܐ	ܡܟܬܒܐ	ܡܬܬܟܬܒܐ
pass. m		ܡܟܬܒ	
f		ܡܟܬܒܐ	
Inf.	ܠܡܬܟܬܒܘ	ܠܡܟܬܒܘ	ܠܡܬܬܟܬܒܘ

II. Third-Yodh (§ 51)

	Pael	Ethpaal	Afel
Pf. sg. 3 m	ܓܠܝ	ܐܬܓܠܝ	ܐܓܠܝ
f	ܓܠܝܬ	ܐܬܓܠܝܬ	ܐܓܠܝܬ
2 m	ܓܠܝܬ	ܐܬܓܠܝܬ	ܐܓܠܝܬ
f	ܓܠܝܬܝ	ܐܬܓܠܝܬܝ	ܐܓܠܝܬܝ
1	ܓܠܝܬ	ܐܬܓܠܝܬ	ܐܓܠܝܬ
pl. 3 m	ܓܠܝܘ	ܐܬܓܠܝܘ	ܐܓܠܝܘ
f	ܓܠܝ	ܐܬܓܠܝ	ܐܓܠܝ
2 m	ܓܠܝܬܘܢ	ܐܬܓܠܝܬܘܢ	ܐܓܠܝܬܘܢ
f	ܓܠܝܬܝܢ	ܐܬܓܠܝܬܝܢ	ܐܓܠܝܬܝܢ
1	ܓܠܝܢ	ܐܬܓܠܝܢ	ܐܓܠܝܢ
Impf. sg. 3 m	ܢܓܠܐ	ܢܬܓܠܐ	ܢܓܠܐ
f	ܬܓܠܐ	ܬܬܓܠܐ	ܬܓܠܐ
2 m	ܬܓܠܐ	ܬܬܓܠܐ	ܬܓܠܐ
f	ܬܓܠܝܢ	ܬܬܓܠܝܢ	ܬܓܠܝܢ
1	ܐܓܠܐ	ܐܬܓܠܐ	ܐܓܠܐ
pl. 3 m	ܢܓܠܘܢ	ܢܬܓܠܘܢ	ܢܓܠܘܢ
f	ܢܓܠܝܢ	ܢܬܓܠܝܢ	ܢܓܠܝܢ
2 m	ܬܓܠܘܢ	ܬܬܓܠܘܢ	ܬܓܠܘܢ
f	ܬܓܠܝܢ	ܬܬܓܠܝܢ	ܬܓܠܝܢ
1	ܢܓܠܐ	ܢܬܓܠܐ	ܢܓܠܐ

II. Third-Yodh (§ 51)

	Peal	Ethpeel
Impv. sg. m	ܒܟܝ	ܐܬܒܟܝ
f	ܒܟܝ	ܐܬܒܟܝ
pl. m	ܒܟܘ	ܐܬܒܟܘ
f	ܒܟܝܝܢ	ܐܬܒܟܝܝܢ
Ptc. act. sg. m	ܒܟܐ	ܡܬܒܟܐ
f	ܒܟܝܐ	ܡܬܒܟܝܐ
pl. . m	ܒܟܝܢ	ܡܬܒܟܝܢ
f	ܒܟܝܢ	ܡܬܒܟܝܢ
pass. sg. m	ܒܟܐ	
f	ܒܟܝܐ	
pl. . m	ܒܟܝܢ	
f	ܒܟܝܢ	
Inf.	ܠܡܒܟܐ	ܠܡܬܒܟܝܘ

III. Second-Waw/Yodh Verbs (§ 53)

	Peal	
Pf. sg. 3 m	ܩܡ	ܡܝܬ
f	ܩܡܬ	ܡܝܬܬ
2 m	ܩܡܬ	ܡܝܬܬ
f	ܩܡܬܝ	ܡܝܬܬܝ
1	ܩܡܬ	ܡܝܬܬ
pl. 3 m	ܩܡܘ	ܡܝܬܘ
f	ܩܡ	ܡܝܬ
2 m	ܩܡܬܘܢ	ܡܝܬܬܘܢ
f	ܩܡܬܝܢ	ܡܝܬܬܝܢ
1	ܩܡܢ	ܡܝܬܢ

[/*p-š*/: Pe. "to remain", Af. "to desist from; to miss, lose.]

II. Third-Yodh (§ 51)

	Peal		Ethpeel
Impv. sg. m	ܒܥܐ	ܐܬܒܥܐ	ܐܒܥܐ
f	ܒܥܝ	ܐܬܒܥܝ	ܐܒܥܝ
pl. m	ܒܥܘ	ܐܬܒܥܘ	ܐܒܥܘ
f	ܒܥ̈ܝܢ	ܐܬܒܥ̈ܝܢ	ܐܒܥ̈ܝܢ
Ptc. act. sg. m	ܡܒܥܐ	ܡܬܒܥܐ	ܡܒܥܐ
f	ܡܒܥܝܐ	ܡܬܒܥܝܐ	ܡܒܥܝܐ
pl. . m	ܡܒܥܝܢ	ܡܬܒܥܝܢ	ܡܒܥܝܢ
f	ܡܒ̈ܥܝܢ	ܡܬܒ̈ܥܝܢ	ܡܒ̈ܥܝܢ
pass. sg. m	ܡܒܥܝ		ܡܒܥܝ
f	ܡܒܥܝܐ		ܡܒܥܝܐ
pl. . m	ܡܒܥܝܢ		ܡܒܥܝܢ
f	ܡܒ̈ܥܝܢ		ܡܒ̈ܥܝܢ
Inf.	ܠܡܒܥܝܘ	ܠܡܬܒܥܝܘ	ܠܡܒܥܝܘ

III. Second-Waw/Yodh Verbs (§ 53)

	Afel	Ethpeel (= Ettafal)
Pf. sg. 3 m	ܐܩܝܡ	ܐܬܬܩܝܡ
f	ܐܩܝܡܬ	ܐܬܬܩܝܡܬ
2 m	ܐܩܝܡܬ	ܐܬܬܩܝܡܬ
f	ܐܩܝܡܬܝ	ܐܬܬܩܝܡܬܝ
1	ܐܩܝܡܬ	ܐܬܬܩܝܡܬ
pl. 3 m	ܐܩܝܡܘ	ܐܬܬܩܝܡܘ
f	ܐܩܝܡ	ܐܬܬܩܝܡ
2 m	ܐܩܝܡܬܘܢ	ܐܬܬܩܝܡܬܘܢ
f	ܐܩܝܡܬܝܢ	ܐܬܬܩܝܡܬܝܢ
1	ܐܩܝܡܢ	ܐܬܬܩܝܡܢ

III. Second-Waw/Yodh Verbs (§ 53)

Impf.		
sg. 3 m	ܢܩܘܡ	ܢܣܝܡ
f	ܬܩܘܡ	ܬܣܝܡ
2 m	ܬܩܘܡ	ܬܣܝܡ
f	ܬܩܘܡܝܢ	ܬܣܝܡܝܢ
1	ܐܩܘܡ	ܐܣܝܡ
pl. 3 m	ܢܩܘܡܘܢ	ܢܣܝܡܘܢ
f	ܢܩܘܡܢ	ܢܣܝܡܢ
2 m	ܬܩܘܡܘܢ	ܬܣܝܡܘܢ
f	ܬܩܘܡܢ	ܬܣܝܡܢ
1	ܢܩܘܡ	ܢܣܝܡ
Impv.		
sg. m	ܩܘܡ	ܣܝܡ
f	ܩܘܡܝ	ܣܝܡܝ
pl. m	ܩܘܡܘ	ܣܝܡܘ
f	ܩܘܡܝܢ	ܣܝܡܝܢ
Ptc.		
act. sg	ܩܝܡܐ ܩܐܡ	ܣܝܡܐ ܣܐܡ
pass. sg.		ܣܝܡܐ ܣܝܡ
Inf.	ܠܡܩܡ	ܠܡܣܡ

III. Second-Waw/Yodh Verbs (§ 53)

Impf.		
sg. 3 m	ܢܩܝܡ	ܢܬܬܩܝܡ
f	ܬܩܝܡ	ܬܬܬܩܝܡ
2 m	ܬܩܝܡ	ܬܬܬܩܝܡ
f	ܬܩܝܡܝܢ	ܬܬܬܩܝܡܝܢ
1	ܐܩܝܡ	ܐܬܬܩܝܡ
pl. 3 m	ܢܩܝܡܘܢ	ܢܬܬܩܝܡܘܢ
f	ܢܩܝ̈ܡܢ	ܢܬܬܩܝ̈ܡܢ
2 m	ܬܩܝܡܘܢ	ܬܬܬܩܝܡܘܢ
f	ܬܩܝܡܢ	ܬܬܬܩܝܡܢ
1	ܢܩܝܡ	ܢܬܬܩܝܡ
Impv.		
sg. m	ܐܩܝܡ	ܐܬܬܩܝܡ
f	ܐܩܝܡܝ	ܐܬܬܩܝܡܝ
pl. m	ܐܩܝܡܘ	ܐܬܬܩܝܡܘ
f	ܐܩܝ̈ܡܝܢ	ܐܬܬܩܝ̈ܡܝܢ
Ptc.		
act. sg	ܡܩܝܡ	ܡܬܬܩܝܡ
pass. sg.	ܡܩܡ	
Inf.	ܠܡܩܡܘ	ܠܡܬܬܩܡܘ

IV. Geminate Verbs (§ 54)

	Peal	Afel
Pf. sg. 3 m	ܬܰܟ	ܐܰܬܶܟ
f	ܬܶܟܰܬ	ܐܰܬܶܟܰܬ
2 m	ܬܰܟܬ	ܐܰܬܶܟܬ
f	ܬܰܟܬܝ	ܐܰܬܶܟܬܝ
1	ܬܶܟܶܬ	ܐܰܬܶܟܶܬ
pl. 3 m	ܬܰܟܘ	ܐܰܬܶܟܘ
f	ܬܰܟ	ܐܰܬܶܟ
2 m	ܬܰܟܬܽܘܢ	ܐܰܬܶܟܬܽܘܢ
f	ܬܰܟܬܶܝܢ	ܐܰܬܶܟܬܶܝܢ
1	ܬܰܟܢ	ܐܰܬܶܟܢ
Impf.		
sg. 3 m	ܢܶܬܽܘܟ	ܢܰܬܶܟ
f	ܬܶܬܽܘܟ	ܬܰܬܶܟ
2 m	ܬܶܬܽܘܟ	ܬܰܬܶܟ
f	ܬܶܬܟܽܝܢ	ܬܰܬܟܺܝܢ
1	ܐܶܬܽܘܟ	ܐܰܬܶܟ
pl. 3 m	ܢܶܬܟܽܘܢ	ܢܰܬܟܽܘܢ
f	ܢܶܬܟܳܢ	ܢܰܬܟܳܢ
2 m	ܬܶܬܟܽܘܢ	ܬܰܬܟܽܘܢ
f	ܬܶܬܟܳܢ	ܬܰܬܟܳܢ
1	ܢܶܬܽܘܟ	ܢܰܬܶܟ

IV. Geminate Verbs (§ 54)

		Peal	Afel
Impv.			
	sg. m	ܬܘܟ	ܐܬܟ
	f	ܬܘܟܝ	ܐܬܟܝ
	pl. m	ܬܘܟܘ	ܐܬܟܘܢ
	f	ܬܘܟܝܢ	ܐܬܟܝܢ
Ptc.			
	act.	ܬܐܟ ܬܟܐ ܬܟܝܢ	ܡܬܟ ܡܬܟܐ
	pass.	ܬܟܝܟ ܬܟܝܟܐ	ܡܬܟ ܡܬܟܐ
Inf.			
		ܠܡܬܟ	ܠܡܬܟܘ

[/*t-k-k*/: Pe. "to oppress", Af. "to do harm".]

V. Regular Verbs with

Pf. Peal	sg. 1	sg. 2 m	sg. 2 f
sg. 3 m	ܩܛܠܢܝ	ܩܛܠܟ	ܩܛܠܟܝ
f	ܩܛܠܬܢܝ	ܩܛܠܬܟ	ܩܛܠܬܟܝ
2 m	ܩܛܠܬܢܝ	—	—
f	ܩܛܠܬܝܢܝ	—	—
1	—	ܩܛܠܬܟ	ܩܛܠܬܟܝ
pl. 3 m	ܩܛܠܘܢܝ	ܩܛܠܘܟ	ܩܛܠܘܟܝ
f	ܩܛܠܢܝ	ܩܛܠܟ	ܩܛܠܟܝ
2 m	ܩܛܠܬܘܢܢܝ	—	—
f	ܩܛܠܬܝܢܢܝ	—	—
1	—	ܩܛܠܢܟ	ܩܛܠܢܟܝ
Impf. Peal			
sg. 3 m	ܢܩܛܠܢܝ	ܢܩܛܠܟ	ܢܩܛܠܟܝ
2 m	{ ܬܩܛܠܢܝ ܬܩܛܘܠܝܢܝ	—	—
f	ܬܩܛܠܝܢܢܝ	—	—
pl. 3 m	ܢܩܛܠܘܢܢܝ	ܢܩܛܠܘܢܟ	ܢܩܛܠܘܢܟܝ
f	ܢܩܛܠܢܢܝ	ܢܩܛܠܢܟ	ܢܩܛܠܢܟܝ

Object Suffixes (§ 56)

sg. 3 m	sg. 3 f	pl. 1	pl. 2 m
ܩܛܠܗ	ܩܛܠܗ̇	ܩܛܠܢ	ܩܛܠܟܘܢ
ܩܛܠܬܗ	ܩܛܠܬܗ̇	ܩܛܠܬܢ	ܩܛܠܬܟܘܢ
ܩܛܠܬܝܗܝ	ܩܛܠܬܗ̇	ܩܛܠܬܢ	—
ܩܛܠܬܝܘܗܝ	ܩܛܠܬܝܗ̇	ܩܛܠܬܝܢ	—
ܩܛܠܬܗ	ܩܛܠܬܗ̇	—	ܩܛܠܬܟܘܢ
ܩܛܠܘܗܝ	ܩܛܠܘܗ̇	ܩܛܠܘܢ	ܩܛܠܘܟܘܢ
ܩܛܠܝܗܝ	ܩܛܠܝܗ̇	ܩܛܠܝܢ	ܩܛܠܝܟܘܢ
ܩܛܠܬܘܢܝܗܝ	ܩܛܠܬܘܢܗ̇	ܩܛܠܬܘܢܢ	—
ܩܛܠܬܝܢܝܗܝ	ܩܛܠܬܝܢܗ̇	ܩܛܠܬܝܢܢ	—
ܩܛܠܢܝܗܝ	ܩܛܠܢܗ̇	—	ܩܛܠܢܟܘܢ
ܢܩܛܠܝܘܗܝ ; ܢܩܛܠܗ	ܢܩܛܠܝܗ̇	ܢܩܛܠܢ	ܢܩܛܘܠ ܠܟܘܢ
ܬܩܛܠܝܘܗܝ / ܬܩܛܠܝܗܝ ; ܬܩܛܘܠ ܠܗ	ܬܩܛܠܝܗ̇ ; ܬܩܛܘܠ ܠܗ̇	ܬܩܛܠܢ ; ܬܩܛܘܠ ܠܢ	—
ܬܩܛܠܝܢܝܗܝ ; ܬܩܛܠܝܢܗ	ܬܩܛܠܝܢܗ̇	ܬܩܛܠܝܢܢ	—
ܢܩܛܠܘܢ ܢܝܗܝ ; ܢܩܛܠܘܢ ܢܗ	ܢܩܛܠܘܢ ܢܗ̇	ܢܩܛܠܘܢ ܢܢ	ܢܩܛܠܘܢ ܟܘܢ
ܢܩܛܠܢܝܗܝ ; ܢܩܛܠܢܗ	ܢܩܛܠܢܗ̇	ܢܩܛܠܢܢ	ܢܩܛܠܢܟܘܢ

V. Regular Verbs with

	sg. 1	sg. 2 m	sg. 2 f
Impv. Peal			
sg. m	ܩܛܘܠܝܢܝ	—	—
f	ܩܛܘܠܝܢܝ	—	—
pl. m	ܩܛܘܠܘܢܝ	—	—
	ܩܛܘܠܘܢܢܝ	—	—
f	ܩܛܘܠܢܝ	—	—
	ܩܛܘܠܝܢܢܝ	—	—
Inf. Peal	ܠܡܩܛܠܢܝ	ܠܡܩܛܠܟ	ܠܡܩܛܠܟܝ
Pael	ܠܡܩܛܠܘܬܢܝ	ܠܡܩܛܠܘܬܟ	ܠܡܩܛܠܘܬܟܝ

N.B. 1. There is an important distinction between the hard and soft pronunciations of /*t*/ in ܩܛܠܬܗ "I killed him" vs. ܩܛܠܬܗ "she killed him", for example.

2. A Begadhkephath as a third radical is pronounced hard in cases like ܐܚܕܗ "he took him", ܢܣܒܘܗ̇ "they took her", Mt 21.46 ܠܡܐܚܕܗ

Object Suffixes (§ 56)

sg. 3 m	sg. 3 f	pl. 1	pl. 2 m
ܩܛܘܠܝܗܝ	ܩܛܘܠܝܗ	ܩܛܘܠܝܢ	—
ܩܛܘܠܝܘܗܝ	ܩܛܘܠܝܗ	ܩܛܘܠܝܢ	—
{ ܩܛܘܠܘܗܝ	{ ܩܛܘܠܘܗ	{ ܩܛܘܠܘܢ	—
ܩܛܘܠܘܢܗܝ }	ܩܛܘܠܘܢܗ }	ܩܛܘܠܘܢܢ }	
{ ܩܛܘܠܝܗܝ	{ ܩܛܘܠܝܗ	{ ܩܛܘܠܝܢ	—
ܩܛܘܠܝܢܗܝ }	ܩܛܘܠܝܢܗ }	ܩܛܘܠܝܢܢ }	
ܠܡܩܛܠܗ	ܠܡܩܛܠܗ	ܠܡܩܛܠܢ	ܠܡܩܛܠܟܘܢ
ܠܡܩܛܠܘܬܗ	ܠܡܩܛܠܘܬܗ	ܠܡܩܛܠܘܬܢ	ܠܡܩܛܠܘܬܟܘܢ

"to capture him" (but Acts 7.5 ܠܡܐܪܬܗ "to inherit it"), Mt 26.4 ܢܐܚܕܘܢܗܝ "they will capture him" (but Jn 19.6 ܙܩܘܦܝܗܝ "Crucify him!").

VI. Third-Yodh Verbs with

	sg. 1	sg. 2 m	sg. 2 f
Pf. sg. 3 m Pe.	ܓܠܢܝ	ܓܠܟ	ܓܠܟܝ
Pa.	ܓܠܝܢܝ	ܓܠܝܟ	ܓܠܝܟܝ
f Pe.	ܓܠܬܢܝ	ܓܠܬܟ	ܓܠܬܟܝ
Pa.	ܓܠܝܬܢܝ	ܓܠܝܬܟ	ܓܠܝܬܟܝ
2 m Pe.	ܓܠܝܬܢܝ	——	——
Pa.	ܓܠܝܬܢܝ	——	——
f Pe.	ܓܠܝܬܝܢܝ	——	——
Pa.	ܓܠܝܬܝܢܝ	——	——
1 Pe.	——	ܓܠܝܬܟ	ܓܠܝܬܟܝ
Pa.	——	ܓܠܝܬܟ	ܓܠܝܬܟܝ
pl. 3 m Pe.	ܓܠܘܢܝ	ܓܠܘܟ	ܓܠܘܟܝ
Pa.	ܓܠܝܘܢܝ	ܓܠܝܘܟ	ܓܠܝܘܟܝ
f Pe.	ܓܠܝܢܝ	ܓܠܝܟ	ܓܠܝܟܝ
Pa.	ܓܠܝܢܝ	ܓܠܝܟ	ܓܠܝܟܝ
2 m Pe.	ܓܠܝܬܘܢܢܝ	——	——
Pa.	ܓܠܝܬܘܢܢܝ	——	——
1 Pe.	——	ܓܠܝܢܟ	ܓܠܝܢܟܝ
Pa.	——	ܓܠܝܢܟ	ܓܠܝܢܟܝ
Impf.			
Pe.	ܢܓܠܝܢܝ	ܢܓܠܝܟ	ܢܓܠܝܟܝ

Object Suffixes

sg. 3 m	sg. 3 f	pl. 1	pl. 2 m
ܓܠܝܗܝ	ܓܠܗ	ܓܠܢ	ܓܠܟܘܢ
ܓܠܝܗ	ܓܠܝܗ	ܓܠܝܢ	ܓܠܝܟܘܢ
ܓܠܬܗ	ܓܠܬܗ	ܓܠܬܢ	ܓܠܬܟܘܢ
ܓܠܝܬܗ	ܓܠܝܬܗ	ܓܠܝܬܢ	ܓܠܝܬܟܘܢ
ܓܠܝܬܝܗܝ	ܓܠܝܬܗ	ܓܠܝܬܢ	—
ܓܠܝܬܝܗܝ	ܓܠܝܬܗ	ܓܠܝܬܢ	—
ܓܠܝܬܝܘܗܝ	ܓܠܝܬܝܗ	ܓܠܝܬܝܢ	—
ܓܠܝܬܝܘܗܝ	ܓܠܝܬܝܗ	ܓܠܝܬܝܢ	—
ܓܠܝܬܗ	ܓܠܝܬܗ	—	ܓܠܝܬܟܘܢ
ܓܠܝܬܗ	ܓܠܝܬܗ	—	ܓܠܝܬܟܘܢ
ܓܠܐܘܗܝ	ܓܠܐܘܗ	ܓܠܐܘܢ	ܓܠܐܘܟܘܢ
ܓܠܘܗܝ	ܓܠܘܗ	ܓܠܘܢ	ܓܠܘܟܘܢ
ܓܠܝ̈ܗܝ	ܓܠܝ̈ܗ	ܓܠܝ̈ܢ	—
ܓܠܝ̈ܗܝ	ܓܠܝ̈ܗ	ܓܠܝ̈ܢ	—
ܓܠܝܬܘܢ ܢܝܗܝ	ܓܠܝܬܘܢ ܢܗ	ܓܠܝܬܘܢ ܢܢ	—
ܓܠܝܬܘܢ ܢܝܗܝ	ܓܠܝܬܘܢ ܢܗ	ܓܠܝܬܘܢ ܢܢ	—
ܓܠܝܢܝܗܝ	ܓܠܝܢܗ	—	ܓܠܝܢܟܘܢ
ܓܠܝܢܝܗܝ	ܓܠܝܢܗ	—	ܓܠܝܢܟܘܢ
ܢܓܠܝܘܗܝ	ܢܓܠܝܗ	ܢܓܠܝܢ	ܢܓܠܝܟܘܢ

VI. Third-Yodh Verbs with

		sg. 1	sg. 2 m	sg. 2 f
Impv.				
	sg. m Pe.	ܓܠܝܢܝ	——	——
	Pa.	ܓܠܝܢܝ	——	——
	f Pe.	ܓܠܐܝ ܢܝ	——	——
	pl. m Pe.	ܓܠܐܘ ܢܝ	——	——
	f Pe.	ܓܠܝܢܢܝ	——	——
Inf.	Pe.	ܠܡܓܠܝܢܝ	ܠܡܓܠܝܟ	ܠܡܓܠܝܟܝ
	Pa.	ܠܡܓܠܝܘܬ ܢܝ	ܠܡܓܠܝܘܬܟ	ܠܡܓܠܝܘܬܟܝ

N.B. 1. Some forms are extremely rare or not attested at all. Hence their absence from the above paradigm.

2. For a discussion of details, see Nöldeke, § 194-98. A fuller paradigm is given by Alphonse Mingana in his *Clef de la langue araméenne ou Grammaire complète et pratique des deux dialectes syriaques occidental et oriental* (Mossoul, 1905).

Object Suffixes

sg. 3 m	sg. 3 f	pl. 1	pl. 2 m
ܓܠܝܘܗܝ	ܓܠܝܗ	ܓܠܝܢ	—
ܓܠܬܗܝ	ܓܠܬܗ	ܓܠܬܢ	—
ܓܠܐܝܘܗܝ	ܓܠܐܝܗ	ܓܠܐ ܢ	—
ܓܠܐܘܗܝ	ܓܠܐܘܗ	ܓܠܐܘܢ	—
ܓܠܝܢܗܝ	ܓܠܝܢܗ	ܓܠܝܢܢ	—
ܠܡܓܠܝܗ	ܠܡܓܠܝܗ	ܠܡܓܠܝܢ	ܠܡܓܠܝܟܘܢ
ܠܡܓܠܝܘܬܗ	ܠܡܓܠܝܘܬܗ	ܠܡܓܠܝܘܬܢ	ܠܡܓܠܝܘܬܟܘܢ

3. It is not certain whether a form like Mt 2.10S, Jn 9.8S ܚܙܘܘܗܝ is phonetically any different from the standard form ܚܙܐܘܗܝ "they saw him".

GLOSSARY

[Verbs are arranged by root, but other words alphabetically.]

ܐܒܐ n.m. (pl. ܐܒܗܬܐ; §30): father, forefather

ܐܒܕ Af. (ܐܘܒܕ): to destroy

ܐܒܝܕ adj.: lost, missing

ܐܓܪ Pe. /o/: to hire

ܐܓܝܪܐ hired labourer

ܐܓܪܐ n.m.: wage, reward

ܐܘ Oh!

ܐܘܠܨܢܐ n.m.: trouble, suffering

ܐܙܠ Pe. (Impf. ܢܐܙܠ): to go

ܐܚܐ n.m.: brother

ܐܢܫ ... ܐܚܘܗܝ each other

ܐܚܕ → ܚܕ

ܐܚܕ Pe. /o/: 1. to seize, grasp (+ ܒ)

2. to shut (door)

Ethpe.: to be captured, caught [אחז]

ܐܚܫܝܪܫ Ahasuerus

ܐܝܕܐ (see under ܐܝܕܐ)

ܐܝܟ 1. prep.: as, like

2. + ܕ and impf.: so that, in order that

ܐܝܟܐ Where?

+ ܕ, conj.: where, wherever ܠܐܝܟܐ Where ... to?

ܐܝܟܢܐ 1. How? In what way?

2. + ܕ, conj.: as (comparison)

ܐܝܢܐ m. sg.: Which? What (sort of)?

ܐܝܩܪܐ (also ܝܩܪܐ) n.m.: glory

ܐܝܬ 1. there is, exists;

2. is (as copula: see §107) [יֵשׁ]

ܐܝܟܘܬ- prep. (w. suf.): like, as

ܐܟܠ Pe. /o/: to eat

ܐܟܡܐ + ܕ, conj.: as

ܐܟܬܐ n.f.: grudge

ܐܠܐ 1. but (after a negative)

2. + ܐܢ : except; 3. unless

ܐܠܗܐ n.m.: god

ܝܠܦ Pe. (impf. ܢܐܠܦ): to learn Pa.: to teach (§49B)

ܐܠܨ Pe. /o/: to force, compel

ܐܡܝܢ truly

ܐܡܪ Pe. (impf. ܢܐܡܪ): to say

Ethpe.: = pass. Pe.

ܐܡܬܝ + ܕ: whenever, when [מָתַי]

ܐܢ conj.: if

ܐܢܗܘ, + ܕ: if

ܐܢܫ 1. (with a negative) nobody (§110)

2. person;

3. ܒܪ ܐܢܫܐ, ܒܪ ܐܢܫ somebody;

ܒܢܝ̈ ܐܢܫܐ people

ܐܢܬܬܐ /'attā/ n.f.: woman; wife

ܐܣܪ Pe. (impf. ܢܐܣܘܪ): to bind, incarcerate

ܐܣܝܪܐ (pass. ptc.): prisoner

ܐܣܬܝܪ : Esther

ܐܦ : also. Sometimes with a superfluous Waw: ܘܐܦ)

ܐܦ̈ܐ n.pl.: face

ܐܪܥܐ n.f.: earth, land [אֶרֶץ]

ܐܬܐ Pe.: to come

Af. (ܐܝܬܝ): to bring

Ettaf. (ܐܬܬܝܬܝ): = pass. Af. See § 55B.

ܐܬܘܬܐ n.f. (pl. ܐܬܘܬܐ): letter (of alphabet

ܐܬܛܦܝܣ See under ܦܣ.

ܐܬܪܐ (ܐܬܪ) n.m.: place

ܒܨܐ Pe. /o/: to examine, study

ܒܕܪ Pa.: to squander, dissipate

ܒܛܠ Pa.: to make void

ܒܝܢܬ prep. (with a pl. noun or pron.): between, amongst

ܒܝܫ adj.: evil, wicked

ܒܝܫܘܬܐ : n.f., wickedness

ܒܟܐ Pe.: to cry, weep

ܒܝܬܐ n.m.: house, home

ܒܝܬ ܐܣܝܪܐ : prison

ܒܠܚܘܕ ܕ 1. (introducing a parenthetical addition) only;

2. (after a noun) only, alone

ܒܣܡ Pe. /a/: to be happy, rejoice

Ethpa: to make merry, to be amused

ܒܥܐ Ethpe.: 1. to be required

ptc. ܡܬܒܥܐ necessary

2. to be requested

ܒܥܘܬܐ n.f.: request, petition

ܒܥܠܦܥܘܪ: Beelpeor

ܒܨܪ Pa.: to detract, take away

ܒܪ n.m.: the outside

ܒܪܐ n.m. (pl. ܒܢܝܐ): son

ܒܪܝܬܐ n.f.: creature

ܒܬܪ prep.: after

ܡܢ ܒܬܪ : after (of time or place), behind

ܒܬܪ ܕ- : conj., after

ܓܐܘܬܐ n.f.: hubris, pride

ܓܐܪܐ n.m.: arrow

ܓܒܪܐ n.m.: man, male

ܓܕܝܐ n.m.: kid

ܓܕܫ Pe. /a/: to happen

ܓܘ n.m.: the inside. Often with prep. such as ܡܢ, ܠ-

ܠܓܘ prep.: inside

ܓܘܒܐ n.m.: pit, cistern

ܓܘܙܠ Pa.intr.: to burn, be in flame

ܓܘܚܟܐ n.m.: laughing-stock

ܓܘܠܒܐ n.f.: cowl

ܓܘܡܨܐ n.m.: pit

ܓܚܟ Pe. /a/: to laugh, make fun of (ܥܠ)

Pa. + ב: to deride, mock [צחק]

ܓܝܪ conj.: for

ܓܝܪܐ n.m.: adulterer

ܓܠܝܐ : ܒܓܠܝܐ openly

ܓܡܪ Pa: to exhaust, consume; to satisfy

Ethpe.: (of a desire) to be satisfied

ܓܢܒܪܘܬܐ n.f.: heroism, manliness

ܓܢܣܐ n.m.: kind (γένος)

ܕ- [= אֲשֶׁר in most uses]

1. (relative pron.) which, who, that
2. (antecedent understood) one who, that which
3. (cause, reason) because, for
4. (linking two nouns or noun phrases) of [See § 86]
5. (introducing direct speech)
6. (+ impf., indicating a purpose) in order that, so that

ܕܒܪ Pe. /*a*/: to lead (away)

ܕܢ [Rt: d-w-n] Pe.: to judge

Ettaf.: = pass. Pe.

ܕܚܠ Pe. /*a*/: to fear

ܕܚܫܐ n.m.: prison guard, warder

ܕܝܠ- w.suf., e.g. ܕܝܠܟ your, yours (§ 16)

ܕܝܠܢܐܝܬ : properly

ܕܝܢ Indicates slight contrast as Gk δέ in μέν … δέ.

ܕܝܢܐ n.m.: judgement

ܕܝܢܪܐ n.m.: dinar

ܕܠܐ prep.: without

ܕܡܐ Ethpa.: to copy, behave like (ܠ)

ܕܡܘܬܐ n.f.: shape, form

ܕܡܟ Pe. /*a*/: (of sexual relationship) to sleep

ܕܪܐ n.m.: conflict

ܗܐ = הִנֵּה

ܗܕܐ f.: this

ܗܘ dem.pron.m.: that

ܗܘܐ Pe. [= הָיָה]: 1. was;

2. enclitic preceded by a ptc. to express a continuous, repeated past action (§ 71)

ܗܝ dem.pron.f.: that

ܗܝܕܝܢ : then

ܗܟܝܠ : (in drawing a conclusion) then, therefore

ܗܟܢܐ : thus, in this manner

ܗܠܝܢ pron.: these

ܗܡܢ : Haman

ܗܢܐ m.: this

ܗܦܟ Pe. /*o*/ intr.: to return, come back

ܗܪܟܐ : here

ܗܫܐ : now

ܙܒܢ Ethpa. (ܐܙܕܒܢ); to be sold

ܙܒܢܐ n.m.: time, occasion

ܒܟܠܙܒܢ : always, all the time

ܙܒܢܬܐ n.f.: (of frequency) time, occasion

ܙܕܝܩ adj.: righteous, just [צַדִּיק]

ܙܗܪ Ethpe: to be cautious, take care

ܙܘܝܬܐ n.f.: corner

ܙܟܐ Pe.: to win, triumph

ܙܟܘܬܐ n.f.: victory

ܙܡܪܐ n.m.: song, singing

ܙܢܐ n.m.: kind, sort, manner

ܙܢܝܬܐ n.f.: prostitute

ܙܥܘܪ adj.: small, young [זְעֵיר]

ܙܩܝܦܐ n.m.: cross

ܚܒ (Rt: ḥ-b-b): Af. (ܐܚܒ) to love

ܚܒܝܒ adj.: beloved

ܚܒܠ Ethpa.: to be impaired

ܚܒܠܐ n.m.: bond, cord

ܚܒܫ Pe. /*o*/: to bind

ܚܕ (numeral): one; the only, sole, single (§ 78)

ܚܕܝ Pe.: to rejoice

ܚܘܐ Pa. (pf. ܚܘܝ): to tell, announce

ܚܒ (Rt: ḥ-w-b) Ethpa.: to be defeated

ܚܘܒܐ n.m.: iniquity, wickedness

ܚܘܒܬܐ n.f.: debt

ܚܘܠܦܐ n.m.: change, interchange

ܚܟ (Rt: ḥ-w-k) Pe.: to rub down

ܚܘܪܒ Horeb

ܚܘܫܒܢܐ n.m.: account, accounting

ܚܙܐ Pe.: to see; Ethpe. = pass. Pe.

ܚܙܝܪܐ n.m.: pig

ܚܛܐ Pe.: to sin

ܚܛܗܐ n.m.: sin

ܚܝ adj.: alive, to live

pl.n. ܚܝܐ : life

ܚܝܐ Pe. (impf. ܢܚܐ ; § 55F): to live, survive; be saved

ܚܝܒ adj.: be in debt

n.m.: debtor, wrong-doer

ܚܝܠܐ n.m.: power

ܚܟܝܡ adj.: wise

ܚܟܡ Ethpa: to conspire, plot

ܚܟܡܬܐ n.f.: wisdom

ܚܠܝܡ adj.: healthy

ܚܠܡܐ n.m.: dream

ܚܠܦ Pa.: to alter, change

ܚܠܦ prep.: instead of

ܚܡܨ Pa.: to hold fast, put one's foot down

ܚܡܬ Ethpa: to be provoked; to be displeased

ܚܡܬܐ n.f.: anger, displeasure

ܚܢܦܐ n.m.: infidel, unbeliever

ܚܢܩ Pe. /o/: to strangle

ܚܣܕ Pa.: to insult

ܚܣܕܐ n.m.: grace, mercy

ܚܣܟ Pe. /o/: 1. to withhold

2. to save

ܚܨܦ Pe. /a/: to overpower, force

ܚܫܒ Ethpa.: to plan, plot

ܚܫܘܟܐ n.m.: darkness

ܚܬܡ Pa. (+ ܥܠ): to prove, confirm

ܛܒ adv.: exceedingly, very

ܛܘܪܐ n.m.: mountain [צור]

ܛܝܒ Pa.: to prepare

ܡܛܝܒ ptc. pass., prepared, ready

ܛܝܒܘܬܐ n.f.: goodness, kindness

ܛܠܝܐ n.m.: boy; servant

ܛܡܪ Pe. /o/: to bury, lay (a snare)

ܛܥܐ Pe.: to forget

ܝܕܐ Af. (ܐܘܕܝ): to admit

ܐܝܕܐ n.f. (also spelled ܐܝܕܐ);: hand

ܝܕܥ Pe. (impf. ܢܕܥ): to know, recognise

Af. (ܐܘܕܥ): to let know, make known; inculcate

ܝܗܒ Pe. (see § 55E): to give

ܝܗܘܕܝܐ adj.: Jewish, Jew

ܝܘܡܐ (pl. ܝܘܡܬܐ) n.m.: day

ܟܠ ܝܘܡ, ܟܠܝܘܡ every day

ܝܘܡܢܐ : today

ܝܘܣܦ: Joseph

ܝܠܦ : See under Alaf.

ܝܣܦ Af. (ܐܘܣܦ): to add (to ܥܠ)

ܝܪܬ Pe. (impf. ܢܐܪܬ): to inherit

ܝܬܝܪ adj.: abundant, excessive

ܝܬܝܪܐܝܬ adv.: especially

ܟܐܒ Pe.: to hurt, be painful

ܟܐܦܐ n.f.: stone

ܟܕ conj.: 1. when;

2. as, while (with a non-past statement and introducing a circumstantial clause)

ܟܘܬܝܢܐ n.f.: a coat, tunic

ܟܝܠ (Rt: k-y-l) Pe.: to measure

Ettaf.: pass. Pe.

ܟܝܠܐ n.m.: measure

ܟܟܪܐ n.m.: talent

ܟܠ / ܟܘܠ : 1. every, all;
2. (+ negative), any

ܟܡܐ : How much?

ܟܢܫ Pa. tr.: to gather, assemble
Ethpa. intr.: to gather, come together

ܟܢܘܫܬܐ n.f.: synagogue

ܟܢܬܐ n.m. (pl. ܟܢܘܬܐ): associate, colleague

ܟܣܝܐ : ܒܟܣܝܐ in secret, unnoticed

ܟܦܢܐ n.m.: famine, hunger

ܟܦܪ Pe. /o/: to deny, disagree

ܟܪܣܐ n.m.: stomach

ܟܬܒ Pe. /o/: to write
ܟܬܒܐ n.m.: writing, document

ܟܬܪ Pa.: to remain

ܠ- prep.: 1. (of destination, recipient, etc.), to
2. introduces a direct object
3. of centripetal force (see on Gn 39.12)

ܠܐ : not

ܠܐܝ Pe.: to be/become tired

ܠܒܐ n.m.: heart, mind

ܠܒܘܫܐ n.m.: garment

ܠܒܢ: Laban

ܠܒܫ Af.: to clothe
ܠܒܫܐ n.m.: garment

ܠܘ : not (§ 110)

ܠܘܐ Pe.: to accompany

ܠܘܚܐ n.f.: tablet

ܠܘܩܒܠ prep.: in front of

ܠܘܬ prep.: (indicating physical proximity, and used with verbs such as "to leave", "to leave sth with sb") beside, with, towards

ܠܚܡܐ n.m.: bread

ܠܝܬ : (negative of ܐܝܬ) there is not; it is not (§ 107)

ܠܒܝܢ : See under ܒܝܢܐ.

ܠܦܘܬ prep.: according to

ܡܐ : + ܕ conj. 1. when;
2. all that, whatever

ܡܐܐ : hundred

ܡܐܡܪܐ n.m.: treatise, section (of a book)

ܡܐܢܐ n.m.: instrument, vessel; garment

ܡܕܒܚܐ n.m.: altar

ܡܕܒܪܐ n.m.: wilderness, desert

ܡܕܠܚܢܐ n.m.: troubler

ܡܕܡ : 1. something; (with negative) anything, nothing
2. (+ sg. noun) some, some kind of
ܟܠ ܡܕܡ : everything

ܡܘܗܒܬܐ n.f.: gift

ܡܘܪܕܟܝ : Mordecai

ܡܚܐ Pe.: to smite, wound
Ethpe.: = pass. Pe.
ܡܚܘܬܐ n.f.: blow, wound

ܡܚܫܒܬܐ n.f.;: thought, counsel

ܡܛܐ Pe.: to reach, to be due

ܡܛܠ, ܡܛܠ ܠ prep. (w. suf. – ܡܛܠܬ) because of
+ ܕ, conj.: because

ܡܝܬ adj.: dead

ܡܟ (Rt; m-k-k) Ethpa.: to be brought low

ܡܟܝܠ : (marking a new turn in speech or narration) now

ܡܠܐ Pe.: to fill

ܡܠܐ adj. (f. ܡܠܝܐ): full

ܡܠܟܐ n.m.: king

ܡܠܟܘܬܐ n.f.: dominion, kingdom

ܡܠܠ Pa.: to speak, talk

ܡܠܬܐ (pl. ܡܠܐ) word

ܡܡܠܠܐ n.m.: speech

ܡܢ prep.: from; (of comparison) than

ܡܢܐ : What?

ܡܢܬܐ n.f.: portion

ܡܣܚܦܢܐ n.agentis: destructive

ܡܣܢܐ n.m.: shoe

ܡܥܦܪܐ n.m.: cloak

ܡܦܩܢܐ n.m.: pronunciation

ܡܨܐ : to be able

ܡܨܝܕܬܐ n.f.: net, snare

ܡܨܥܝܐ adj.: middle (grammatical t.t.; see Text no. 11)

ܡܨܪܝܐ adj.: Egyptian

ܡܪܐ n.m.: master, husband

ܡܪܝܐ n.m.: the Lord (= God of Israel or Jesus Christ)

ܡܪܬܐ n.f.: mistress

ܡܬܘܡ : ܡܡܬܘܡ ever

ܢܓܕ Pa.: to beat, scourge

ܢܘܪܐ n.f.: fire

ܢܛܪ Pe. (impf. ܢܛܘܪ) to observe, keep

ܢܟܠܐ n.m.: treachery, guile

ܢܟܣ Pe. (impf. ܢܢܟܘܣ): to slaughter

ܢܟܦ (ܢܟܝܦܐ) adj.: modest, chaste

ܢܡܘܣܐ n.m.: law (Gk νόμος)

ܢܣܒ Pe. (impf. ܢܣܒ): to take

ܢܣܝܘܢܐ n.m.: temptation

ܢܦܠ Pe. (impf. ܢܦܠ): to fall

ܢܦܩ Pe. (impf. ܢܦܘܩ): to go/come out

Af. ܐܦܩ : to bring/take out

ܢܦܫܐ n.f. (pl. ܢܦܫܬܐ) 1. soul; 2. (+ suf., as reflex. pron.), -self

ܢܩܕ (ܢܩܝܕܐ) adj.: thin, weak (gram. t.t.: see Text no. 11)

ܢܩܦ Pe. (impf. ܢܩܘܦ): to consort, become associated with (– ܠ)

Ethpe.: to adhere, cleave to (– ܠ)

ܢܫܒܐ n.m.: noose, net

ܢܫܩ Pe. /*o*/: to kiss

ܢܬܠ Pe. impf.: he will give (§ 55E)

ܣܒܪ Pe. /*a*/: to think

ܣܓܐ Pe.: to be many, multiply

Af.: to increase, multiply

ܣܓܝ adj.: many, much

ܣܗܕܐ n.m.: witness

ܣܘܟܠܐ n.m.: prudence

ܣܘܢܩܢܐ n.m.: need

ܣܘܦܐ n.m.: end, extinction

ܣܛܪ : + ܡܢ, except, but for

ܣܡ Pe. (impf. ܢܣܝܡ): to place, put

Ettaf.: = pass. Pe.

ܣܝܦܐ n.m.: sword

ܣܟ: (not …) at all, altogether

ܣܟܘܠܬܢ adj.: prudent

ܣܟܠܘܬܐ n.f.: wrong-doing

ܣܟܪܐ n.f.: shield

ܣܢܐ Pe.: to hate

ܣܩܒܠ Ethpa. (ܐܣܬܩܒܠ): to happen, occur

ܣܩܘܒܠ adj.: averse, contrary

ܥܒܐ adj. (ܥܒܝܬܐ): thick, (litera) aspirata (gram.t.t.)

ܥܒܕ Pe. /e/: to do

Ethpe.: = pass. Pe.

ܥܒܕܐ (ܥܒܕ) n.m.: servant

ܥܒܕܐ n.m.: work

ܥܒܕܘܬܐ n.f.: servitude

ܥܒܪ Pe. /a/: 1. to cross over, move to (ܠ–)

2. to depart

3. to transgress (+ ܥܠ)

ܥܒܪܝ adj.: Hebrew

ܥܓܠܐ n.m.: calf

ܥܕ ܠܐ conj.: before (= while ... still not)

ܥܕܡܐ 1. + ܠ, prep. until

2. + ܕ, conj. until

ܥܗܕ Pe /a/: to remember

ܥܗܪ Pe.: to be furious

ܥܘܠܐ n.m.: iniquity, injury

ܥܘܬܪܐ n.m.: wealth

ܥܙܩܬܐ n.f.: ring

ܥܣܩܬ adj.: grievous

ܥܝܢܐ n.f.: eye

ܒܥܝܢܝ in the eyes of

ܠܥܝܢ in the sight of

ܥܠ Pe. (Rt: ʿ-l-l; impf. ܢܥܘܠ): to enter (– ܠ a place; ܠܘܬ a person's presence)

Af.: to lead into

ܥܠܝ adj.: upper

ܥܠܡ n.m.: aeon

ܠܥܠܡ ܥܠܡܝܢ: for ever

ܠܥܠܡ: *do.*

ܥܠܬܐ n.f.: cause, occasion

ܒܥܠܬ on account of

ܥܡ prep.: with

ܥܡܐ n.m. (pl. ܥܡܡܐ): nation, people

ܥܡܘܪܐ n.m. (agentis): resident

ܥܡܠܐ n.m.: labour, toil

ܥܢܢܐ n.f.: cloud

ܥܣܪܐ m.: ten

ܥܪܘܩܝܐ n.m.: fleeing, escape

ܥܪܦܠܐ n.f.: mist

ܥܪܩ Pe. /o/: to run away

ܥܬܕ Pa.: to bring about

ܥܬܪ Pe. /a/: to become rich

ܦܘܛܝܦܪ : Potiphar

ܦܘܡ n.m.: mouth

ܦܘܩܕܢܐ n.m.: commandment

ܦܘܪܩܢܐ n.m.: salvation

ܦܚܐ n.m.: snare

ܦܛܡܐ n.m.: fattening

ܦܝܣ Ettaf. (ܐܬܬܦܝܣ): to consent

ܦܟܪ Ethpe: to be bound

ܦܠܓ Pa.: to divide

ܦܠܚ Pe. /o/ or /a/: to serve, work for (ܠ–)

ܦܠܛ Pe. /o/: to lead to (ܠ)

ܦܨܐ Pa.: to rescue, deliver

ܦܩܕ Pa.: to command

ܦܩܩ Pa.: to chatter, prate

ܦܙܪ Pa.: to squander

ܦܪܣ Ethpe.: to be spread; to spread (oneself)

ܦܪܥ Pe /o/: to requite, repay
ܦܪܩ Pe. /o/: to save, rescue
ܦܬܓܡܐ n.m.: matter, event; one of the Ten Commandments

ܨܒܐ Pe.: to wish, desire, want; + neg.: to refuse, decline
  ܨܒܝܢܐ n.m.: will, desire
ܨܘܕ Ettaf. (ܐܬܬܨܝܕ); to be caught
ܨܘܡ Pe.: to fast
  ܨܘܡܐ n.m.: fasting
ܨܘܪܐ n.m.: neck
ܨܠܐ Pa.: to pray
ܨܠܘܬܐ n.f.: prayer
ܨܠܚ Af.: to prosper, make successful
ܨܠܡܐ n.m.: image (for worship), idol
ܨܢܥ Ethpa.: to act artfully
ܨܥܪܐ n.m.: ignominy
ܨܦܪܐ n.m.: morning

ܩܒܠ Pa.: to receive, accept
ܩܕܡ Pa.: (joined directly to a following verb): formerly, previously, earlier (§98b)
ܩܕܡ prep. (w. suf., ܩܕܡܘܗܝ): before, in front of
  ܩܕܡܝܐ adj.: first
ܩܕܫ Ethpa.: to be hallowed
ܩܡ Pe.: to stand, stand up
ܩܘܪܒܢܐ n.m.: offering
ܩܛܠ Pe. /o/: to kill, murder
  Ethpe.: = pass. Pe.
  ܩܛܠܐ n.m.: murder

ܩܝܛܘܢܐ n.m.: bed-chamber (κοιτών)
ܩܝܡܐ n.m.: covenant, treaty
ܩܠܐ n.m.: voice, sound
  ܒܪܬ ܩܠܐ : word
ܩܠܝܠ adj.: (of amount) little
ܩܢܝܢܐ n.m.: possession, property
ܩܥܐ Pe.: to shout, yell
ܩܪܐ Pe.: to call, summon
  Ethpe.: = pass. Pe.
ܩܪܝܒ adj.: near
ܩܪܝܬܐ n.f.: field
ܩܫܝܫ adj.: old, aged, elder
ܩܫܬܐ n.f.: bow קֶשֶׁת

ܪܒ adj.: great
  n.: chief, master
ܪܒܐ Pa.: to bring up (a child), rear
ܪܒܘ : ten thousand
ܪܘܓܙܬܢ adj.: angry
ܪܓܙ Pe. /a/: to be/become angry
ܪܗܛ Pe. /a/: to run [רָץ]
ܪܘܓܙܐ (ܪܘܓܙ) n.m.: anger
ܪܘܡ Af. (ܐܪܝܡ): to raise, lift
ܪܚܝܩ adj.: distant, remote
ܪܚܡ Pe. /a/: to love, like
  Ethpa.: to have pity
  ܪܚܡܐ (Pe. ptc.): friend
  ܪܚܡܐ n.m.: mercy
ܪܗܝܒܬܢ adj.: eager
ܪܡ adj.: high
ܪܡܐ Af.: to cast; show (mercy)
[1] ܪܥܐ Pe.: to shepherd, tend (a flock)
[2] ܪܥܐ Ethpa.: to get reconciled
ܪܦܐ Af. (ܐܪܦܝ): to let go, leave
ܪܫܐ (also ܪܝܫܐ) n.m.: head

ܪܓܝܓ adj.: choice, best
ܪܫܝܥ adj.: evil

ܫܐܠ Pe. (impf. ܢܫܐܠ): to ask for
Pa.: to ask, enquire
ܫܒܗܪ Ethpa. (ܐܫܬܒܗܪ): to glory, boast
ܫܒܗܪܢܘܬܐ n.f.: vainglory, boastfulness
ܫܒܩ Pe. /o/: 1. to leave, let go
2. to forgive (– ܠ pers.)
Ethpe.: to be forgiven
ܫܕܐ Pe.: to throw, cast
ܫܕܪ Pa.: to send, dispatch
ܫܘܐ Pe.: to be equal, worthy
ܫܘܒܩܢܐ n.m.: remission, forgiveness
ܫܘܠܛܢܐ n.m.: dominion, realm
ܫܘܦܝܢܐ (or ܫܘܦܝܢܐ) n.m.: file
ܫܘܦܪܐ n.m.: beauty
ܫܘܩܐ n.m.: street
ܫܟܚ Af. (ܐܫܟܚ): 1. find;
2. to be able, can
Ethpe.: to be found
ܫܠܛ Af. (+ ܒܝܕ): to entrust with
ܫܠܡ Pe. /a/: to be fulfilled; be at peace
Af.: to hand, entrust
Ethpe.: to be handed, delivered
ܫܡܐ n.m. (pl. ܫܡܗܐ): name; substantive
ܫܡܝܐ n.: sky, heaven
ܫܡܥ Pe. /a/: 1. hear;
2. to heed
3. to consent
Ethpe: to be heard; get heard
2. to yield to (–ܠ)
Af.: to declare
ܫܢܐ n.m.: tooth
ܫܢܬܐ (pl. ܫܢܝܢ, ܫܢܝܐ) n.f.: year
ܫܘܦܠܐ n.m.: (in pl.) foot (of a mountain)
ܫܪܐ Pe.: to acquit
Pa.: to begin
ܫܪܪܐ n.m.: truth

ܬܒܥ Pe. /o/ or /a/: to demand
ܬܒܪ Ethpe.: to be broken
ܬܘܒ adv.: 1. again:
2. now (introducing a new chapter or a new document in a manuscript containing more than one piece of literary composition)
ܬܘܢܐ n.m.: inner chamber
ܬܚܘܝܬܐ n.f.: illustration, example
ܬܚܬܝ adj.: lower
ܬܠܐ Ethpe.: to be hanged
ܬܠܡܝܕܐ n.m.: disciple
ܬܡܢ adv.: there
ܬܩܢ Pa.: to construct, fashion
ܬܪܝܢ m.: two
ܬܪܥܐ n.m.: door
ܬܪܬܝܢ f.: two
ܬܫܒܘܚܬܐ n.f.: glory, praise